THEORY Q

*A series edited by
Lauren Berlant and
Lee Edelman*

MELODRAMA

· · ·

AN AESTHETICS OF IMPOSSIBILITY

· · ·

Jonathan Goldberg

DUKE UNIVERSITY PRESS

Durham and London   2016

© 2016 Duke University Press
All rights reserved
Printed in the United States of
America on acid-free paper ∞
Designed by Amy Ruth Buchanan
Typeset in Whitman and Gill Sans Std.
by Tseng Information Systems, Inc.

Library of Congress Cataloging-in-Publication Data
Names: Goldberg, Jonathan. author.
Title: Melodrama : an aesthetics of impossibility /
Jonathan Goldberg.
Description: Durham : Duke University Press, 2016. |
Series: Theory Q |
Includes bibliographical references and index.
Identifiers: LCCN 2016000376
ISBN 9780822361756 (hardcover : alk. paper)
ISBN 9780822361916 (pbk. : alk. paper)
ISBN 9780822374046 (e-book)
Subjects: LCSH: Melodrama—History and criticism.
Classification: LCC ML2050.G65 2016 |
DDC 809.2/527—dc23
LC record available at http://lccn.loc.gov/2016000376

Cover art: *All That Heaven Allows*
(dir. Douglas Sirk, 1955). Courtesy of Photofest.

FOR MARCIE FRANK

CONTENTS

Preface ix

Acknowledgments xvii

PART I · THE IMPOSSIBLE SITUATION

ONE Agency and Identity:
The Melodram in Beethoven's *Fidelio* 3

TWO Identity and Identification:
Sirk–Fassbinder–Haynes 23

PART II · *MELOS* + DRAMA

THREE The Art of Murder:
Hitchcock and Highsmith 83

FOUR Wildean Aesthetics:
From "Paul's Case" to *Lucy Gayheart* 133

Coda 155

Notes 169

Bibliography 187

Index 197

PREFACE

Peter Brooks's *The Melodramatic Imagination: Balzac, Henry James, Melodrama, and the Mode of Excess* (1976) remains in print and has been influential in discussions of melodrama for an entire generation (or two) of scholars. It provides a place to start as I briefly lay out what this book aims to do and how it relates to work that precedes it. In his preface to the 1995 edition, Brooks argues that melodrama is "central to our modernity," a mode that makes available "large choices of ways of being" shorn of any transcendental guarantee.[1] Melodrama, he claims, pits exaggerated forms of good and evil in Manichean struggle in ways that promote the reader's reassuring perception of various cosmic forces and "latent moral meanings" (9), a thesis he seeks to capture in the phrase "moral occult" (5). This thesis is historicized through an account of the role of melodrama (a post-Revolutionary theatrical form first named as such in the late eighteenth century) in nineteenth-century novels that counter that genre's claims to realism. History moves in the direction of a formalism as Brooks engages a "mode of excess" in which writing exceeds the literality of the real to usher in a metaphoricity that he finds "noumenal" (54), spiritual, and primal, an ur-language not confined to language (indeed, gestural and silent), psychic and yet not a personal truth—Truth with a capital *T*.

In a word, Brooks offers melodrama as a key to literariness. In the excess to which he points, he gestures to a beyond the letter and the literal that, I will argue, must also go beyond (or come short of) moral clarity and the clear choice between polar opposites that he claims melodrama makes available. Tellingly, that availability Brooks poses as a scene of recognition. The bearer of Truth may insist on the Truth but is nonetheless powerless to make it happen. Rather, Truth must be witnessed and recognized, and thus hailed by the very forces that seek to deny it. In the coming discussion, I follow Brooks but linger on a fundamental contradiction: it is the (im)possibility of recognition that makes melodrama a generative form rather than one that offers happy endings that confirm the ability of the social as presently constituted to make good on goodness. If indeed this is ever possible, it would be because the social, the real, already is a site of excess different from the "moral occult," which after all occults what is desired as good; this excess houses what Lauren Berlant and Lee Edelman describe in the closing words of their preface to *Sex, or the Unbearable* as "the metamorphic potential that the sameness of things contains," a potential that "can never be predicted or controlled" because sameness does not preclude self-difference.[2] Or, to put this beside the related claim of Rei Tereda in *Looking Away*, melodrama testifies to the "wish to be relieved for a moment of the coercion to accept what one does not dispute," claims of necessity (social, natural) with which, she goes on to say, "we're within our rights to feel uncomfortable" and voice a dissatisfaction that she calls queer.[3]

In the pages ahead, I will open queer contradictions glossed over by Brooks. Take, for example, the fact that for Brooks, more often than not, the disempowered/empowered Truth figure is a woman (melodrama itself is feminized). Brooks acknowledges this gender plot, but not in any consequential way. (When melodrama came under the scrutiny of film critics, this situation was central to feminist analysis.) Without a pause, he notes that the scene of recognition—the unveiling of female virtue—can take the form of hailing a woman as "above her sex" (27). This is an occultation, to be sure, but not one that works to reveal the secure and conventional truth of gender difference assumed by Brooks, and certainly not mobilized toward critical recognition of the sex that is not one. So, too, when villainy is unveiled as a "hideous Moor" (19) a racialized category of difference is imbricated and unremarked, yet it calls the very metaphoricity of Brooks's "pure and polar" (xiii) opposition into question.

The fundamental contradiction in Brooks that requires further attention has to do with the form and history of melodrama: Is melodrama a distinctively modern genre, or is it a "mode" arguably always already available? Melodrama is a genre that is not one, thereby troubling the fundamental moral difference that Brooks nonetheless wishes to insist that melodrama clarifies. At more than one point, Brooks allies the Truth of melodrama to a "love that cannot speak its name" (73, 93), yet that telling phrase for non-normative desire is never pursued as

X PREFACE

such and always is located in a heterosexual matrix (this remains the case for virtually all the work done on melodrama).[4] In considering the not-to-be-named, as I will do in this book, I do not mean to arrive at some truth allied to (homo)sexual identity; rather, by way of contradictions—in race, gender, and sexuality; in formal and historical situation—I aim to relocate the impossible place that Brooks occults and yet glimpses, and in so doing to throw the transcendental as much as historical and empirical determination into question. Like Lauren Berlant, I have "a commitment to maintaining contradiction."[5]

In his 1995 preface, Brooks notes the strange confluence that just as he was starting to publish work toward his book, in 1972, Thomas Elsaesser published an essay on family melodrama ("Tales of Sound and Fury: Observations on the Family Melodrama") that proved influential to film studies as the field began to explore the gendered implications of melodrama. Brooks hails this development as pointing to a postdisciplinary future; the future of melodrama is not only the novel, but film, especially so-called silent film, intent, on the one hand, on frozen gestures, offering, on the other, brief bits of interpolated text, and yet, on a third hand, accompanied by continual live music, which Brooks claims at several points enhances the "legibility" (48) of melodrama. Although Brooks privileges the novel, he points to something I will examine ahead: the remediated, mixed-media form of melodrama. If music, text, and image enhance each other, they baffle literary legibility. My analysis of remediation is indebted to Marcie Frank's exacting and illuminating work in progress on dramatic melodrama and the novel. My prompt for attention to formal questions also comes from Elsaesser; following the etymology of the word "melodrama," he posits an originary impulse in its combination of *melos* and drama.

Brooks takes 1995 as a year in which a convergence of disciplines seemed incipient. That's not the story one finds, however, in John Mercer and Martin Shingler's Short Cuts volume, *Melodrama: Genre, Style, Sensibility* (2004), a guide to "the melodrama debate" in film studies, a debate that is itself melodramatic (in conventional uses of the term) in its posing of insuperable oppositions.[6] Trying out first the notion that melodrama names a genre, Mercer and Shingler light on the historical problem that films first dubbed "melodrama" tended to be action pictures, while films called melodrama by critics following Elsaesser tended to be devoted to suffering: male versus female names the ge-

PREFACE xi

neric (and gendered) impasse. Deeming genre definition irresolvable, Mercer and Shingler turn to "style" and to Douglas Sirk, a key figure in Elsaesser's essay and to his definition of family melodrama: they tick off Sirk's stylistic features as a Hollywood style, then worry the question whether Sirk's work is subversive or conservative, only finally to note that Rainer Werner Fassbinder and Todd Haynes follow Sirk; since neither of them counts as a Hollywood filmmaker, another definitional impasse is reached. Looking for "a more encompassing and progressive theoretical framework" than either style or genre afford, Mercer and Shingler opt for "sensibility" (their word for "mode"), seeking a term that can make manifest the movement "across genres" that defines melodrama.[7] Arriving here, they land belatedly in the very terrain that Brooks enunciated in 1976, returning to the developments that Brooks hailed in his 1995 preface as having been inaugurated by his work and Elsaesser's in the 1970s. This book, too, returns to those ur-moments of theorization. They seem inescapable.

Brooks hailed developments in film studies for ushering in a possibility of interdisciplinarity. Mercer and Shingler instead detail the internecine squabbling as film studies established itself as a discipline seeking univocal terms that would found it as a field. As their book closes they affirm that melodrama somehow speaks the unspeakable and represents the unrepresentable, yet they also cling to it as a site of the repressed, of the unspeakable unspoken and the unrepresentable unrepresented.[8] In their closing pages they glance at developments in "gay" cinema and gay criticism as still "marginalized" areas in film studies.[9] If this is the case, it is because of a blindness in film studies to queer work. Mercer and Shingler's Short Cuts volume is indebted to work by two percipient film critics of melodrama, Linda Williams and Christine Gledhill. In her essay "Melodrama Revisited" (1998) Williams acknowledges but refuses the limitation of melodrama to the terrain of female gender, opting instead to read it as a mode that serves to index American culture, especially American false consciousness and guilt, a thesis pursued in *Playing the Race Card: Melodramas of Black and White* (2001). Nonetheless, in her move to name a specific modernity, and to think of melodrama not as a genre, but as a mode, Williams is, as she acknowledges, belatedly following Brooks. She also follows Gledhill, who likewise follows Brooks in her important introduction to *Home Is Where the Heart Is*, "The Melodramatic Field: An Investigation" (1987), and in

xii PREFACE

her essay "Rethinking Genre" (2000). Gledhill historicizes melodrama, going back to divided theater worlds of the eighteenth and nineteenth centuries, and from them to a sense that the reception of melodrama cannot be univocal. Nor, she writes in her 2000 essay, can the form be seen as univocal either: "Melodrama is not nor ever was a singular genre."[10] So, too, Williams, following Gledhill, insists that the "feminine" relation to melodrama must be a double one, a conflicted identification with both Pathos and Action. Yet, for Williams and for Gledhill, what the form or mode of melodrama reveals is cultural contradiction. This is certainly a position I endorse insofar as it takes us past Brooks, past clarity, past the transcendental. But it also is a position I question if it means that a reading of melodrama must ultimately be an account of the social, one in which aesthetic form simply mirrors the real.

Melodrama, Gledhill affirms, rather than being a genre, operates at the borders of genre; rather than demarcating a territory, it ignites sites of desire at its places of crossing: "Melodrama, as an organizing modality of the genre system, works at western culture's most sensitive cultural and aesthetic boundaries, embodying class, gender, and ethnicity in a process of imaginary identification, differentiation, contact, and opposition." Thus, she continues, "melodramatic modality, personifying social forces as psychic energies and producing moral identities in the clash of opposites, is committed to binaries which bring the 'others' of official ideology into visibility."[11] Gledhill's condensed conclusions work from Brooks—from the polarities and opposition of a mode—but in a dialectical analysis of the social. Aesthetics and the social may mirror each other, but ideology is not secure enough to be able to repress what it suppresses; the reception of melodrama is a complex mix of repudiation and identification. These powerful insights into the form grant melodrama the force to unveil the social, but only, finally, to see it as a site of willed, if limited, coercion and domination. The small o "other" is relegated to the minority status of an identity rather than explored as a queer lever in the modality Gledhill describes so compellingly. This book seeks to open what Gledhill's formulations seem to foreclose.

In moving this discussion in that queer direction, I want to further something like Foucault's unsettlement of power—"Power is everywhere," he writes in *The History of Sexuality: An Introduction*[12]—rather than a map of oppositions in dialectical struggle. This means, also, not wanting to start from the notion of the categorical. Replacing abstracted black and white with male and female or Caucasian and African American may still be exercises in elaborating rather than metamorphosing the same. Replacing the literary with the historical, the author with the audience, production with reception — moves that film studies has performed to establish itself as a field — may be too costly short cuts if they involve ignoring the ways in which filmmakers work as I do in the chapters that follow, tracing a line from Sirk to Fassbinder to Haynes, or tracing crossings from Patricia Highsmith to Alfred Hitchcock. Brooks puts melodrama with its multimedia ambitions — of gesture, spoken words, music — in relation to the novel, which is silent (all there is to see on a printed page is black marks against a white background; everything else we see and hear is not there). The "occultation" of melodrama lies in this remediated relationship. It is akin to what Linda Williams studies in her endless fascination with the "money shot" in her book on pornography, *Hard Core: Power, Pleasure, and "the Frenzy of the Visible"* (1989): male ejaculate proves that sex has happened, yet proves it in the absence of what usually counts as sex (intercourse, where semen is not seen) and with no equivalent available to register female sexual pleasure. "The frenzy of the visible," like the "excess" of melodrama, attempts to register what cannot be seen and yet is. As Gledhill writes in "The Melodramatic Field: An Investigation," "Taking its stand in the material world of everyday reality and lived experience, and acknowledging the limitations of the conventions of language and representations, [melodrama] proceeds to force into aesthetic presence identity, value and plenitude of meaning."[13] But if so, the meanings it reveals no longer are fully determined by and limited to the terms of everyday reality, lived experience, the bounded significance of conventions, of language, of "realistic" representation. As Brooks noted of Sirk, his films represent "the refusal of the dailiness of the everyday" (ix). Or, as Hitchcock wrote, in an early affirmation of his own practice as melodrama, "I use melodrama because I have a tremendous desire for understatement in film-making."[14]

This book follows Brooks to the extent that it begins with a post-Revolutionary moment before moving to Hollywood melodrama and on to some twentieth-century novels. It is willing to imagine that such violations of form and history can take us to a place that defies the making of boundaries and that refuses to hand over to the real a straitened version of reality or a straightened version in which the miseries of heterosexuality for women who suffer the "female complaint" can be resisted only by voicing suffering within the constraints of the desires it produces, or where minorities suffer and suffer the desire to be the majority. It is against and "across" these impasses that I seek to move, putting "across" in quotation marks to telegraph Eve Kosofsky Sedgwick's queer lexicon in essays gathered in *Tendencies*. Her work is coincident with but not acknowledged by Brooks as he tallies happy coincidences circa 1995. At the end of his 1976 preface, Brooks does, however, remark on two students who deserve special mention. One of them is named David A. Miller (xx); D. A. Miller is important in this book as I follow him on questions of denotation and connotation that Brooks opens as well in his pursuit of metaphor. "Beside" was a later formulation of Sedgwick's to complement "across," akin to her impulse to add "others" but not in some infinitizing gesture—to mark thereby the capacities and affordances of the real without being unaware of its limits, perhaps thereby summoning up what Berlant calls in *The Female Complaint* "unlived better survival" as something other than utopic fantasy or sentimental attachment to sites of irremediable loss.[15] Melodrama remediates: I depend on the double implication of the verb as a way to gesture toward the (im)possibility of melodrama. This doubleness resonates with Sedgwick's discussion in the opening pages of *Tendencies* on the resources that queer inquiry finds when things—and persons—do not line up to mean one thing. "What if the richest junctures weren't the ones where *everything means the same thing*?" Sedgwick asks.[16] Melodrama may be the form or mode that demonstrates the point.

....

Melodrama: An Aesthetics of Impossibility is divided into two parts. The first is titled "The Impossible Situation," quoting a phrase that Douglas Sirk used in his book-long interview with Jon Halliday to describe the productive impasses that melodrama thematizes. The second part, "*Melos* + Drama," also draws on this interview, as Sirk underlines the formally remediated nature of melodrama.[17] These questions of form and theme are, of course, ultimately inseparable, as is clear from where the book starts, with the section of Beethoven's opera *Fidelio* labeled "Melodram," and where it ends, with Willa Cather's *Lucy Gayheart*, her late novel about musicians. Discussion of *Fidelio* is followed by an analysis of Sirk's *All That Heaven Allows* (1955) and the two films widely recognized as being in its immediate orbit, Fassbinder's *Ali: Fear Eats the Soul* (1974) and Haynes's *Far from Heaven* (2002).[18] Putting these films in relationship to Beethoven's opera enables a backward glance at the moment of melodrama's generic inception and the complications involved in a mode that may exceed historical determination. The impossible situation in Beethoven opens questions of gender and sexuality that call the categorical into question. These are related in *Fidelio* in its various conjunctions of drama to music. To that question I return in the second half of this book, working from music in Hitchcock (*Rope* [1948] and *Strangers on a Train* [1951] are my prime examples) to its thematization in Highsmith (her *Strangers on a Train* [1950] and the five Ripley novels are my focus) and Cather as a way of metaphorizing the aesthetic realm of melodrama — a realm to which, at various points in the book, I attach the name of Oscar Wilde as a kind of *point de capiton* for my exploration of melodrama. Wilde's name is not meant to carry the normative and ideological force that the upholstery button can convey in its Lacanian usage. This figure of attachment comes to mind thanks to the emerald brooch Todd Haynes pins on the infant Wilde delivered from outer space at the opening of *Velvet Goldmine* (1998); passed down over time, this jewel might figure the aesthetic vitality of melodrama.

ACKNOWLEDGMENTS

I am grateful to Lauren Berlant and Lee Edelman for welcoming this book into Theory Q, and to *Sex, or the Unbearable* for inspiration. I thank Lee and Joseph Litvak as well for a response to my monograph on *Strangers on a Train* that prompted my return to Hitchcock and Highsmith in this book. I am indebted to those who commented on the chapter on Beethoven when I delivered it at Concordia University or read the version of it that appears as "*Fidelio*: Melodramas of Agency and Identity" in *Criticism* 55, no. 4 (fall 2013): Meredith Evans, Esther Frank, Bonnie Honig, Stephen Orgel, James Kuzner, Joe Quinn, and Sharon Cameron among them, and to Adam Frank, who heard it and read much of the manuscript as it was being written. My thanks to Aaron Goldsman for a stimulating response to the chapter on Cather that I circulated for a workshop at Emory, and to Paul Kelleher and Pat Cahill for their engagement. Sharon Cameron also read the coda with enthusiasm, and it pleases me to think that this book echoes some of the remarkable work she has done on impersonality. Brent Dawson was my able research assistant on this project, and I thank him especially for traveling to the Warner Bros. Archive on my behalf; I also thank Jonathon Auxier, the archivist there, for his unfailing assistance. I am indebted to Hal Rogers for helping me think through this project on many occasions. Michael Moon has read it over and again with his loving and caring eye, on which I depend. This book would never have been written had not Marcie Frank invited me to take part in a workshop and conference on melodrama. Her illuminating thoughts about that endeavor and Michael's response to it are found in the issue of *Criticism* on melodrama she edited that includes my *Fidelio* essay (fall 2013). I dedicate this book to her, not just because she is behind it, has read the entire manuscript in draft, and encouraged me through the writing, but also for the inspiring conversation and friendship we have had for years and I hope will have for many more.

PART I · THE IMPOSSIBLE SITUATION

ONE

AGENCY AND IDENTITY

The Melodram in Beethoven's Fidelio

In the score of *Fidelio* (1814), Beethoven's only opera, the duet between Leonore and Rocco in the second act is preceded by what the heading for musical number 12 calls a "Melodram."[1] This is the appropriate technical term for this brief two-minute stretch of the opera: the two characters speak, their utterances punctuated with musical phrases. Beethoven's opera is formally a singspiel or opéra comique; everywhere else in the score, we find either speech or concerted numbers. If the orchestra is playing, the singers will be singing. If not, the singers speak. Music and speech never interact except in this Melodram. This raises some obvious questions: Why does Beethoven introduce melodrama into his opera? Why at this point in his score does he violate the rules of composition about speech and song that he follows everywhere else? In "Tales of Sound and Fury: Observations on the Family Drama," Thomas Elsaesser pointed to melodrama of the kind we find in *Fidelio* as a "system of punctuation" through which the emotional weight of the moment is underscored.[2] For Elsaesser, this formal feature lies at the heart of all melodrama and is notably present in the twentieth-century work most immediately associated with melodrama, the films of Douglas Sirk. What it might be doing in an opera, where, it is easy to presume, the singing voice heightens emotion, is a question that Elsaesser does not ask.

Although Elsaesser's point is not about opera, it does

help to remind us how much the plot of Beethoven's opera and the moment at which it arrives in its dramatic-musical Melodram brings his score into the orbit of a family drama. Leonore is, in this scene, descending into the lowest reaches of a prison in the company of Rocco, the jailer in charge of the prison. In male disguise and bearing the name Fidelio, she has insinuated herself into Rocco's company by winning the affection of his daughter Marzelline away from Marzelline's previous lover, Jaquino. Now engaged to Marzelline, she has persuaded her future father-in-law to allow her to be a fuller partner to him in his job, his assistant in the most arduous tasks. The job before them is to dig the grave of a long and unjustly held political prisoner whom the commandant of the prison, Pizarro, is about to murder. This prisoner may be Florestan, Leonore's husband, as she suspects, and as we, well before she does, will know it is. This is why she has disguised herself—to find him, to save him. At this melodramatic moment of disguise and blocked knowledge, at this moment when Beethoven writes a Melodram, discoveries of identity—his, hers—are incipient. Will all be revealed, or will she be there only to witness his death, to prepare his grave?

Beethoven's Melodram begins with a brief descent partway down a scale, ending with a tremolo punctuation on a diminished seventh chord. After this moment of musical descent and suspension, Leonore speaks in a voice that, the stage direction indicates, is "halb laut," mezza voce: she remarks how cold it is this deep underground. Rocco responds by commenting how natural this is since they are down deep ("Das ist natürlich, es ist ja tief").[3] Rocco's common sense is belied by the unresolved musical descent down the scale and by a tremolo chord that changes from a seventh to a diminished seventh. However much one can name these musical elements, the line of music is anything but predictable: its effect is to open a space of irresolution. The music is not there merely to illustrate the downward movement of the characters, as commentators claim it does. When the music stops on the tremolo, it opens the way for a voice that is only half-voiced, and in a space that, however much it may be located in this world, is nonetheless below the earth, "unterirdisch" (164) underground: hell, a grave, another world. As André Lischke comments, the music that accompanies this scene of underground cold and the imminence of death produces an effect that we might expect today in a horror movie.[4] It intimates that alongside the everyday world there is another.

When the music resumes after this initial exchange about depth and cold, it repeats the descending motif, starting anew, but a half step lower, a key change that has nothing to do with the key anticipated by the suspended seventh chord. This descent is a truncated version of the initial musical line. The descent this time is sudden and interrupted, landing precipitously on a chord that is, this time, sustained; but once again, it is, like the earlier tremolo conclusion, augmented, producing yet another change in key and further irresolution. Leonore's words at this point — "I never thought we would find the entrance" ("Ich glaubte schon, wir würden den Eingang gar nicht finden," 164) — might describe the music seeking resolution as easily as it does the terrain they are exploring as they look for the cell that holds the prisoner. But does it find resolution? In what key is the Melodram written? There is no answer to that question, it seems, until three chords in quick succession that follow Leonore's observation disrupt that supposition. The tempo changes at this point as well, from the Poco sostenuto of the first two descending phrases to an Allegro. The music, for the first time, arrives somewhere harmonically; the three chords resolve in D major. "There he is" ("Da ist er"), Rocco says, as if the arrival in a key were the equivalent to the discovery of the man. "He seems totally motionless" ("Er scheint ganz ohne Bewegung"), Leonore responds. To Rocco's commonsense observation — "There he is" — Leonore offers a chilling rejoinder. Is he there if he is not moving — if, that is, this means he is not alive? Does the D-major resolution underline his identity, that he is there, or does it mark his end, that he is not there? Leonore's observation all but says that he is dead. The equivocation of appearance — "he seems" — seems overridden in the chordal progression that follows: the Allegro continues, the D-major chord replaced by a D-minor chord underscoring the ominous possibility that they have found him dead already. Rocco gets the point: "Perhaps he's dead" ("Vielleicht ist er todt," 164), he says, but, once again, the statement is not definitive: "Perhaps."

The music continues, two more chords follow, once again moving to a diminished seventh, opening musically the possibility in the "perhaps" of moving forward, beyond the life-death quandary. Leonore questions Rocco, "really dead?," and the music answers when the diminished chord is followed by a passage in F major marked Poco Adagio; an arpeggio ascends in the key of F, descending in the C_7 that is its harmonic partner. This is the second time in the Melodram that we experience an expected harmonic progression; this time it is prolonged. For the first time, speaking voice and music overlap and coincide, for, at the same time that the music plays, Rocco speaks. "He is asleep" ("Er schläft"), he says. The music continues, again changing speed, again changing key, prompting Rocco to speak again in the interval opened: it's time for them to get to work, he urges. The opening—the discovery of the sleeping man—gives them an opportunity that must be seized. But when the music resumes, it does so only to come to an immediate halt. A staccato C-major sequence is replaced with a sustained C-minor chord that then modulates into a series of more-than-measure-length chords that come to a halt on yet another seventh. As it sounds, Leonore speaks: "It is impossible to distinguish his features" ("Es ist unmöglich seine Züge zu unterscheiden," 164). The chord continues with an additional note, and she speaks over it again: "May God help me if it is he!" ("Gott steh mir bei, wenn er es ist!," 165).

That it *is*, and that her wish may be answered, seems indicated by the Andante con moto that follows in the key of E-flat that resolves the chord on which Leonore hung. But the musical phrases keep passing in and out of the minor; Rocco again enjoins them to seize the moment and begin to dig. The melody resumes, this time punctuated by tremolos that Rocco translates quite literally into an observation about his companion: "You're trembling," he says. "Are you afraid?" he asks. Leonore denies it, after a brief Allegro passage moves away from the major/minor theme to a series of chords that appear to be heading for G-flat major; the answer to Rocco's question is couched in his naturalizing language. "It's so cold," she says, that's why she is trembling—as if the temperature could explain her affect, as if there simply was an outer cause for her inner turmoil. Not that Fidelio could say to Rocco: "I'm Leonore, not your future son-in-law; that man might be my husband." To the kind of explanation possible to be uttered, Rocco can respond in his usual commonsensical way—work will warm you up, he promises. After she speaks, the key changes, however, to A major for three measures before arriving at A minor, the key in which the duet is set. Speech is replaced by singing; the Melodram is over.

Why is this melodrama here? What has happened in it? Outwardly, nothing. Leonore still does not know if the man she sees is Florestan. Rocco sees beside him a trembling young man, his future son-in-law Fidelio, apparently cold, perhaps afraid of the job to be done. He does

6 CHAPTER ONE

not know Fidelio is Leonore. Florestan does not know his wife is there. The melodrama, half-voiced, spoken at cross-purposes, is remarkable (as Daniela Kaleva notes in an essay titled "Beethoven and Melodrama" that has helped guide my musical analysis) for how various its uses of musical punctuation are, sometimes used between utterances, sometimes alongside them. Sometimes speech occurs while music plays, sometimes as a chord or pedal point is sustained, sometimes in the silences between which the music keeps reinventing itself in its extraordinary series of key and tempo changes. "The harmonic language relies on prolongation of dissonance, tonic-dominant progressions, and major-minor relationships for illustrative purposes," Kaleva writes.[5] But illustrative of what? Kaleva notes Leonore's agitation, anxiety, and fear, along with Rocco's impatience. She assumes that the music underlines the dramatic tensions of the scene. This is true, as far as it goes, but more than that kind of underlining is involved.

Kaleva assumes we are to read Fidelio as Leonore, that the truth behind disguised and unknown identity lies beneath the surface, and that music underscores such singular truths. I would suggest, however, that this melodramatic passage is a very unsettled and unsettling interval and that that is what it is about—not some underlying truth waiting to be revealed, but an inhabitation of the irresolutions, the what-ifs and as-ifs: Who is it? Is he alive or dead? Why is s/he trembling? These hesitations, suspensions, and doubts play out in the words spoken and in musical passages that are themselves sometimes at cross-purposes, resolving, unresolving. These relationships undermine the kind of naturalizing understanding of the scene that Rocco is prone to offer and that musicologists tend to echo; they suggest the limits of an analysis of the music as simply underscoring some singular point of reference (descending scale = descending stairs; tremolo = shivering). Whatever this Melodram is about, it's not simply the temperature that's making Fidelio tremble, not a matter of a young man not up to the man's work Rocco has been sent to perform. (Earlier, when Rocco had hesitated when Pizarro wanted him to kill the prisoner, Pizarro had asked him, "Are you a man?" ["Bist du ein Mann?," 91] before staking his own manliness on the murder.) Nor is the scene merely about the question of the identity of the prisoner or his rescuer. For Leonore to know she has found her husband, for Florestan to know that Leonore has found him, for Rocco to know that Fidelio is Leonore and that the young man is a woman:

such knowledge certainly could and will dissipate some of the tension in this scene. As this knowledge surfaces, the strict decorum of speaking and singing will be resumed.

The question not asked in assuming that these suppressed revelations of identity are the underlying truth of the Melodram is this: Will identity revealed in itself produce a solution? Such a supposition is certainly in play in Peter Brooks's theory of melodrama in *The Melodramatic Imagination*, that there is some moral clarity and force in the distinctions represented by characters, that to reveal those distinctions is the aim of melodrama. For husband and wife to know each other would be tantamount to salvation. Marriage would secure the social and political order. But if Florestan is in prison precisely because he is Florestan, how would knowing he is Florestan lead to his freedom? And if he knew that Leonore was there, how would such knowledge of her identity have salvific force? Brooks supposes that some form of self-identical goodness triumphs in melodrama. But are these characters simply to be understood as themselves? Is it who they are that enables the resolution of the dilemma of unjust imprisonment? Is that political situation solved by a domestic revelation? To suppose a seamless connection between the dilemma of unjust imprisonment and revelation of identity is to imagine that the lifting of the veil empowers action, indeed explains why and how action is possible. To assume a correlation between action and identity relegates melodrama to an impasse to be overcome; it assumes that embodiment and visceral experience serve as hindrances to the achievement of identity. This is the idealizing and ideological plot that lies behind the kind of literariness that Brooks accords melodrama.

Melodrama offers more than such an either/or in which disguise, opacity, and impasse must be exchanged for identity, knowledge, and action. Beethoven's Melodram, however much it involves disguise and uncertain knowledge, is not simply some false state that would be relieved by true knowledge, nor is it in the service of the equation of such supposedly true knowledge with power. We can see this formally if instead of understanding the Melodram as a violation of the rule of the opera's separations of speech and song that needs to be repaired, we view it as a moment dense with musical invention, filled with experiments in the relationship between speech and music. These various states of hesitation, musical irresolution, cross-purpose, key change, suspension, and half-voicing are themselves kinds of knowledge. They point in fact to something that exceeds the rule that keeps music and speech separate. In its plotting, too, the Melodram continues the opera's exploration of states of possibility marked by disguise. It is, after all, *as* Fidelio that Leonore has arrived where she is, as male and marriageable (rather than as female and married); it is *as* Fidelio that she has been able to act. That doing may be tied to a false identity, but it is nonetheless real action. It may thereby call into question the assumption that action is tied to true identity. It calls into question, moreover, the singularity of identity.

To assume that Leonore is the truth of the character, that the basis of what is happening is tied to the fact that "underneath" Fidelio there is Leonore, makes everything—all possibility—hinge on the revelation that Fidelio is Leonore. It makes that identity her only identity, her one true identity. This Melodram is just about the last moment that Fidelio can be Fidelio: in the next musical number she will know who the prisoner is; he will be Florestan, not merely an unjustly imprisoned man, and once he is Florestan, she will be Leonore. But these true names, and the knowledge of them—the knowledge that might be supposed to be that of true identity—are something more than the truth of personal identity. "*Fidelio* is based on the French drama, *Léonore, ou L'amour conjugale* by J. N. Bouilly," as Kaleva reminds anyone unfamiliar with the basic information.[6] Beethoven first called his opera *Leonore* before settling on *Fidelio*. The moment that she is "herself," that is, Leonore will be Florestan's wife. "First kill his wife!" ("Tödt' erst sein Weib!") is the tremendous line she sings when she stands up to Pizarro and reveals who she is. "His wife?" ("Sein Weib?"), asks Pizarro; "My wife?" ("Mein Weib?"), asks Florestan. "Yes, Leonore is here. Look!" ("Ja, sieh' hier Leonore," 194), she says, speaking in propria persona, as his wife, as Leonore.

"Yes, Leonore is here. Look!" she says, and melodrama is over. Beethoven has not used it for the revelation of identity, nor for the resolution of action, but to sustain irresolution. Nonetheless, if we return to the score of the Melodram, we can see that it more than hints where it is going—toward a resolution that will remove Fidelio and reveal Leonore but, in so doing, will reveal her only as Florestan's wife. The Melodram suggests this from its first note, an F in the cellos and double basses that points to the key of the aria Florestan has sung just before at the opening of act two of *Fidelio*. Florestan's aria closes with the C7–F-major harmonic resolution to be expected for an aria in the key of F. When the F sounds in the strings at the beginning of the Melodram, we are, musically, still in his world. The tremolo, which Kaleva follows Erich Schenk in calling a "shiver motif"[7] — as if Leonore's remark about the cold is only to be taken at face value — recalls the tremolo heard toward the end of the first part of Florestan's aria when he sings about the chains that are his unjust reward for his commitment to the truth (158). If the tremolo functions in his aria in what is usually taken to be the melodramatic mode of underscoring his words, and if, at the same time, it is supposed to imitate the clinking sound of his chains, it carries two meanings at once — naturalistic imitation of the sound of chains and unnatural imprisonment. This double meaning has the effect of making the natural sound unnatural; the music means more than the literal because the literal is not univocal. The tremolo captures this as it oscillates between two notes; rather than simply fitting the situation, it marks a lack of fit and serves as a critical comment, another language. These effects are further complicated when Florestan's music, including the tremolo, are heard again in the Melodram. Quotation does not bear the same meaning in that scene. Identical notes do not carry identical meanings.

In the Melodram, when Rocco pronounces the calming news that the prisoner is not dead but asleep, the music plays on a C7–F-major resolution, as we've observed. It does not merely echo the identical harmonic resolution we hear at the end of Florestan's aria; the oboe that traces the melody of the broken chords plays the very same notes that Florestan sings to the words "Leonoren, di Gattin, so gleich" (162; "Leonore, my wife, so like"). He sings of Leonore and identifies her in a series of likenesses. The likeness of which he sings may start with a picture of Leonore that he holds in his hand; Florestan's hope of freedom fastens on her. He expresses a desire for a literal reunion but, he intimates, even more, a heavenly one, for alone in his cell before she arrives there, he thinks he sees her, or thinks he sees an angel that looks like her. Likenesses proliferate. At the moment that Rocco confirms that the prisoner is asleep, not dead, the music plays the tune that keeps him alive: the dream of Leonore as rescuing angel. This dream of a wife represents her husband's freedom. Erich Schenk calls this oboe melody the "Leonore-motif" without mentioning that it is sung by Florestan;

the motif is attached to the fantasy-wife figuration. It identifies her as his. The music that bears the identity of Leonore is music that belongs to Florestan.[8]

This is the melody resounded in the Melodram, the one attached to Leonore as she is for Florestan, the Leonore that would make him whole, who would remove his chains (as she actually will do in the closing moments of the opera). Leonore is Florestan's wife: beneath the disguise is not Leonore in herself; her identity is bound to her status as his wife. A parallel can be drawn to "Fidelio"; the name allegorizes him—as fidelity, and in the masculine. What truth of identity this entails can be seen through another musical quotation in the Melodram: its final 6/8 section recalls an earlier duet between Fidelio and Rocco from the finale to act one (127). There Fidelio pledges to aid Rocco in digging the grave of the unjustly imprisoned man, a commitment that parallels what Fidelio has done just before when the prisoners were let out of their cells to enjoy a bit of sunlight that their rousing chorus addresses as "Freiheit." That word ecstatically ends Florestan's aria; freedom, the central value of Beethoven's opera, is played out on gendered terrain. What conjugal love can perform politically can be done only in the masculine. This is not the gender situation usually supposed in analyses of melodrama that attach its truth to the suffering woman, to oppressed forces of goodness and innocence that somehow overcome the oppression gendered masculine. For Leonore to act, she must act in the masculine. Fidelio lets the prisoners out of their cells. Fidelio descends to dig the grave. When Fidelio declares herself Florestan's wife, she has come to the end of this possibility. A trumpet sounds, a benign political figure appears; only he can do what a wife cannot.

....

In *Fidelio* we are in the world of the prisons of the ancien régime as seen in the post-Revolutionary period; the modern prison system—and with it, the system represented by Foucault as the new regimes of discipline and new regimes of identity—has yet to appear. Florestan's life is about to be taken in an act of punishment supposed possible only under tyranny. The opera represents this political plot in combination with a conjugal plot that looks ahead to modern regimes of identity. This domestic terrain complicates a clear cut before and after. As Isabel V. Hull argues, whereas marriage in the older system had reenacted forms of political domination, the modern separation of the domestic from the political institutes new regimes of identity that nonetheless function more as displacements than as replacements of the earlier regimes.[9] "We still have not cut off the head of the king": Foucault's pithy sentence in *The History of Sexuality* suggests that more is needed than cutting off the sovereign's head to end domination.[10] The prison in *Fidelio* is the immediate site of social injustice, not the social management of 1950s Hollywood melodrama, to be sure. But in both forms the relationship between the domestic and the political is not a matter of simple translation; the truth that speaks in melodrama is marked by the title Beethoven finally chose for his opera. In the duet with Rocco that follows the Melodram, Fidelio commits himself to the prisoner whose grave they have come to dig: "Whoever you are," she sings, "I will save you" ("Wer du auch sei'st, ich will dich retten," 171). However fleetingly, she commits herself at this moment not as a wife come to rescue her husband and restore him his freedom but as someone committed to freedom for anyone unjustly deprived of it. Anyone male, that is. The commitment voiced here is one only a man can make and act on. Through "Fidelio," the opera attempts to finesse the difference between the freedom Leonore can give her husband and the freedom Fidelio espouses. This universalizing "anyone" could be the expression of the hope that the new regime that replaces ancient tyranny will be one in which gendered difference will be no bar to freedom. If so, it founders: the erasure of gender difference imposes masculinity as if it were the absence of gender, thereby reimposing the problem it sought to solve.

The way that Leonore can secure her husband's freedom fulfills a Kantian paradigm of marriage: his freedom lies in the public sphere; her place is the domestic sphere to which the man relegates his sexual desire precisely so that he is free to act in the world.[11] Fidelio's ability to act, and to act on behalf of any man, is set within an understanding of gender difference that allies activity and political efficacy with men. Fidelio is not exactly a man, of course, although he is engaged to a woman and has been empowered to act alongside his future father-in-law precisely by securing himself a wife. (Marzelline's aria [no. 2] is about the hope for fulfillment in marriage, which, again, in a Kantian vein, represents the freedom a woman can have—to reign supreme at home.) The opera locates its action in the impossible space in which it might be possible for a woman to act in the public sphere; this is not

12 CHAPTER ONE

the space of clear-cut difference that Peter Brooks imagines as the force underlying the moral truth that melodrama reveals, and certainly not a space of clear-cut difference between male and female gender identity. The opera imagines the possibility of female heroism and of female agency and does that most gloriously musically in Leonore's big act one aria (no. 9, "Abscheulicher! Wo eilst du hin?"), in which, appalled by the monstrous villainy of the tyrant, she soars, for the first time, ferociously into soprano territory, freed from singing the alto line to Marzelline's soprano. These heroics, the aria concludes, are in the service of an inner drive ("inner'n Triebe") equated with the true love of a wife ("treuen Gattenliebe," 109–10). That inner drive, however, is a force that ultimately must divide the spheres of husband and wife, of female and male, differences that are suspended as long as the melodrama lasts. The thrill of hearing Leonore's voice ascend into soprano range has a great deal to do with its escape from confinement to the alto register. This vocal reversal of masculine and feminine could be compared to the musical inventiveness on display in the Melodram.

The ideological restrictions of *Fidelio*—the naturalization of Fidelio's love as wifely love — does not match what the music conveys in the exultant conclusion of the act one aria. Similarly, when Leonore and Florestan rejoin in act two, they sing of a joy without a name ("namenlose Freude," 210) constituted in their reunion; they sing of each other as husband and wife, but they do so singing exactly the same notes. At a moment like that, the music attempts to equate the two, making "nameless" the differentiating names of wife and husband, identifying them by way of an identification with each other in a shared joy-without-a-name. In their duet, the usual procedures of naming and differentiating that obtained in the first scenes of the opera, in which soprano and alto lines marked difference, are suspended. This is not the end of the opera, however, and such differences will recur as the opera comes to a close and Leonore is restored to wifely subordination even as she is hailed as savior of her husband's life.

The music continually offers a counterplot that exceeds the ideology of the opera. Thus, in her act one scene and aria, the ("male") heroism of Fidelio has to do with her transgression of the alto limit. This must remind us of the fact that, at least when the opera begins, the audience does not know that the woman singing a male part, wooing a woman, is someone else's wife. Indeed, the audience would not know whether the fact that a woman is singing means that the character is to be understood as female. A long-standing tradition of operatic casting is involved, one familiar to modern operagoers from Mozart's Cherubino or Strauss's Octavian. This is the convention of the so-called trouser role. This convention provides a critical reflection on gender difference and the nature of sexual desire, often infusing ostensible heterosexuality with a same-sex lesbian suggestiveness. The Melodram in *Fidelio* is the last moment in the opera fully to sustain the gender ambiguity of Fidelio. When Leonore stands up to Pizarro, thrusting herself before Florestan, offering her body to his blade, the gesture of declaring herself a wife also marks her limits as a wife: she can die for him; she cannot, by herself, rescue him. A trumpet sound stops Pizarro from killing Florestan. A deus ex machina is the only way out of the impasse.[12]

Jacques Derrida contemplates a version of this political dilemma in *Politics of Friendship*, deploring the equation of liberty, fraternity, and equality that works only in the masculine and which, according to him, taints the revolutionary promise with a suspect "virile homosexuality" that he hopes will not obtain in the heterosexual democracy of which he dreams.[13] Feminist music critics such as Susan McClary and Lawrence Kramer have deplored Beethoven for a mastery that they equate with a hypervirility; Adrienne Rich's powerful poem "The Ninth Symphony of Beethoven Understood at Last as a Sexual Message" could join this company.[14] There, the shouts of joy accompanying the call for brotherhood are read by Rich as an impotent and infertile cry of a man wrapped up in himself, hating women, loving men as he loves himself.

Introducing his Cambridge Opera Handbook on *Fidelio*, Paul Robinson lauds "the only opera by a composer, Beethoven, universally considered among the greatest in Western music" for its ability to transcend "the frivolity and exhibitionism endemic to opera." He writes: "Every listener senses the discrepancy between the domestic comedy (and light-weight idiom) with which the opera begins and the emotionally charged, musically resplendent political allegory with which it ends."[15] Robinson conveniently forgets how closely tied the allegory of political freedom is to a domestic situation, a domestic resolution that saves Fidelio from the same-sex frivolity of marriage to Marzelline by hitching Leonore to Florestan. Or, to be more exact, when he develops his point in "*Fidelio* and the French Revolution," the essay he contributed to the volume, Robinson does not forget this; rather, he insists

14 CHAPTER ONE

that the marriage of Leonore and Florestan is desexualized, "utterly untouched by eroticism. . . . Leonore and Florestan are well past the ardours of the first love. Theirs is essentially a companionship of the spirit. . . . In every meaningful musical and dramatic sense Beethoven treats her exactly as if she were a man. More precisely, he treats her as a generic human being."[16] It is not difficult to imagine what Rich would make of Robinson's analysis. And, given the fact that Robinson is not at all closeted (his most recent book is an unsympathetic account of gay conservatism and a brief for the politics of gay liberation), it is not difficult to see Derrida's thesis seemingly demonstrated as well. Robinson's "generic human" is nothing more than a universalized masculinity.[17]

Robinson's remarks echo the Kantian view of marriage as productive of an essential humanity that depends on a masculinized desexualization. He is certainly not offering a feminist critique of this paradigm. Nor does he seek to suggest a homoerotic possibility in what he calls the "generic human." Indeed, he insists that Leonore's transvestite performance is devoid of sexual interest, and rules out any possibility that Beethoven might be identifying his love for his nephew with her same-sex situation. Political liberation is, for Robinson, the real subject of Beethoven's opera—that is Leonore's true "ardour" and it has nothing to do with sex. Yet one has to wonder at this claim: it can't be just political ardor to which Marzelline responds, for example. Moreover, both Leonore and Florestan end their big arias by invoking the other in the most musically exultant passages. Is Leonore really bent on saving Florestan only out of a political commitment? Is there any way to separate her desire to free an unjustly imprisoned man from the desire to save her husband?

Robinson wants to void all questions of sexuality from the politics of the opera precisely so that the liberal political commitments he values can be extended to gays in a way that would evade Derrida's critique of a damaging homoerotics in liberal politics. If there is no sexual motivation for freedom, then brotherhood cannot be sexual either. Derrida distrusts such a claim because he assumes that a heterosexual democracy will preserve gender difference even as it will disable invidious hierarchies; translations of liberty and equality into the masculine are suspect not only because gender difference is erased but because that erasure glimpses the possibility that male same-sex desire could translate across gender. Robinson shares this worry: political desire, for him, needs to be desexualized so that homosexual and heterosexual desires remain distinct. He follows Kant, who desexualizes marriage and deplores same-sex sex; Kant fails to see the connection between desexualization (a universalism in the masculine) and same-sex sex that Derrida exposes.

There is a way around this impasse, but it depends precisely on a universalism that refuses the absolute difference of genders, the absolute difference of hetero- and homosexuality that Derrida and Kant and Robinson all suppose. This solution is glimpsed in the Melodram in *Fidelio*. Melodrama in general may depend on it. Robinson supposes that gay affirmation is a separatist, minoritarian, political position. For him all universalizing understandings of sexuality are politically conservative, voiding gay identity and identity politics; he is unable to grasp a nonidentitarian position or a politics that has broken with liberalism. To save the value of "freedom" for gay liberation that is separate from the sphere in which Beethoven's opera operates, Robinson denies any homoeroticism in Beethoven's opera, neither same-sex male nor same-sex female. But this places him in the contradictory position of affirming a liberal universalism that denies the very difference (majority/minority) on which it depends. Eve Kosofsky Sedgwick deftly parses this paradox in her essay "Making Gay Meanings": movements attached to identity politics "claim the right of seamless social assimilation for a group of people *on the basis* of a separatist understanding of them as embodying a stable ontological difference."[18] These complex relations between sexuality and politics underlie the exploration of melodrama that follows, in which, Sirk and Fassbinder and Haynes, I argue, move in the direction that Robinson cannot countenance — beyond minority, separatist identity; beyond liberalism as the model for politics. That movement presses on the contradictions in liberal ideology in which Beethoven's opera operates.

The Melodram is one privileged place in *Fidelio* in which we can see its contradictory seams quite fully exposed. Another locus might be the quartet in the first act (no. 3), composed in strict canonic form. Formally, that is, the four singers — bass Rocco, tenor Jaquino, alto Fidelio, and soprano Marzelline — must repeat each other. There is no room for them to diverge and thereby express what we might assume to be their individual true selves, their real and conflicting emotions. As everyone writing about the opera notices, the canon breaks away from the lighter musical modes that characterize the opening numbers, in which the love triangle of Marzelline-Jaquino-Fidelio is vocalized: noteworthy is the stillness and solemnity of the music along with its insistence on a form that refuses to individualize the singers. The spoken prompt into the quartet is Rocco's claim to be able to see what is in the hearts of the young people. He presumes, that is, the kind of equation between "inner drive" and heterosexual desire that we find explicitly stated at the end of Leonore and Florestan's arias later. But, as we have already seen, those desires seem denaturalized in the opera. The canon denaturalizes that assumption musically as well; Jaquino's disappointment at having lost Marzelline's affections, and Fidelio's dilemma, having succeeded with her, get expressed identically; they are in line with Marzelline's opening of the canon as she expresses her wonder at having gotten just what she desires, and with Rocco's complacent vision of their forthcoming marriage.

What gets voiced in the quartet in repeated soundings of the same musical line is something like the impossibility that Elsaesser notices in Sirk's *Written on the Wind* (1956), where "Dorothy Malone wants Rock Hudson who wants Lauren Bacall who wants Robert Stack who just wants to die."[19] In the canon, impossible realization and the impossibility to realize are voiced as if they were identical. The wonder of getting what you think you want and the misery of not getting it are equated. There is no bottom-line real in such an equation. The hollowness of human experience is nonetheless borne by a musical form rich in its complexity and sonority. Its stillness seems to glimpse another world, possibilities that go beyond the impasses and show them not to be impasses. Whereas the Melodram brings music to a crisis of continual reinvention, the canonic form of the quartet makes resolution and impossibility coincide.

....

At this moment, I am reminded of Anne Carson's brief essay "Why I Wrote Two Plays about Phaidra by Euripides" (2006), included in *Grief Lessons*, her translations of four Euripides plays.[20] In her essay, Carson ventriloquizes Euripides, who attempts to fathom the nature of desire: "What is the question of desire? I don't know. Something about its presumption to exist in human forms. Human forms are puny. Desire is vast. Vast, absolute and oddly *general*."[21]

In his book-length interview with Jon Halliday, Douglas Sirk notes that several of his own 1930s German films were "melodramas in the sense of music + drama." Sirk claims that a precedent for his 1950s Universal Studio melodramas can be found as far back as classical Greek drama: "Aeschylus and Sophocles wrote plenty of melodramas."[22] This observation about plot, as Kaleva notes in her essay on Beethoven and melodrama, also applies to the formal structure we have been exploring: "The underlining of dramatic text with music had been part of theatrical performances before the eighteenth century, the earliest example of which is a form of melodrama in Greek drama called *parakatalogue*."[23] (In this context it is worth recalling that the earliest films—so-called silent movies—were accompanied by music.) Sirk does not mention this formal feature in Greek tragedy, nor does he have much more to say about Aeschylus and Sophocles. The dramatist that claims his attention is Euripides, and the play that comes to his mind more than once is *Alcestis*. "Let me just refresh your memory about the play," he says to Halliday: "a king is about to die; his wife, Alcestis, who loves him very much, offers herself instead. Death is satisfied. The husband hesitates. If he accepts he is ruined. If he doesn't he is dead. It is an impossible situation."[24]

Sirk's plot summary (which is not quite accurate) must remind us of *Fidelio*, although he has in mind his own melodramas, *Magnificent Obsession* (1953) in particular. There, playboy Bob Merrick (Rock Hudson) is first responsible for the death of a Dr. Philips, then for the blinding of his wife, Helen (Jane Wyman). Impossibly, Hudson and Wyman's characters fall in love; impossibly, Merrick reforms, becomes an eye surgeon, and restores her sight. The impossible situation for which Sirk appeals to Euripides for a precedent is this: to accept love from the person responsible for such grief. In Euripides, as Sirk points out, the solution to the dilemma that Admetus faces in accepting his wife's sacrifice is found when "the god steps out of his machine" and restores her to him.[25] In his own films, Sirk says, the happy ending tacked on to *Magnificent Obsession*—and not just that film, but *All That Heaven Allows* (1955), *Written on the Wind* (1956), and *Imitation of Life* (1959) as well— is just such a deus ex machina; if some in the audience are happy for the promise of happiness, those in the know know better. Much the same

18 CHAPTER ONE

can be said for the ending of *Fidelio*. The joyful reunion of the couple and the freeing of Florestan returns Leonore to a future in which she will be his faithful wife, celebrated for her willingness to sacrifice her status and gender. The freedom that the opera extols returns her to her place.

Euripides's *Alcestis* illuminates this ending. In the play, King Admetus has been spared from dying thanks to the gratitude of Apollo to his "host / and friend, Admetus" (7–8), who "revered [his] sacred rights" (11).[26] Admetus has extended hospitality to Apollo, and Apollo repays him by striking the bargain that Death accepts, allowing someone to die in the king's place. It is not Apollo, however, who brings Alcestis back from death, but Hercules, and, again, in thanks for an act of hospitality. Admetus is thereby saved from the consequence of allowing Alcestis to die in his place, the shame of having accepted her sacrifice. Only after she dies does he see this, voicing it as what others will say about him: "Look at the man, disgracefully alive, who dared / not die, but like a coward gave his wife instead / and so escaped death. Do you call him a man at all?" (955–57).

The glory of Alcestis is to be a wife who would die for her husband; what she would do, she does, dying a third of the way into the play. At just that point, Hercules arrives, seeking hospitality; Admetus is in a difficult position since the death of his wife precludes the offer of hospitality, but to deny hospitality to Hercules would only add to what might be said against him and would, moreover, not relieve him of his loss, as he tells the Chorus: "My misery would still have been / as great, and I should be inhospitable too, / and there would be one more misfortune added to those / I have, if my house is called unfriendly to its friends" (555–58).

His solution is to prevaricate with Hercules, keeping him from knowing who has died, and thus opening a space between his wife's promise to die for him and its accomplishment. "Being and nonbeing are considered different things," Hercules insists to him (528), but Admetus denies the difference. Later, after Admetus experiences the shame of letting his wife die, Hercules learns that Alcestis has died and decides to defeat death in order to reward Admetus for his extraordinary hospitality. He gives Admetus a veiled woman he has won for him, a woman who, when uncovered, looks exactly like Alcestis — she is Alcestis, Hercules insists. The woman remains silent as the play ends.

Richmond Lattimore, in the preface to his translation of the play, claims that its theme "is not 'if a wife dies for her husband, how brave and devoted the wife,' so much as 'if a husband lets his wife die for him, what manner of man must the husband be?'"[27] The solution of the play rewards Admetus for *xenia*, Lattimore explains, a term that refers to his civilized, hospitable, and reverent behavior. What Lattimore does not say is that this form of sociality is one that takes place between men; a wife could be sacrificed for this, and she could as readily be saved as a token of what men will do for each other. What form is Euripides's drama? (It is his earliest extant play, we might note.) Lattimore calls it a tragicomedy.[28] In the preface to her radically stripped-down translation of *Alkestis*, Anne Carson does not settle on a name for it. Comparing the play to Hitchcock's *Shadow of a Doubt* (1943), she writes that "both works explore the psychological weirdness of ordinary people and everyday existence by jarring comic and tragic effects against one another as if they belonged to the same convention. In fact no one knows what convention *Alkestis* belongs to."[29] Perhaps "melodrama" is the name of the convention. At the end of *Alkestis*, as Carson goes on to say, we do not know whether or not the woman brought to Admetus is his resurrected wife, nor, if she is, whether a happy ending lies ahead.

Swept up into the political joy of the final measures of *Fidelio*, with everyone extolling the wife who has saved her husband and won him his freedom, Leonore savors the extraordinary moment at which she has arrived. Her love has been rewarded by God, she believes. Florestan is hers again; everyone celebrates the freedom she has given him. As much as in Euripides, the solution of the play, while couched in the tones of comedy — Beethoven hammers out C-major chords with abandon — remains disquieting when one thinks about what lies ahead. "In the Hollywood melodrama characters made for operetta play out the tragedies of humankind," Elsaesser comments.[30] The formula is perhaps reversed in Euripides. Beethoven begins his opera in the world of operetta, formally in its speech-song separations, and in its plot, where a woman has unknowingly become betrothed to another woman; marriage is being played for laughs or for untoward titillation. *Fidelio* concludes with the happy ending that marks the end of the trouser role of Fidelio, marriage played for keeps, the male drama of freedom and humanity sutured onto domestic propriety. Leonore assumes the fantasy position of savior, when the force she calls God, and who, in the opera, is represented by the minister Fernando, has saved Florestan and ended the reign of political tyranny. The formal use of melodrama in the opera brings to a point of crisis the ideologies of gender and sexuality that the happy ending glosses. In the Melodram, neither speech alone nor song is apt; resolution is momentary. The ending of the opera leaves ahead the possibility of reflection and critical distance that Sirk claimed for melodrama by way of Euripides:

> Many are the shapes of things divine.
> Many are the unexpected acts of gods.
> What we imagined did not come to pass—
> God found a way to be surprising.
> That's how this went.[31]

TWO

IDENTITY AND IDENTIFICATION

Sirk–Fassbinder–Haynes

"It is an impossible situation," Douglas Sirk says to Jon Halliday, glossing his melodramatic practice by way of the example of Euripides's *Alcestis*.[1] Sirk was attached to this example; in an interview with Mark Shivas he quickly alludes to *Alcestis* in discussing what he terms the metaphysical quality of the theme of one person dying for another in *Magnificent Obsession* (1953).[2] Theorizing his film practice by way of an example from literature points to Sirk's literariness, but, even more, it points to the remediated nature of his melodramatic practice. With Halliday, he lists novelists he considers to have influenced him: Melville, James, Faulkner, Nabokov, Kafka, and Flaubert, among others. Plays abound, too. Before he became a film director, Sirk worked in the theater, directing contemporary plays (Brecht, for example) along with classics such as Shakespeare. (In 1922 he translated Shakespeare's sonnets into German.) "For some time I didn't know whether I wanted to be a painter, a theatre man, or a writer" (18), he explains, tallying his multiple ambitions.

Rainer Werner Fassbinder sustained a similar range; like Sirk, he was a theater director. He also wrote his own screenplays and acted in many of his films. Todd Haynes, too, writes his own screenplays. He made a film when he was in high school, *The Suicide* (1978); in college at Brown, he was known as a painter.[3] Nonetheless, in 1985, the year he graduated, he made what is usually considered his first film, the twenty-minute *Assassins: A Film Concerning Rimbaud*—by its title, a literary venture as well.

For Sirk, sustaining all these possibilities was not possible. In an interview from 1980 included in Eckhart Schmidt's documentary *From UFA to Hollywood: Douglas Sirk Remembers* (1991), Sirk insists on their differences, intent especially on the different kind of acting required in theater and film; with Halliday he insists that film is ultimately a visual and not a literary endeavor: "You have to write with the camera" (97). Likewise, talking to Schmidt, he details how certain scenes in *Written on the Wind* (1956) or *The Tarnished Angels* (1957) had to be wordless in order to convey better what he aimed at.[4] Even though Sirk distinguishes film and theater, writing and filming, his metaphor of the writing camera suggests the intermediate, intermedial conjunction of film and writing in his melodramas, a quality I consider crucial to melodrama. "[Camera] angles are the director's thoughts. The lighting is his philosophy," Sirk avers to Halliday (40). Drawing a parallel between his distrust of language and Wittgenstein's, filming becomes a way of philosophizing. Sirk's acute awareness of the relations—antithetic and not—between and among media connects the "impossible situation" central to the thematics of his melodramas to their stylistic aims, which involve the impossible task of overcoming differences that remain insuperable. As he says in his interview with Schmidt, doing this created his style. Declining to define it any further, he notes that Fassbinder got it (indeed, Sirk claims, shared this aesthetic): it amounts to a certain "imponderable quality."

Sirk offers an instance of what shaped his aesthetic when he describes to Halliday his own experience with *Magnificent Obsession*. Handed this studio assignment, his first response was "bewilderment and discouragement," but then "something irrational" in it grabbed his attention. He found himself compelled by the "structural irony" of the "blindness of the woman," blind to the fact that she loves the man responsible for her husband's death. Her blindness is literalized and ultimately cured by the man who caused it, delivering her finally to the "happy ending" of knowingly accepting that impossible love, a love founded in an antipathy from which it cannot be separated. "Antinomy" (95) is Sirk's word for this compelling structure, a metaphysical term that applies both to what happens in the film and to Sirk in his double response to its plot. Its metaphysics is immanent, conveyed by the motion of the camera, which, Sirk claims to Halliday, is emotion (43). This correlates with his use of objects in his films — statues and mirrors, for example: "The point is there is no such thing as a dead thing and a live thing" (79). The point about this point about objects, persons, and the camera's correlation of them is that it posits a relationship between the absolute opposition of life and death; this is the metaphysical location of the impossible situation.

"People shouldn't be what in German is called *eindeutig*," Sirk said (Halliday, 70). *Eindeutig*: unequivocal, unambiguous, unmistakable, singular in meaning, self-identical. It seems significant that Sirk describes his notion of identity through a German word, as if what he has to say escapes the singularity of a language.[5] "Intermediate" is the English term perhaps used most often in conversation with Halliday, although "split" and "in-between" also recur as terms for nonsingular identity. He exemplifies this type in conversation with Schmidt through his first star, Zarah Leander: she presented an overwhelming feminine, maternal quality coupled with a deep masculine voice and raunchy talk that nonplused him. In her gendered contradictions Sirk saw Leander's star quality. So, too, when he discovered Rock Hudson, he found that the camera could hold before the film viewer a lived impossibility. To Sirk's eye, Hudson was not much more than handsome, "but the camera sees with its own eye. It sees things the human eye does not detect. . . . And it was not wrong about Hudson" (Halliday, 86–87). Sirk does not say what the camera saw, although presumably it was akin to what Sirk discerned in Leander. More than that, it sees what would go unnoticed; the camera catches a life best apprehended by its nonhuman eye. The camera can see this best because this is the life it shares, one that refuses the alive/dead distinction. A moving connection, a life in which humans participate but which exceeds the human. Melodramas may convey the message that "you can't escape what you are" (130), but what you are is not one thing.

Sirk felt that Fassbinder understood these antinomies. In the obituary he wrote for the young filmmaker, dead at thirty-seven, Sirk celebrated him in just these terms.[6] Hailing the "indestructible" creativity that survives his untimely death, Sirk spends most of the obituary recalling his first meeting with Fassbinder a decade or so before his death in 1982. He recounts their conversation about the astonishing productivity of Lope de Vega and Calderon coupled with their scrupulous attention to form and language and Fassbinder's response: "That's the kind of creativity I'm after, too." Fassbinder achieved that goal, Sirk avers, making some forty films in about a dozen years "as great in form as they are in theme." The theme to which Sirk points, "the human being, in all his contradictions and wounded grandeur," names through contradiction the shared terrain of the two filmmakers. That's what may guarantee their afterlife: "Only work that is able to stand up to controversy has the strength to endure. The drama inherent in this counterpoint of controversy and contradiction is what gave birth to and is able to explain the great passion of his work." The antinomies that give their films form and theme live beyond them in the failed reception that is the sign of success. Such life inhabits the constrained possibilities that determine social life or the life span of an individual. Sirk, over eighty years old, hails his colleague, dead at less than half his age, for a career of contradiction and controversy that he hopes will prove inextinguishable.

What Sirk saw in Fassbinder, Fassbinder saw in Sirk.

In "Imitation of Life: On the Films of Douglas Sirk," Fassbinder wrote about the six films of Sirk that he had seen at a recent retrospective.[7] He opens his essay alluding to Sirk's notion that camera angles are a philosophical expression, struck, too, by Sirk's metaphysical idea that it is from things and people that films get at the truth about life. As he reviews each of the films, Fassbinder lights on fundamental productive contradictions. Thus, of *All That Heaven Allows* (1955), he writes: "Human beings can't be alone, but they can't be together either" (79). *Written on the Wind* he sums up as a series of encounters at cross-purposes and deflections; *Interlude* (1956) reveals that "the only one who has experienced fulfillment is done in by it" (84). *The Tarnished Angels* offers nothing but defeats and therefore the grounds for a life of illusion, a theme heightened in *A Time to Love and a Time to Die* (1957) — "without war there wouldn't be any love" (87). This is a point consolidated in the last film Fassbinder discusses, Sirk's final Universal melodrama, *Imitation of Life* (1959); its title names the double prospect of impossible life: "The mother who wants to possess her child because she loves her is brutal. And Sarah Jane is defending herself against her mother's terrorism, the world's terrorism. That's cruel; you can understand both of them, and both of them are right, and no one will ever be able to help either of them. Unless, of course, we change the world" (89). Changing the world opens the critical relationship to

26 CHAPTER TWO

the real that the film makes available. As Fassbinder notes about *All That Heaven Allows*, Sirk rarely invites identification by way of close-ups or the convention of shot/reverse shot that affirms point of view. Rather, it is mise-en-scène — music, color, lighting — that makes manifest the strangeness of what otherwise might be supposed the naturalness of social life. By having us see what the camera sees, "Douglas Sirk's films liberate the mind" (83). They show the constraints of the life seen as all constraining. Such films defeat the viewer's expectations and create a dissatisfaction for those who expect mimesis and reality confirmation. Out of that dissatisfaction, thinking arises. Indeed, thinking is to be seen in Sirk's films, Fassbinder insists, most notably in their women: "In Douglas Sirk's movies the women think" (81).

These claims about Sirk also articulate Fassbinder's aims as a filmmaker: what he says in an interview about his first feature-length film, *Love Is Colder Than Death* (1969), could be said about any of his films: "My film isn't supposed to let feelings people already have be neutralized or soaked up; instead, the film should create new feelings" (7). The point about these new feelings must be that they can be had even by people who don't know they have them; new feelings become possible by inducing discomfort with the familiar, by refusing those neutral and naturalized reactions." What is "new" is, at the same time, always already there.

Such relationality bound Fassbinder and Sirk. From his encounter with Sirk, Fassbinder saw that he could make personal films that might nonetheless claim a public: "Anything that I pass on truthfully has to be valid for other people, because my way of seeing things may have a different setting from other people's, but ultimately they're the same experiences" (41). The discovery of sameness in difference (Sirk's and Fassbinder's) is explicitly posed in the name of the personal and against a universalism of sameness without difference, the regimentation of the social. This "personal" is curiously impersonal. It is key to the stylistic identification of Sirk and Fassbinder. It is key to melodrama.

Finding terms for this relationship, Fassbinder rejected the notion that he and Sirk formed some kind of a father-son pairing. As with style, here, too, explicit terms are not offered. We might find them in how Fassbinder described his relationship to Alfred Döblin's *Berlin Alexanderplatz* (1929), a book Fassbinder read first in adolescence and that was the basis for his late project, a fourteen-episode TV version of the novel. On first reading, the novel helped him deal with his same-sex desires, he reports; reading it again several years later, Fassbinder recognized it had done more than that: "It became clearer and clearer to me that a huge part of myself, of my behavior, my reactions, many things I had considered part of me, were nothing more than things described by Döblin in *Berlin Alexanderplatz*" (162). This realization upset him at first—the recognition that his life was an imitation—and then had just the opposite effect, offering a key to what might be termed identity in an identification that exceeds self-identity. Fassbinder explicitly registers this in his films when he plays the parts of characters named Franz, sometimes indeed bearing the full name of Döblin's protagonist Franz Biberkopf. What this identification amounts to Fassbinder suggests best in parsing the relationship between Biberkopf and Reinhold. It is not a homosexual relationship, he insists, even if Reinhold does have sex with boys when he is in prison: "No, what exists between Franz and Reinhold is nothing more or less than a pure love that society can't touch" (161). Except, since the two are creatures of society, they are unable to realize this love for which terms are necessarily lacking. It is this love without a name that also is the basis of the identification of Fassbinder and Sirk, I would venture.[8]

Concluding his essay on Sirk, Fassbinder writes: "I've seen far too few of his films. I'd like to see all thirty-nine of them. Then maybe I'd be farther along, with myself, with my life, with my friends. I've seen six films by Douglas Sirk. Among them were the most beautiful in the world" (89). I don't know whether Fassbinder ever saw them all, but I'm struck by the odd coincidence that he and Sirk made roughly the same number of films. It is entirely likely that Todd Haynes has seen them all, fulfilling Fassbinder's desire. Indeed, if you have read Haynes on Sirk and Fassbinder, you might think he wrote the discussion you just read. That shared critical project—that sameness in difference—is what preoccupies me in the opening section of this chapter as I begin to articulate what ties together the melodramas of Sirk, Fassbinder, and Haynes through these overt gestures of identification.

In an interview with Haynes in *Bright Lights Film Journal*, Julia Leyda quotes sentences from Fassbinder's account of *Imitation of Life* that I just quoted, on the impossible situation that binds Annie and Sarah Jane. "That's one of my very favorite passages," Haynes tells her.[9] Leyda might have known that it was a favorite, or known to quote the passage, be-

28 CHAPTER TWO

cause Haynes himself does that in the "Director's Statement" about *Far from Heaven* (2002) that he included in the publication of the screenplay. With Leyda he adds the affective charge: "You do understand all the sides, and it kills you." But, however much it kills you, it doesn't stop there: "Society is not let off the hook." As Haynes avers—by way of Thomas Elsaesser (his essay on family melodrama guides Haynes as much as it does me)—melodrama shows us people not up to the situations in which they are caught. And the effects of this are complicated as Haynes outlines in his "Director's Statement": social constraint and yet "something larger"; social critique and yet recognition; intellectual distance and yet empathetic identification.[10] Neither being caught nor escape is possible. Both are.

Haynes has read the same theorists I have, consulted the same sources, and is struck, as I am, by the productive possibilities in the impossible situation that remains impossible. The "Director's Statement" exemplifies this when Haynes quotes Fassbinder on Sirk's ability to show women thinking. "Fassbinder . . . also loved Sirk," Haynes remarks, introducing the citation, and it is clear that he does, too, and not just from *Far from Heaven*, which was conceived as a tribute to Sirk.[11] Nonetheless, asked by Noel Murray in a 2007 interview what filmmaker he would like to have been if he could have been any, Haynes replies, Fassbinder, "his career blows my mind."[12]

Haynes, who writes his own screenplays, also offers commentary about them as well as about films by Max Ophüls and Fassbinder on DVDs and in his numerous interviews. He writes (and talks) in an academic vein; this is not at all surprising given his education in what was then called the semiotics program at Brown. His introduction to three of his screenplays closes by quoting one of his teachers there, Mary Ann Doane—a theorist, of course, of women's films (the classification that Sirk's melodramas fall under in feminist film theory). Haynes quotes her writing about him in the introductory essay she contributed to an issue of *Camera Obscura* devoted to Haynes: "Mise-en-scene, music, and lighting absorb the function of signifying interiority."[13] Here she might be quoting Fassbinder on Sirk, "The moviegoer's intense emotion doesn't come from identification but from the montage and the music" (80). Haynes's own comment on Doane points in this direction: "The best melodramas reveal how social—how 'political'—our feelings can be." That's how Fassbinder understood Sirk. But like him he also testifies to the unutterable beauty of his films. Haynes ends his "Director's Statement" contemplating "the most beautiful melodramas," in which Sirk's are to be included.[14]

This circuit of cross-citation conjures up citations in my discussion so far. It is not just that we are all trying to say the same difficult thing. For one thing (and by no means a small thing), Sirk, Fassbinder, and Haynes are not just theorists of film; they are filmmakers. Besides their words there are their films, and they don't simply translate into the words that they — or anyone — might write. Moreover, these gestures toward a terrain of complex intellectual, emotional, visual, social, and political relationships (the relationality that is encompassed in "love" in all the registers in which it is invoked), however much they share in linguistic formulation, are not identical — neither verbally nor as verbal equivalents for the films they seek to describe. Nor is "theory" one thing. A striking instance to put beside the remarkable theorization that Haynes displays in recent interviews and writing might be his one academic publication, an article titled "Homoaesthetics and *Querelle*," published in 1985 (at the end of his undergraduate years) in the third issue of *subjects/objects*, a short-lived journal produced under the aegis of the Brown semiotics program.[15] The *Querelle* in question is Genet's novel and, even more, Fassbinder's film, his last. Haynes, writing just a few years after Fassbinder's death, works in this essay to articulate an aesthetics that, arguably, remains his, and that also is Fassbinder's and Sirk's.

In this piece, Haynes was trying to articulate a homoaesthetics that had not yet emerged "despite the fact that much European theory has come from (predominantly male) homosexual writers," he notes.[16] Haynes names no names but presumably has Barthes and Foucault in mind; if such theories were already articulated, it would take work written later — D. A. Miller's *Bringing Out Roland Barthes*, for instance — to show that. That "later" is incipient in 1985; to unearth this earlier moment when his writing touches on Fassbinder, who was already mesmerizing him — this moment when Haynes is barely a filmmaker, more a committed abstract painter, and, at least in this essay, a budding academic — might be valuable, since in trying to find terms for what does not yet exist his essay perhaps suggests what still remains now "after queer theory." What remains is a radical theory, radical in the sense of a root. "Something about *queer* is inextinguishable," Eve Kosofsky Sedgwick wrote in the foreword to *Tendencies*, at the first moment when the term was gaining currency; its passing, its dispersal from its root attachments, therefore, also could be glimpsed, as Haynes himself did in his 1993 interview with Justin Wyatt.[17] To go back to Haynes in 1985 provides a way here to theorize melodrama as homoaesthetics; it lets sexuality enter the conversation a bit more overtly, if still within the necessary obliquities of 1985, an obliquity that is not tied to that date, however.

The Haynes struck by Fassbinder's claim that in Sirk women think seeks to articulate a theory of homoaesthetics (and of homosexuality) by way of feminist theory (Julia Kristeva especially, Luce Irigaray as well) and by way of elisions and provocations in the work of Gilles Deleuze and Félix Guattari and Jean-François Lyotard. From Kristeva's parsing of the possibility that feminism might do more than claim for itself the power it decries in the masculine — the possibility, that is, that feminism might do more than reinscribe or simply reverse binaries — Haynes seizes on what he nonetheless finds disturbing in her radical provocation; he describes it as "a sort of religious submission to certain governing divisions by way of an identification with division itself." What is disturbing about this, as Haynes notes toward the end of his essay, is the danger that it might reinscribe real women in a position of submission identical to their placement in the systems of domination feminism opposes. The possibility in this impossibility, however, lies in overcoming difference (sexual difference, gender) by seeing that the poles of domination and submission are not simply a reiteration of the difference male/female. Homoaesthetics would begin, Haynes avers, by seizing on "the discovery of an interiorized difference within all subjects."[18] Against the absoluteness of the binarisms, there would be the division in the terms themselves. Identification would be not along the lines of identity but in the track of those divisions.

Haynes thus argues for a disengagement of the term *woman* from its referent "woman" ("her *real* social existence") and its transfer to the male — to Querelle in Fassbinder's film — as he is put in the female position, as object of the gaze, male and female, the one to be fucked. (Such arguments might recall Judith Butler or Leo Bersani, but Haynes couldn't have read *Gender Trouble* or "Is the Rectum a Grave"; they had not yet been published.) For male to become female is not to become woman but to enter into the differentially shared space of self-division.

This embrace of the non-self-identical is reminiscent of Sirk's refusal of the eindeutig. Haynes attaches his theory of becoming-woman to Guattari's, "a state of *always* becoming and *never being* a woman," a state of *real* impossibility for a man and yet an ineradicable possibility because of a foundational self-division. Guattari's theorization of this, Haynes notes, reinscribes binarisms (including the hetero/homo divide) that Haynes seeks to radicalize — and to metaphysicalize: "*Being*, that infamous human catastrophe, is nonetheless an unavoidable catastrophe." So becoming must *always* be becoming: "Binarisms are neither collapsed nor separated, but *swallowed whole*, identified with according to their duality, their split." Rather than the embrace of a dualism, Haynes advocates a necessary identification with the split, with division.[19]

Equations within a same that is self-different further explains Kristevan submission: this quasi-religious submission to the overwhelming force that is represented by the desire to dominate or be dominated may look like the familiar terrain of sadomasochism, of male domination of the female, but, as Haynes notes by way of Lyotard — who offers male exemplars of this supposed female submission (Jesus, for a prime example; Schreber, for another) — it is, rather, what it means to submit to desire. This further explains why Haynes is drawn to that moment in Fassbinder when he distinguishes Sirk as a filmmaker whose women think. For it is by thinking "woman" that Haynes arrives at the homoaesthetics of Fassbinder: "In Fassbinder . . . women are consistently of central concern, and homosexuality, rarely asserted" (*Querelle* is one of those rare exceptions). "Everyone — women, men, gay or straight — is subject to the same." So the scene of sadomasochism is that of the child being beaten with its mobile identifications. Domination of the symbolic order (to speak in the psychoanalytic register in which Haynes writes) is inevitable. But that order also fails to secure the differences on which it rests. Hence the doubling in the film; hence the dividing of the subject. So, anticipating Lee Edelman's *No Future*, Haynes delivers his queer and now by way of the death drive. It tells us "there is no me, no ego." Identification without an I: *I'm Not There*.[20] Instead of Bob Dylan, Fassbinder sets Oscar Wilde to music, "Each Man Kills the Thing He Loves," and has the one actual woman in the film sing those lines. Haynes thinks her song marks her exclusion, but the logic of a homoaesthetics of identification through difference well might put that reinscription of sexual difference into question.[21]

It certainly raises questions central to melodrama. Identification is the nexus of complication in melodramatic representations as well as in their reception. As Haynes remarks in his interview with Julia Leyda, melodrama may be assumed to feature a split between the dastardly villain and the innocent woman tied to the railroad tracks (the Peter Brooks scenario, not that he is mentioned), but that is not the kind of melodrama Haynes makes; nor did Sirk, he goes on to say (following Elsaesser)—nor did Fassbinder, I might add, sure that Haynes would agree.[22] Manichean division is not what melodrama offers, but rather the refusal of the eindeutig, the singular. If so, identification is never simple. Introducing the book that contains his screenplays of *Far from Heaven*, *Safe* (1995), and *Superstar: The Karen Carpenter Story* (1988), Haynes quips, "These are my women's films." He pauses to note the importance of feminism that his undergraduate essay documents, to note it lest we think his remark smacks of appropriation—*my* women's films—or because of just the opposite, an ironization of *my* in his further description of the three films as "sisters" to each other, testaments to *their* feminism, a lesbian utopics not his own. He continues: "For me, everything that I questioned about what it meant to be a man—and how much my sexuality would perpetually challenge those meanings—could be found in arguments posed by feminists. What can I say? I identified."[23] That sentence is as disarming as the claim that these are his "women's films." What does it mean to identify?

As Haynes goes on to say (and reiterate in interviews), this is the crucial question in his films, and a crucial question in melodrama. Personal questions that don't exactly remain personal. The question is not simply how he identifies or how we identify, "but identification itself."[24] Identity, Haynes reminds his reader, comes from identification. This is what psychoanalysis insists; feminist film theory as well. Mirror stages. Identification along the lines of identity is, for Haynes, as bleak a prospect as the human catastrophe of being inscribed in Being. As he told Justin Wyatt, this is what we experience in most films (the ones that have the largest audiences), those that give in to "this awful sick need to replicate yourself and make a double in the creation of a narrative. It's the horrible mirroring of the need to affirm who we are." He hates it, and it is inescapable. The answer to this (and to the theory that finds no possibility in impossibility) is a question: "What would happen if this procedure were interrupted"?[25] That is what he does in his films.

In his first feature film, *Poison* (1990), three narrative lines, in three different styles and genres, complicate each other. Haynes might well have included the screenplay along with the three so-called women's films: its Genet-inspired section also is inspired by Fassbinder's *Querelle* and by the becoming-woman of its homoaesthetics. *Superstar*, included as a "women's film," is also the first in a trilogy of "musicals" that includes *Velvet Goldmine* (1998) and *I'm Not There* (2007); their music makes overt a remediation that affects the generic and gendered definitions of melodrama. (I discussed this topic in chapter 1, on *Fidelio*, and will turn to it again in the second part of this book.) Moreover, in *Superstar*, Karen Carpenter's story is told by Barbie dolls, an effect of distantiation that reinvents the possibility of "investment" by holding firm to a story line that demands it, "carefully embracing a well-known genre . . . the desire to identify could even succumb to an ensemble of plastic."[26] Plastic: the utterly artificial, the totally nonliving. In this film, that is where life and art meet. *Safe*, in contrast, refuses to play it safe by using genre against itself, making utterly opaque how to read the film and its (and our) investments. It prompts the other questions Haynes raises about interrupted identification: Will stopping or impeding that automatic and inescapable process allow us to see it happening? Will it enable a critical distance from the inescapable process? Can we go on feeling—identifying and therefore being—even as we are thinking? Haynes writes, "But what would happen if this procedure were interrupted, if the narrative gears subsumed by our identification were quietly revealed? Would blowing their cover necessarily destroy our emotional connection? Or is our need to identify strong enough to bend, strong enough even to allow a glimpse of *how* we're feeling what we're feeling—even while we're feeling it?"[27]

These are the self-reflective, self-dividing questions melodrama addresses, and that Haynes, in his various experiments with the form, explores. As Haynes formulates it (in terms that can't help but remind us of Sirk and Fassbinder, can't help doing that if only because Haynes repeatedly invokes them as exemplary), identification is located at the complicated nexus where submitting to the inexorable is coupled with resistance. Identification involves a process of coming to identify by experiencing ourselves located outside us: this process of feeling-with, of identifying-as, thus involves being ourselves by not being ourselves. We are made by and in the "narrative gears" in which the very force that creates identity by identification is strong enough to dismantle itself along the route of the non-self-identical through which identity is made. In *Far from Heaven*, as Haynes tells Julia Leyda, the way to do this lies in a "diagrammatic narrative" whose very geometries belie what otherwise looks like nothing more than a remake in the classic style of Sirk's Hollywood melodrama.[28] "Style," however, as Haynes affirms in the introduction to his three women's films, is the word for melodrama's way beyond words. "In *Far From Heaven* the love and pain depicted is almost too big for any single character to contain. So it spills into the music, the wardrobe, the decor, the colors and shadows on the screen."[29] What it spills into is where it arises from, something impersonal, relational, nonverbal.

This is the life that film attempts to grasp, a life beyond the limits and constraints of the social—our constrained social existence, bound to the categories of identity: "I've always felt that viewers of film have extraordinary powers. They can make life out of reflections on the wall."[30] Haynes testifies to a belief he shares with Fassbinder and Sirk. This extraordinary power is what melodrama offers in its view of the impasses of the ordinary. This is the life too large for anyone to endure. Sex, or the unbearable, we could say with Lauren Berlant and Lee Edelman, insofar as sex—in its refusals of identity, in its utopic attempts at relationality—names the locus for the discovery of what we want and its impossibility. Sex exceeds the identities that constrain us and mark us as social beings to which "our need to identify" clings. Melodrama, Haynes avers with Fassbinder, can't change the world, but it can change our perception and experience of the world. "If it has a message to proclaim it's always, at the very least, a supremely mixed one." Our succumbing and submission to the social is "supremely mixed" with submissions to excessive desires that exceed even those constraints: "The most beautiful melodramas, like those of Sirk and Ophuls, are the ones that show how the worlds in which those characters live—and the happy endings foisted on them—are wrong. And like all those shimmering objects crowding the screen, the answer always lies in what's missing."[31] What's missing? Haynes declines to say. If it is missing there is no word for it. Melodrama inhabits this locale, a space in whose extraordinary negations arise further questions, inarticulate inextinguishable feelings, the possibilities of impossibility.

Melodramatic Relations and the Real

"Revolution doesn't belong on the cinema screen, but outside, in the world." Haynes endorses this quotation from Fassbinder on the final page of the introduction to his three women's films.[32] Fassbinder does not aim to show how things should be, but to reveal the mechanisms of the real. He eschews didacticism. What the screen shows is neither a realistic view of the world nor some utopic projection of a world transformed. "Movies are basically nothing until we bring an emotional life to them," is how Haynes has put the point in an interview with Amy Kroin.[33] Neither filmmaker is interested in making films that look "real": filmic realism is itself a set of conventions (embodied in method acting and its supposition that everything arises from the individual psyche); Haynes, like the filmmakers he follows, aims for another kind of real, the real that melodrama plumbs by its immersion of characters and their interiority in a mise-en-scène that exceeds the individual.

The three films that most overtly declare the relationship between Haynes and Fassbinder and Sirk—the series *All That Heaven Allows, Ali: Fear Eats the Soul (Angst Essen Seele Auf*, 1974), and *Far from Heaven* that will concern me in the rest of this chapter—exemplify this shared aim. Commentators have been hard-pressed to settle on a term for this relationship: homage? imitation? remake? update?—all terms entertained by Salomé Aguilera Skvirsky in an essay on the three films. Following Linda Williams following Peter Brooks, she assumes that melodrama offers moralistic solutions parsing good and evil; for her, this scenario cannot produce political solutions, which must involve a recognition more complex than one of innocent victims. So far, so good. However, even though Haynes eschews identity politics and does not offer the melodrama of the moral occult, for Skvirsky his attachment to Sirk represents a "nostalgia for the moral righteousness" of the form. (Following Fredric Jameson, nostalgia is a worrisome affect for Skvirsky.) "*Far from Heaven* is mired in the nowhere place of 'left melancholy,'" she concludes, "nostalgic for the galvanizing moral outrage of an activist past, but unable to mount a political strategy for the present, not even in the realm of the imagination."[34]

Skvirsky wants melodrama to provide political solutions that fit her left convictions: since Ron (Rock Hudson) isn't merely a working-class

36 CHAPTER TWO

gardener "but also a successful small businessman," *All That Heaven Allows* is not about genuine class conflict but a critique of one group of the bourgeoisie for its prejudice against another.[35] It blames individuals, but not the system. Fassbinder rectifies this, she claims, by offering a kind of rainbow alliance of black and white working-class subjects who come together to create class solidarity. Because Fassbinder knows that class is not some automatic effect joining the victims of capitalism, his solution is political, not merely a moralistic parsing of good and evil.[36] For Skvirsky this means that Fassbinder has transcended the limits of melodrama's support of a truth-in-victimage that underlies Williams's definition of melodrama, and which, following her, Skvirsky attributes to Sirk. Her analysis, couched entirely in terms of class and race, ignores the sexual dimensions of these relationships.

The loss of social salience of the kind of subject matter Skvirsky thinks film must engage explains why for her melodrama is no longer a viable form in Haynes. "Unpleasant social realities" that once "seemed visible" no longer are. Now they are covered over with a liberal rhetoric of the acceptance of difference that makes prejudicial behavior incompatible with the "ideals of American democracy."[37] She supposes that no one now could yell out "Boy" at a black man in the company of a white woman as happens in the 1957 of *Far from Heaven*. This argument seems to depend on a dubious notion of social progress: we now have no trouble accepting cross-class relations; we are working toward full acceptance of race and sexual difference. Melodrama simply charts such social issues and becomes increasingly outmoded as the issues fade. But, more interestingly, Skvirsky also seems to be saying that it is not so much that the issues fade as that they persist, hidden under the shield of neoliberal disavowals. We know now to conceal behavior that once could be open. Melodrama, however, for her, is tethered to the visibility of such social issues.

It is certainly true that melodrama seems entranced by surfaces. But the mise-en-scène of melodrama does not simply reflect the real. Nor is history a progressive story that leaves Haynes behind. I'm taken by what J. Hoberman wrote at the conclusion of an admiring *Village Voice* review of *Far from Heaven* when it first screened. Insisting on how close Haynes is to Sirk (this extends to many technical features of the film's cinematography), Hoberman describes the film as a "full-bodied simulation of a genre that, historically speaking, should no longer exist."[38]

IDENTITY AND IDENTIFICATION 37

Hoberman titled his review "signs of the times" pluralizing an identification between past and present. What should no longer exist still does. Those times and these times are not as different as Skvirsky presumes. Moreover, as Geoffrey O'Brien comments in a review that appeared at the same time as Hoberman's piece, in *Far from Heaven*, "we have the vertiginous experience of being dropped back into a past all the more welcoming for having never existed in the first place."[39] The past in the film exists in 1950s film. O'Brien titled his piece "Past Perfect," not to declare nostalgic attachment to the past, but to affirm a past that remains present. Despite the ways in which events are datable in *Far from Heaven*, historical referents do not stop signification. This is, as Marcia Landy underlines, the point about "the *persistence* of melodrama": what persists beyond historical explanation suggests the limits of historical explanation, for both the form and the content of melodrama.[40] This ahistoricity makes a time for the (im)possibility of melodrama.

Thus the very inability of most film critics to find the right word for what Haynes is up to — slavish remake, condescending update, archeological pastiche, camp send-up (these are among the characterizations that have been offered) — may be more to the point than deciding on one or another term as the right one for his melodramatic practice. The difficulty in naming the form of *Far from Heaven* is not just a historical problem; it inheres in melodrama as a form — or is it a mode or style? — and does so precisely because the visible realities that it seizes for its plots, the impossible situations that animate its impasses, are the means to suggest impossibilities that exceed those represented. These impossibilities are not confined to the realistic details and issues of these films — foreign workers in Fassbinder's Germany; race antagonism and homophobia in 1957 Hartford supposed missing in Sirk's vision of 1950s suburban middle-class society. Whatever we may take as real and referential is illuminated in these films by camera work, by effects of non-naturalistic lighting and color, by the music, by the mirrors and thresholds and other recurring features of the mise-en-scène (the kinds of effects 1970s theorists seized on in revaluing Sirk); these visibilia exceed mimetic realism and point to the invisible as the motor of melodrama. As Haynes avers, there is nothing but surface to be seen onscreen, a nothing that is nothing until the viewer grapples with it.

Glyn Davis comes to a similar conclusion in his monograph on *Far from Heaven* when he argues that Haynes offers a simulation of Sirk that de-authorizes his own practice.[41] Melodrama exceeds individual identity and agency. John Gill, in his monograph, gets to a more humanistic version of this point when he proposes that melodrama seeks to expose what he calls the "human condition." Although Gill pins impossibility to sociohistorical limitations, his generalization of the situation could suggest that it is not so tethered. "Everyone seems to be following an imagined script of their lives," Gill writes; this scriptedness — call it "Imitation of Life" — exceeds the particulars of any instantiation.[42] For O'Brien, this is what constitutes the triumph of Julianne Moore's performance: "She plays her part as someone who reads the lines she's been given as if she senses their falseness but can't come up with an alternative," an acting style appropriate when false scripts are all that there are.[43] Under Haynes's direction and his script, Moore copies from models in Sirk — or from the style of delivery in Fassbinder. "Ali" (El Hedi ben Salem) speaks a foreign tongue with an impoverished vocabulary and grammar; Emmi, his charwoman lover (Brigitte Mira), speaks a German marked by her class; Cathy speaks English the same way. It is not psychology that melodrama exposes so much as the placement of its characters in a mise-en-scène that exceeds them: "their" words don't belong to them. It is that alienating situation that also affects the audience and provides an emotional connection beyond language, identifications of a shared situation that exceed identifications based on identity.

To sum up: melodrama may batten on the timely and the social but always to explore something that exceeds the immediate and the historical, a relationality that exceeds the life of the individual film or filmmaker, a life that passes through each film in its relationship to each other. These are relationships beyond an individual life, possibilities of survival, of living on and living after. To think this way could make a "revolution," but not necessarily in the overturning of one political regime with another, with the utopic dream, inevitably shattered, of the decisive replacement of one way of living with another deemed capable of solving every problem once and for all. Rather, in filmic crossings and attachments like those that Jane Bennett unearths to argue for the material basis for "the enchantment of modern life," an ethics that makes it possible to see and live life differently could emerge into visibility.[44] It is that other life that runs alongside this one that melodrama glimpses.

Most critical parsings of the relationship between *All That Heaven*

Allows, Fear Eats the Soul, and *Far from Heaven* are on the lookout for didactic instruction in political desire. Cross-class impasse becomes cross-racial; same-sex desire interferes with the machinery of hetero-sexual fulfillment. Omissions, lacks, occlusions are cleared away, Davis says. "Fassbinder's film recuperates the absences of the Sirk text: the urban space, the working class, and the racial minority," he continues (as if these don't appear in *Imitation of Life*; as if Haynes does not draw on that film as he reimagines *All That Heaven Allows*).[45] In each case, replacement is seen as a kind of updating of no longer relevant social concerns; alternatively, replacements are said to get closer to truths hidden earlier, capable only now of being revealed, another presentist assumption of social progress. Haynes, Sharon Willis tells us, "lavishes an obsessive attention upon moments when the 1950s 'unspeakables,' the loves that dare not speak their names, homosexuality and inter-racial sex, body forth in all their scandalous effects."[46] He can make explicit what only is implicit, restoring a fullness (Willis calls it mater-nal) to the past lacking such representations. For her, *Far from Heaven* aims at the historical truth of Hartford 1957. For Willis, as for Skvirsky, Haynes is inscribed in a historical progression. For both, Haynes none-theless fails politically to bring political truth to light.

Willis equates same-sex love with cross-racial desire (in the citation just given by way of a Wildean locution) only to insist on the falsity of that equation. Just as Haynes has insisted that Hartford 1957 is where his film is located only if we recognize it as the 1957 of films, not of the historical, so, too, has he refused the equation that Willis makes and then takes Haynes to task for making: "It became clear to me as I was writing the script that the theses of sexuality and race were counter-balances, with the woman as the force separating them. One was con-demned to secrecy and the other to a public backdrop; one was buried within the domestic setting and the other was visible and open to ram-pant projection."[47] Willis contextualizes the film against the burgeon-ing civil rights movement that Frank (Dennis Quaid) sees on the TV screen, Eisenhower sending troops into Selma. Given this truth, the film fails, she argues, by treating the African American man—the gar-dener Raymond (Dennis Haysbert)—as a stick figure, a good father, a cultivated, soft-spoken black who is there to counter the racist articu-lation that calls him "boy" and thinks it has said everything. She espe-cially bridles at Haynes's showing black-against-black violence, sure that is not historically true to the solidarity of movement politics, sure that it is politically regressive to suggest otherwise. Claiming to want history, Willis wants the film to reflect the liberal ideology that Skvirsky thinks is the source of the political failure of melodrama (it certainly is the limit of most analyses of melodrama). We say we are past the past, but are we?[48]

Not surprisingly, each of the recent critics reading these three films decides on which character gets closest to the happy ending the critic desires as a form of social justice. For Willis, Raymond is most bereft. Gill, on the other hand, thinks that Raymond emerges "as the least damaged of the three central characters . . . , the only one with any chance of rebuilding his life." For him, and for Davis, Cathy is the one most devastated. Willis, in contrast, sees her as oppressive, "both disappointed and disappointing in her knowledge of Raymond's world," the only world Willis seems to value.[49] Skvirsky glimpses a happy ending for Emmi and "Ali" in Fassbinder's film precisely because they have agreed on their need for each other. In each case, it is the politics of the critic that determines what they see (race is determinate for Willis; class for Skvirsky). This is true for me, too, of course: I write from what I take to be the position that Sirk and Fassbinder and Haynes theorize, one that will not countenance the happiness of the happy ending, a position that has broken with liberalism and identity politics. There are no happy endings; history is not simply moving ever forward. As Vance Comeau suggests in his resolutely and limited formalist analysis of mise-en-scène in the three films (mirrors, unnatural colors, and the like), the three women boxed in by their societies are all "different incarnations of the same character."[50] Something does not change even though history and society do. What does not change is the notion that identities are determinate, that differences are insuperable.

The resuscitation of 1950s melodrama by Fassbinder and Haynes is a way of showing what does not change: we are placed in a life not made for us. Where we are will not be remedied even when some perceived social injustice is seen and supposedly resolved. (I'm thinking of the nonsensical claims made these days that we live in a postracial United States or that, with the success of gay marriage politics, homophobia no longer has any political or social force.) If life is not made for us, and if we cling to identity as our way of affirming who we are, these affirmations can stand in the way of the crossings of identity, of identifications that go beyond us and that also place us all in the same position of alienated existence whose remedy will always be impossible when it is at the expense of others. To say this is not to preach quietism or defeatism but to look for what binds us to others, what makes us, in Jean-Luc Nancy's term, "singular plural." Beyond, within, the categories of human difference is the impersonal in the personal that we all share. As bodies we are all mostly water. We all die.

Even at the simplest level of social existence, what critics think no longer possible remains all too possible: Gill recalls Harvard professor Henry Louis Gates Jr. being arrested as an intruder in his own home in fashionable Cambridge, Massachusetts, as one sign that things have not changed; Matthew Shepard tortured and exposed to die, James Byrd dragged to his death.[51] Glyn Davis mentions the waves of anti-Muslim sentiment that have swelled in the United States against fellow citizens in the past decade, and which indeed preceded the 9/11 attacks often taken as their origin. One need not cite individual examples (white police killing unarmed blacks most recently in the news) to make the point; the increasing disparity between rich and poor in the United States, the growing prison population, all attest to a society scarcely accommodating difference. The seeming triumph of gay politics through the gay marriage agenda has been affirmed by an extremely conservative Supreme Court. Melodramas may fasten on social problems that reflect the historical moment of a given film's creation, but their gestures toward the sociohistorical do not simply mean they believe that solving a particular problem would instigate a revolution that would decisively change the world. No doubt the desire for change is a part of the appeal of melodrama, but it remains utopic, impossible by definition; the social is not the cause or the site of a permanent solution to the problems that melodrama engages. There is no permanent solution. Recognizing that is a way to finding what is possible.

That the social is not the ultimate quarry of melodrama is registered to some extent when critics regard these films as failures—Haynes's, especially, as he is the filmmaker contemporary with film critics and therefore expected to reflect their desire for social progress. Willis ends her essay by allying Haynes and Sirk as mirrors of their characters, left in "lovely and compelling disappointment."[52] She wants the satisfaction of a happy ending; for her, the closest *Far from Heaven* gets is when Frank is allowed the emotional and erotic outbursts that the

42 CHAPTER TWO

constrained Cathy and Raymond never experience. Does she think the gay filmmaker simply identifies with the gay character? Gill is sure that Frank's happy ending will be short lived; there is no world for gays, and that's why the film disappoints him. Indeed, his disappointment with the film goes further than its not supplying the gay affirmation he desires; its narrative lapses bother him, and especially its failure to fill in the blanks: how did Frank so quickly progress in his flirtation with Blond Boy to be ready to couple with him and leave the security of marriage as a cover for his gay extramarital sex life? In his impatience with the non-Hollywood aesthetic Haynes practices, Gill sees that Haynes's film only looks like a seamless narrative. He is unhappy with what he calls a "semiotic cocktease" equivalent to dabbling in the realm of the "empty sign" (Barthes is the instigator pronounced guilty of this crime).[53]

Davis also is perturbed by Frank. For him, too, queer film should show the truth and deliver an uncloseted homosexuality. Queer theory shows that identity is constructed; gays know that best from the experience of the closet. Once gay people can stop pretending they are straight, then there will be no more performances, just the real that queer melodrama should reveal. Amelia DeFalco writes in a similar vein about Haynes's queer use of previous melodramas: "The absurdity of the suffering engendered by prejudice (racism, homophobia, sexism) is accentuated by its artificiality and constructedness and the frustrating knowledge that things don't have to be this way."[54] They don't have to be, but they are. They do have to be, and there is no getting past that. Constructedness does not mean there is some real that escapes or is occluded by construction. Construction is not repression; it is reality. If so, and if that is what melodrama "knows," it seems possible to imagine that melodrama was always already queer. It was always allowing audiences the possibility of seeing and knowing that there is more to see than the most visible abuses that are so clearly false or artificial dilemmas, but not thereby easily remedied.

Critics are unhappy with Sirk because he is constrained, they think, by history, by the 1950s, by the Hayes Code, by a melodramatic world of black and white (though this is not at all how Sirk imagines the form); but then, when Fassbinder and Haynes say and show what it is supposed that Sirk could not, they don't seem to be telling the just-so stories that the critics want. Why do these later filmmakers cling to an outmoded form? Why does Haynes indulge in what Gill calls a "pre-/post-feminist/gay conceit."[55] Even worse, these preposterous "pre-/post-" styles may reflect back on Sirk, presumed innocent (or is it guilty?) of the feminist and proto-queer theory that Haynes started articulating in 1985. They are sure, with Barbara Klinger (in the only book-length critical treatment of Sirk yet written), that such notions only come to 1950s melodrama retrospectively, through a "retrospectatorship" that Willis and Davis both claim from Patricia White, privileging a knowing now against past impercipience.[56] It is as if the desires that move characters are real only when they become identities that have a name and a politics, only when they are stigmatized — or affirmed — as such. But what if who we are does not go by one name?

We can get further with this question by turning now to look at each of these three films for the ways in which the impossible situation is housed in couples that would form sexual relations. Race and class are the most visible social axes on which these films turn; this justifies the emphasis in most criticism. Sexuality, because it is not so readily seen, comes closer to what melodrama probes — that is, so long as sexuality is not viewed only as a matter of an identity politics that will allow people to be what they are and have what they desire. Not that there is anything wrong with that, of course, or with ameliorating the oppressions still attached to class or race or gender. Politically what this has meant, however, usually involves not letting others have what "we" do, or allowing them to have it only if in the same way we do, at someone else's expense.

Queer Relations: *All That Heaven Allows*

Haynes has been said to have uncovered what Sirk could not show: interracial and same-sex desire.[57] Yet the focus on passing in *Imitation of Life* is entangled with sexuality, as when Sarah Jane (Susan Kohner) is beaten by her white boyfriend Frankie (Troy Donahue) when he discovers that her mother is black; or when she performs in a girlie show or in a night club. Her passing always involves the sexual allure and danger associated with cross-racial sex; she is placed on a "sexual conveyor belt," as Lauren Berlant puts it.[58] Nor is it the case that same-sex desire can be represented only now. In 1957, when Eric Rohmer and Claude Chabrol took stock of Hitchcock's films to that date, they seized on *Mur-*

der! (1930), *Rope* (1948), and *Strangers on a Train* (1951) as constituting what they dubbed a "homosexual triptych."[59] Thus, in the very real 1957 fictionalized in *Far from Heaven*, these nouvelle vague filmmakers had no trouble seeing or naming same-sex desire, however invidiously, in Hitchcock films, including two from their own period, the same time frame as Sirk's Universal melodramas. Barbara Klinger makes an opposing argument in her book about Sirk's melodramas, claiming that they look campy only after gay liberation, but could not possibly have been viewed that way back before Stonewall, or before Rock Hudson revealed that he had AIDS. Klinger even suggests that the "self-reflexive [element] and distancing" of Sirk films are aftereffects of such revelations.[60] Her historicism, for all its dialectical trappings, confines singular meanings to historical periods. She acknowledges the double entendres in Hudson's sex comedies with Doris Day—*Pillow Talk* (1959), *Lover Come Back* (1961), and *Send Me No Flowers* (1964)—but is confident no one at the time noticed them. Richard Dyer has called such suppositions into question by suggesting that these plots (when manly Rock pretends not to know what to do with Doris, a gag in both *Pillow Talk* and *Lover Come Back*; or when he seems to think he is pregnant, or appears clothed only in a woman's mink coat) reflect an epistemology of the closet.[61] He is certain that Sirk's melodramas, in their failure to deliver a happy ending through the marriage plot, blow the cover on the pretending manliness of a gay man. Richard Meyer furthers such claims but counters the supposed impossibility of being openly gay in the 1950s with the likelihood that everyone involved in making films with Hudson knew he was gay.[62] Made for the camera's eye, Hudson is put by Sirk in the place Laura Mulvey claimed was reserved only for the female star—that of being looked at. "Part of the appeal of Rock Hudson's body," Meyer writes, "was that it seemed somewhat immobile, available as an object of erotic delectation but without the threat of male action."[63]

This different form of masculinity was perhaps first caught by Sirk's camera in *Taza, Son of Cochise* (1953). In *Sirk on Sirk*, he describes the lead character played by Hudson as "my most symbolic in-between man" (Halliday, 92). In the revised 1997 edition of the book, Halliday follows Sirk's 1970 instruction "to hold off writing about the fact that Rock Hudson, who was then still alive, was homosexual, until all concerned were dead."[64] Sirk knew about Hudson's sexuality. In the revised text, discussing the role of the gay producer Ross Hunter in promoting Rock Hudson in the part of Bob Merrick in *Magnificent Obsession*, which assured his stardom, Sirk claims: "I sometimes think Ross Hunter played a part in pushing Rock towards being homosexual. At first Rock seemed to me to lie near the middle of the sexual spectrum, but when he met up with Ross, that was it. The studio had a heck of a time trying to hide Rock's homosexuality" (107). The performances Hudson gave for Sirk, through Sirk, were performances of the open secret; these are, as well, performances of the in-between, the middle. As William J. Mann puts it: "Rock Hudson projected an on-screen gayness different from any who came before," not effeminate or delicate and ambiguous, but masculine.[65]

This image was achieved for the first time in *Taza*, the second film Hudson made with Sirk. The first, *Has Anybody Seen My Gal?* (1951), a conventional boy-meets-girl story, has a number of plot elements that suggest something equivocal in Hudson's part in the heterosexual romance. He does not hold the screen in his first Sirk film and is palpably acting in a way he will not in the later melodramas; busily emoting, he is expressive in a manner quite unlike his rocklike, impassive style there (which extends to his comedies with Doris Day). In *Taza*, Hudson plays the lead, an Indian who allies with the U.S. Army. He is invariably bare chested and bronzed, except when he is with the army (Hudson's "in-between" role), at which times he dresses as a soldier. His Indian plot is a continuously interrupted heterosexual romance; his cross-race plot involves bonding with and (cross-)dressing as a white man. Critics who claim that cross-race desire was impossible in 1950s film seem only to have white–African American relations in mind and forget that many westerns are about nothing if not cross-race relations. In *Taza*, questions of racial identity are complicated beyond a black/white binary. Not only is Taza divided; the Indians themselves are divided within themselves, Apaches versus Apaches. Some, following Taza, hold to the legacy of Cochise, of peace with the so-called white eyes; others side with Geronimo, who espouses war. At the end of the film, betrayed by his army allies, Taza takes off his military costume and returns to native undress, seemingly to fight with his fellow Indians; instead, he fights against them, in the name of a peace that refuses the white/native divide.

A similar cross occurs in Taza's relationship with Burnett (Gregg Palmer), the U.S. captain with whom he allies and who also represents a division within the whites, sometimes following his superior officer, sometime siding with Taza. Taza calls Burnett "nantan," an Apache term for chief. He explains to Burnett that it is a native term of endearment that means he is a great leader and a good friend, and he looks deep into the eyes of his friend as he says this. They are face-to-face, close up and filling the screen in the kind of two-shot that often signifies heterosexual romance. Hudson's otherwise stolid delivery of lines melts for a moment as he pronounces "nantan." The film careens from one side to the other in this two-sided relationship. Along the way, too, Taza courts Oona (Barbara Rush), who is simultaneously courted by his brother Naiche (Bart Roberts). Taza never kisses Oona, barely embraces her, and keeps deferring their wedding until peace has been made. Naiche, on the other hand, violently attempts to rape Oona and is given her by a father who beats her. Oona wavers back and forth between obeying her father and betraying his plans to Taza. Hudson's masculinity, although supposedly made visible in his powerful physique, is not like that of his rivals.

Sirk does not often deploy close-ups of Hudson, although there are moments when his body fills the screen. More characteristically, the film — shot almost entirely outdoors in Arches National Park in Utah — features towering mountains in the background, big skies filled with clouds. In scenes of plot complication, a dark filter creates an ominous mood that alternates with brilliantly lit sunlit scenes. In either of these, however, human bodies, faces, and identities may be obscured. Just as white/native difference is subsumed by the questions of war and peace, human bodies are usually dwarfed by the mountains, framed by trees in the foreground of beautifully composed scenes, or shadowed in filtered light that make bodies indistinct. Hudson no longer acts his lines; he reads them as if reading a script. He is given lines to read that are sententious, portentous: "We will not talk of right or wrong. We will talk of peace." What Mann says of Hudson's performance in comedy is true in this melodramatic western: "He was comfortable with the camp of *Pillow Talk* and yet never campy."[66] This acting style involves going native; crossing race carries sexual implication. Sirk's western, like those of Budd Boetticher, whom he admired, is an exercise in the most precise kind of formal plotting, testing oppositions and dissolving them in a wider framework of setting and lighting. It anticipates his Universal melodramas and Rock Hudson's performances in them.[67]

Indeed, the character of Ron Kirby in the Edna and Harry Lee novel *All That Heaven Allows* on which the film is based provides an explicit link: "sun-browned shoulders beyond a clump of rhododendron" is all of him that Cary sees at first; a few pages later, when he agrees to join her for lunch she thinks that he looks "rather like an Indian."[68] Sirk keeps Hudson's Ron clothed, but, as in the novel, he is initially part of the landscape: in the first shot of him he is up a tree, a tan smudge against a tree trunk, lost in its leaves. A bit later, when we do see his face, his skin is tanned, while Cary's (Jane Wyman) is makeup face-powder white. His work clothes — khaki pants and shirt — match the autumnal tones of the bushes; her grey outfit blends with the outside of the house and, moments later, echoes the blue light with which her bedroom is flooded.[69] She may not be quite the walled-up Egyptian widow that her daughter, Kay (Gloria Talbott), invokes, but her skin and clothing make her appear lifeless compared to Hudson's bronzed Ron.

By way of stereotypical Indian allusions, the novel provides racialized terms for Cary and Ron's natural/social difference: "Working in the open with growing things, his activity imposed by the changing seasons, he would be close to the deep reality of life, as a wood creature or a savage was close to its source."[70] "The deep reality of life" names, however, a theme that goes beyond racialized difference to a fundamental sameness. In their first meeting in the film, only when their talk turns to trees does his face light up; the camera engages it. When he cuts a branch from the Koelreuteria, a connection is made — with Cary, with us. He is animated, smiling, talkative. The next scene opens with the cut branch in a vase beside Cary's face in the mirror, an intimation of the impossible project of bringing the outside in, the inside out, the project of being one with nature that unmakes social relations and self-relation as well.

In the novel Cary comes to a self-realization about her nature (her sexuality) in tune with figurations of the gardener as a Native American: "She was unprepared for the discovery of a creature that was part of her and yet somehow independent, a being who scoffed at conventional considerations; who was as ignorant of shame as any amber-skinned, savage woman with a sarong about her hips and a scarlet

48 CHAPTER TWO

flower in her hair."[71] Sirk's film does not follow this racialized plot in quite these terms (for savages he substitutes the bohemian company at Ron's friends Mick and Alida's), but he is intent on his own version of the unsingular, the other who is part of and yet apart from one's self, in both the relationship between Cary and Ron as well as in each of them.

This plot of self-division for most recent critics of the film is pinned to social terms, personal desire versus the "conventional considerations" to which the novel alludes. As individual versus society, this is the recognizable liberal dilemma cogently critiqued by Skvirsky. The novel's savage within could easily suggest psychological terms for self-division, including the pop-psychology ascribed to Freud that Kay spouts. We can't take her analysis seriously, but the antipathy of the children to their mother's desire to marry Ron does point to an overlap of an oedipal situation with class division. Her son, Ned (William Reynolds), and Kay would be happy to have their mother marry Harvey, because he's the right age (and class) to have learned the lesson Kay ascribes to Freud early in the film, that "at a certain age, sex becomes incongruous." (Does "incongruous" imply a union akin to one across species or races?)

Recent critics have tended to ignore sexuality as the domain of impossibility in *All That Heaven Allows*, unlike Laura Mulvey, whose brief and acute analysis of Sirk and melodrama zeros in on the topic. Sexuality for Mulvey is the operation of heterosexuality in patriarchal society. Cary's dilemma lies in her placement between male predation (the truth about men) and domestic confinement to a sphere in which men have been tamed and women are thwarted. In Mulvey's analysis, Harvey is "impotent and decrepit" and Ron offers more of the same. He may look as if he is outside the norm — not the country club type and with no desire to fit in — but union with him is equally impossible. (Mulvey sees well what Sirk affirmed — that his happy endings are delusional.) For Mulvey, the film asks: "How can natural man and woman re-establish the values of primitive economy and the division of labour when the man is bedridden and incapable? How can a mother of grown children overcome the taboo against her continued sexual activity in 'civilized society,' when the object of her desire is reduced to child-like dependence on her ministrations?"[72]

Mulvey's primitivism is not what the novel means by the term; "primitive economy" offers a Marxian naturalization of heterosexuality (the division of labor according to a division in gender). The relationship in the film between the institutionalization of heterosexuality (social convention) and "natural" desire can be seen when Cary shares Ron's excitement about the tree that grows in her garden. When the branch he cuts is put into the vase and shot next to her face in the mirror, any simple opposition of nature and society is complicated by that doubling. "With a picture like that," Sirk says to Halliday, "your only saving point is to take a tree out of the garden and put it down in a salon. It's antinomy again" (99), the antinomy of the natural and the social.

This question of identity Fassbinder acutely identified as the impossibility of coupling or of being single. Wanting social approval and failing to get it certainly is part of the dilemma, an impossibility rooted in perceived social differences that extend from the threat of a difference within to differences that move in the direction of racial and species difference. Sexuality as "incongruous" at a certain age also is part of the way the film registers impossibility. As Mulvey sees well, "Cary's transgression of the class barrier mirrors her more deeply shocking transgression of sexual taboos in the eyes of her friends and children."[73] Is her transgression simply a violation of the rules of patriarchal heterosexuality? Indeed, how committed is Sirk to those norms? "Impotent" Harvey, Mulvey almost sees, might be a desirable mate precisely because he is not heterosexual. In the novel, that is close to explicit: Harvey is an available bachelor because his mother has just died. "He gave his whole life to her," Sara remarks to Cary; when Cary turns up at Sara's country club party, her husband, George, tells her he doesn't think Harvey is the man for her, there's "something of an old woman about him."[74] Is the underlying impossibility in the romance between Cary and Ron inviting us to recall that the actor playing his part was gay? That is what Laura Cottingham suggests: "Careful viewing of *All That Heaven Allows* reveals that Hudson's face does not always look right. He is not really interested in Jane Wyman."[75] Mulvey's analysis of "impotence" might suggest this, yet her analysis of heterosexuality also problematizes such a reading: the ideological solution of patriarchal heterosexuality requires its impotent masking in the domestic sphere in order to grant women the illusion that their cage is a domain in which they exercise sexual power, Mulvey supposes.

Is it just an illusion? Women have the power to ostracize Cary from the country club or to welcome her back into the fold. They are intent

50 CHAPTER TWO

on each other and indifferent to their husbands, some of whom, like Howard, are expected to be predators since they don't get what they want at home. In the novel Sara complains about her husband from the opening page (the complaints are muted but voiced in the film as well). In the film she confides to Cary that her clubwoman duties are compensation for what her marriage lacks (they don't have children; in those terms, it is a sexual failure). Sara is played by Agnes Moorehead, identified compellingly by Patricia White as an actress who always conveys a lesbian charge that exceeds whatever her role may be.[76] Moorehead plays the part of Jane Wyman's nurse companion in *Magnificent Obsession*, her best friend in *All That Heaven Allows*: these films are not only reprising a Wyman-Hudson pairing.

The bonds between women may not simply signify their patriarchal cooption. Beneath the opening titles of *All That Heaven Allows*, we see a woman wheeling a baby carriage; her companion is another woman. In the sequence that follows, Sara arrives to break her lunch date with Cary (Ron will substitute for her to the extent of eating two ladylike rolls). Sara and Cary walk hand in hand past Ron, oblivious of him. Sara calls Cary "darling," and will again; it is also the term used later between Hudson and Wyman.[77] At the end of the novel, Cary almost suffocates; Sara rescues her, and she comes to another realization: "She realized that she loved Sara."[78] Does the film allow this other love — of women for each other — into the presumptively heterosexual world? Is the love that flows between Ron and Cary a "natural" desire (it begins with the silver-tip spruce) ill suited to heterosexual union — perhaps, indeed, to any socially sanctioned human relation? White says that the "lesbianism" conveyed by Moorehead is always a force of negativity. This might also be the case with the homosexuality conveyed by Hudson. Does Ron seem at all interested in Cary, or is it his negativity that attracts her? Are they joined by negativity? A close look at dialogue and shots in their scenes together suggests this.

At their first meeting Cary asks Ron, "Do you think you'll finish today, or will you have to come back?" She looks face forward at the camera. He looks aside, up and back, not at her, as he answers, "Probably will." Probably will what? Finish today, or come back? He says yes and no to her question, and this is key to their relationship as it develops in the film. He is not facing her but nonetheless onscreen with her; this exchange sets many of the themes that bind and separate the two, that constitute the double binds of their impossibility. The next time they are onscreen together, the film seems to be starting again. Sara's blue car drives up, this time letting Cary out. The first time, Sara had complimented Cary on her timeliness in having her trees pruned. This time, seeing Ron again up in the tree, she asks, "how long has this been going on?" as if Ron had never left the tree. "I almost gave him up for lost," Cary tells Sara, saying more than she might be supposed to mean. "The independent type," Sara responds, continuing the double entendres.

Are they starting again, or coming to an end? Cary once again offers him coffee. This time he refuses. Shot-/reverse shot establish that they may be facing each other, but they are each separate. He's finished, he tells her. The camera catches Cary's face and her disappointment as she says, "That means we're not going to see you again til next spring." A slight smile flickers across his face. Nature boy (tree man, as the novel wishes to call him) may not be tied to this calendar. He won't be coming back, he says. They change position; now we see his back, her face, pensive. "Don't worry," he tells her, "I'll find someone for you." Now she begins to smile, but it's not pleasure at the thought of a replacement; it's bitter, sardonic, as she thanks him, adding, "I guess this is good-bye."

At this impasse Ron plucks the silver-tip spruce out of thin air and invites her to come see it at his place. She refuses, then accepts. Once there, they go through the same routine: his silver-tip trees don't engage her: she wants instead to see the old mill he is reluctant to show her. A bird frightens her into his arms, and she imagines him coupled to some appropriate girl and wonders whether or not he is susceptible. "No, I don't think that," he replies laconically. At their next visit to the mill, he has made it the home she wants and offers marriage. She says it is impossible. He has repaired the Wedgewood pot she had found. She breaks it. When she finally returns at the end of the film, he is comatose. She sees the beauty he has made, and she sees as well that what has been between them is herself. When he wakes, he says they are home, but he had told her before that home is where you are yourself. Home is separateness, within yourself, where you live with another, your stranger self. Coupling is impossible because no one is single, each one is divided. But it also is in division that coupling resides. Even Ron, the unmovable rock, is beginning to sense that Cary might change him. Every one is two. And every couple cannot be one. Differences that can be marked as if they are the effect of social divisions (of race, of class, of gender, of age, of sexuality) are the effect of divisions that don't originate in the social: this is the impossible situation of melodrama.[79]

The negativity in this relationship is treated as if it were a social negativity—as if, that is, everything might be possible were there not socially made differences. Ron is disparaged by the country club set as a Nature boy. Although the film does not repeat the novel's racialized terms for difference, it finds what it means by nature in Thoreau; Sirk tells Halliday that he insisted the shot of the cover of *Walden* remain visible, much to the bafflement of the studio. It's Mick's Bible, Alida tells Cary. It's Ron himself, she says; he doesn't have to read it, he is it. Cary opens the book just before the company of bohemians arrive. They include the only non-Anglo couple in the film, as well as a "spinsterish" single woman (a birdwatcher and head of the Audubon Society), and a single man dubbed "Grandpa," a beekeeper and an artist of self-identified "primitive" paintings. This group may be meant to translate Thoreau's love of nature into a social group that has broken with the all-white entirely heterosexual country club world (For Members Exclusively, the sign reads). Nonetheless, Sirk does not make this bohemian gathering all that outré; this is still a group in which nature has been cut to fit a salon. Mick and Alida's house, like Ron's, has lots of glass, letting the outside in; they live in a nursery. They are also a happily married if childless couple; Mick is presumably devoted to plants, a nurseryman like Ron—and devoted to him, too (he is his "master"). Alida is a homemaker. It is certainly possible to imagine that Sirk was oblivious to the reinscription of conventional marriage in this alternative world, but it seems just as possible that it is there to suggest the limits of this (of any) translation of Thoreau.

Cary reads from a copy of *Walden* that has been opened to a page on which, in fact, passages from different parts of the book have been spliced together. "The mass of men lead lives of quiet desperation" from "Economy" precedes sentences from "Where I lived and what I lived for": "Why should we be in such desperate haste to succeed? If a man does not keep pace with his companions, perhaps it is because he hears a different drummer. Let him step to the music he hears, however measured and far away." Thoreau's antisocial message is the strongest element in sentences that Cary proclaims "beautiful"; they clearly match Mick's decision to leave the "rat race" and adopt his new lifestyle. Sirk's Thoreau resonates with his queer reception by Michael Warner and Peter Coviello, unlike *Walden*'s reading by Perry Miller, the major Americanist of Sirk's time, who found Thoreau perverse, queer, uncomfortable (Sirk presumably found admirable his aversion to society, especially as determined by heterosexuality; Mick's misogyny is Thoreau's).[80] Thoreau has been read by some gay critics as gay, but neither Warner nor Coviello is making that argument, even as both register the fact that the strongest human attractions that Thoreau records are for other men, especially woodsmen and farmers. These are not quite the same as the domesticated nurserymen Ron and Mick, and I take Sirk to be pointedly indicating the limitations of their translation of nature into society.

Loving trees, growing them, and selling them is not quite what Thoreau did at Walden. But Thoreau, too, as Warner and Coviello both mention, draws back from identification with rough farmers and woodsmen, measuring his distance from them even as he makes his attempt at total immersion in nature. For Warner that immersion is a kind of utopic solitariness, a zero-sum game in which one is at once entirely lost to and yet entirely one with nature. Coviello's argument fastens on an insistence that Thoreau's sexuality cannot be translated into identitarian terms. Coviello is not making the familiar gay studies argument (its weak reading of Foucault) that gay identity does not yet exist in his time, so he can't really be who he is. Rather, Coviello insists that identity formation is a process of consolidation that also entails a refusal of self-difference, a refusal of what does not add up to an identity. For Coviello, Thoreau remains valuable for us now precisely because he models another way of being than subscription to a regulatory regime of identity. In his chapter "Disappointment, or Thoreau in Love," he shows how the impossibility of relationship is infused with a yearning for connections that go beyond those shaped by conventions of identity. This is a union that does not have to do with ownership; it involves giving up the "liberal self's secured properties."[81] Perhaps crucially, Thoreau is Sirk's model for the impossible project of an identification with nature in which the self is reflected in something that exceeds oneself, something that refuses to reflect back oneself as a self, that instead embraces us (if it does) only insofar as we are part of something that is not us, or that stares at us, measuring the distance. This

54 CHAPTER TWO

nature points to the underlying negativity through which Ron and Cary join and separate in Sirk's film; it is the insecurity they embrace, the "home" they make. It is fraught with difficulty. The picture window in which a tamed deer puts in a final appearance suggests that the dissolve into nature that Thoreau claims for himself is not achieved. But it also suggests a desire to go beyond Alida's clichéd translation of the Thoreauvian message of Ron into the bathos of "to thine own self be true."

Thoreau's "different drummer," Coviello notes, is also a figure in his journals, where the different tune and measure heard are the measure of a different temporality. Time is not one. Cary and Ron cannot find a time. The novel explicitly fetches its title from a libertine poem by Rochester that acknowledges at best the momentary possibility of synchronicity: "If I can be / This live-long minute true to thee; / 'Tis all that Heaven allows" (this is Mick's poem in the novel; it is his bible).[82] The film is banking on it. Jane Wyman, at the end of her career, is an older woman. In fact, she is only eight years older than Rock Hudson; but he is a new star, just at the beginning. In 1955 Wyman is making one of her last films; she is about to become a TV star—the television set given her in the film glances at this, relegating her to this diminished existence. (It will mark Hudson's career end, too, but not for twenty more years.) In 1955 Hudson had just married; Wyman had famously divorced Ronald Reagan as he moved from minor stardom to a political career. Hudson is as close in age to William Reynolds, the actor who plays Wyman's son, as he is to her. And "decrepit" Harvey, Conrad Nagel, was, in the silent film era, a matinee idol, a heart stopper. When talkies arrived, he switched to character parts, then went on to radio and TV. His role as Harvey marks the end of the life of a film actor (he is almost sixty years old), which is a different life than life itself, if there is such a singular thing. The film is a star vehicle but also wishes to vehiculate its stars and us into the glasshouse where we might lie in bed and see the stars; where the wall between us and nature might dissolve. But it knows that's a dream of taming nature that is just that, a dream, not a way of being one with nature. The deer at the end, like a pun in a Sir Thomas Wyatt poem, is also the dear who remains savage if only because it is not oneself.

Queer Relations: *Angst Essen Seele Auf*

According to Michael Töteberg, Fassbinder had sketched a scenario for a film that was much closer to Sirk's film than the one he ultimately made in response to *All That Heaven Allows*.[83] *Fear Eats the Soul* certainly evokes Sirk's film without being a remake, most obviously in its focus on another impossible situation, a couple divided by age difference and, this time, by race and nationality as well. (Recalling Sirk's phrase, the trailer for the film ends by announcing it as a story of an impossible love, "Die Geschichte einer unmöglichen Liebe.") Impossibility lies in a sexual relationship that is despised, as in Sirk's film, by those others that constitute the social world of the couple, including the woman's family.[84] Although the dynamics of Fassbinder's film match those of Sirk's, the setting is not the affluent suburbs where nature is just a short drive away, but urban Munich. At the end of each film, the lover who might "rescue" the lonely woman lies bedridden; Ron's condition is supposedly temporary, a concussion from which he will recover, and he is already speaking at the film's close. Ali's condition will recur and is pronounced incurable by a doctor whose affect veers from a neutral professionalism to a final, sadistic gaze at the bedridden, unconscious Moroccan and the aging German woman weeping and stroking his hand.

This change in the final scene may reflect the difference Fassbinder announced at the opening of his essay comparing Sirk's "tender films" with his own: they show "a man who loves human beings and doesn't despise them as we do" (77). If so, it suggests how small that affective distance is. Sirk perhaps continues to love humans because he countenances the yearning for what is outside the window, for some relationship to something beyond the human — call it nature — that might bind humans to each other and take them past the inevitability of decisive division. Ali's condition is irremediable. It is born of a difference that seems most immediately that of being a foreign worker, away from home.[85] Yet, as in *All That Heaven Allows*, a social explanation goes only so far. Stated even in the terms of "foreign" versus "home," that antinomy is generalizable: Who is at home in the world? There still is a wall of glass between Ron and Cary and a nature beyond them. If humans are fundamentally unlovable for Fassbinder, it is in part because humans can't be at home with each other and yet can't be alone either. This is, of course, what Fassbinder saw in *All That Heaven Allows*: "human beings can't be alone, but they can't be together either" (79), and it is what we can see in his film as well.[86]

Chris Fujiwara has noted that Fassbinder intensifies what he saw in Sirk.[87] One way he does this is through his focus on characters who seem so socially disempowered that one might think they could do what they wanted in their private lives and no one would care. Fassbinder dismantles any notion of the private in his numerous shots of staring. There is no being alone, and the glance of one human upon another is enough to set up disabling difference. No category of social difference is a necessary trigger for this. Toward the end of the film, Emmi's fellow workers, who had first turned against her for her relationship with Ali, bond with Emmi against a new member of their cohort, whose difference from them seems first to arise from her nationality (she is from Yugoslavia) but seems triggered even more by the fact that she makes less money than they do. They want to keep her in that position. Fassbinder films Yolanda (Helga Ballhaus) sitting on the stairs during a lunch break in exactly the same place and configuration in which Emmi had been shot earlier in the film when her fellow workers had ostracized her. Yolanda is abjected because the members of any group need to abject someone. The fact that she is young and attractive (blonde and white) provides a catalyst for these older women, if not its driving force. Or perhaps it is the fact that Yolanda wants to be part of the group. Emmi finally bonds with these women who had acted as though their job as cleaning women was to rid the world of filthy foreign workers and the German women who sleep with them, starting with Emmi.

What in Sirk might be diagnosed as the indulgence of "bourgeois" problems is extended by Fassbinder to workers low on the social scale. They are the same problems. In the hallway of her apartment house, where her every move is watched by the other women who live there (Frau Karges [Elma Karlowa] is this film's Mona), Emmi confesses her secret shame to Ali: she is a cleaning woman. No sooner has she confessed than she adds her pleasure in being chauffeured to work by a rich client. She is self-divided by her class position and identifications. Her security in feeling that it is safe to tell Ali her secret, that he won't scorn her or laugh at her, stems from the possibility that his own divisions will somehow track alongside hers. Indeed, all the characters are crossed in ways that undermine the singularity of categories of identity, whether of race, class, gender, or sexuality.[88] In this film, any group that might be assumed to identify as a group is shown also to be divided. The film itself breaks in two, reversing its supposed governing binarisms. Fujiwara posits this as a break between opposing forces outside and inside the couple; however, the parallelism throws the binary inside/outside into question: Has the outside been internalized, or is the outside the externalization of what already is within?

The category difference inside/outside is further violated in the casting of the film in ways that might recall the part Rock Hudson's sexuality plays in Ron. El Hedi ben Salem M'Barek Mohamed Mustafa plays Ali; when he tells Emmi his name at their first meeting, that is the name he gives. Laura Cottingham takes this to mean that the film is to be translated to its referent: since El Hedi ben Salem was Fassbinder's lover at the time the film was made, the film must be a disguised version of their affair, Brigitte Mira a stand-in for Fassbinder, her heterosexual relationship in the film a cover for Fassbinder's homosexuality. Fassbinder, however, made the film for his lover and as a way of ending their relationship.[89] The complexity of this double gesture — filmic permanence is granted to real relations at their end — raises questions for Cottingham's literal translation.

Perhaps the most provocative instance of this referentiality effect in the film can be seen in the role (uncredited) that Fassbinder plays: Eugen, Emmi's son-in-law. This is the kind of part Fassbinder often assigned himself, one that exemplifies and enacts why he considered humans hateful. "Swinish, barbaric, sadistic" is how Cottingham describes Eugen, who is married to Krista, played by Irm Herrman (Fassbinder had a long sexual history with the actress, which seems to be reenacted in their abusive relationship in the film).[90] "Swinish, barbaric, sadistic": Cottingham treats Eugen as if he were not human but an animal, as if he were not civilized; she pathologizes and racializes him, describing his hatefulness in just the way others disparage others in the film. Various forms of the terms "swinish" recur throughout the film — it is applied to foreigners by Eugen, who rails at his "Turkish" boss; Emmi uses it to refer to fellow Germans who shun her and also for the shopkeeper who won't serve Ali. Fujiwara calls Eugen "the most swinish racist" in the film. Like Cottingham, he deploys a term that the film puts into everyone's mouths. Cottingham and Fujiwara think they are making a moral, political distinction by condemning Eugen, but they use the racist language of the character they condemn as racist. Playing the part of Eugen, Fassbinder invites such responses and opens the possibility of recognizing them as akin to behavior the film asks us to deplore. Casting himself as Eugen, he does not exempt himself from human hatefulness nor hold out much hope for the process of recognition and radical change. Playing Eugen, Fassbinder makes possible the showing of impossibility.

Sirk punctuates his film with visits to the mill that Ron is making a home for Cary; the place of possibility, out in the country, its picture window open to the world outside. He is prompted by her when he doesn't want to do it, then refused by her when he has; it is at the mill that Ron and Cary wrestle with each other to see if there is a place people can make that opens them to something beyond themselves, that might overcome what divides them from each other, what divides them from themselves. The equivalent place in Fassbinder's film might be the Asphalt Bar, where the first scene is set and to which the couple return, early in the film to celebrate their plan to marry, and at the end, when they replay the scene of their meeting until Ali collapses on the dance floor and is rushed to the hospital. The bar is "outside" of constituted sociality; it is not a workplace for anyone except its owner, nor where the family is holed up or meets for ritualistic gatherings. It is, instead, a place where strangers meet. The clientele is mixed; the music on the jukebox is Arabic and German. The Arabs, however, are all men, while the Germans are women; what brings the two groups together is the desire of Arab men for their own company and a desire for heterosexual sex, which it seems only German women will fulfill.

Fassbinder may be following Fanon in *Black Skin, White Masks* on the kind of alienation that makes for cross-racial desire. German women who sleep with foreign workers are called whores throughout the film, Emmi included. What the women in the bar want from these men may be sex, and some of them may be paid for it. Yet Barbara (Barbara Valentin), the owner, offers to make couscous for Ali after Emmi refuses to and tells him that he should eat German food. It is not clear whether any of the women in the bar want the kind of domestic relationship that Emmi and Ali attempt, including Barbara, who has sex with Ali. One woman labels the relationship between Ali and Emmi "unnatural," but Barbara diagnoses her opposition as based in envy. One can want what one doesn't want because another desire is even greater: to have someone rather than no one; to have someone by taking that person away from someone else. Does anyone want anyone else, or do they really want to annihilate everyone else and be alone?

As everyone stares at them in the café in the park, Emmi says to Ali that she wishes they could be the only couple in the world. But once that comes true and they are isolated and only have each other, she turns on him. Indeed, from the moment she begins to imagine she can be with him in any way, she starts attempting to have him. In her hallway, just after they have met, she tells him he should wear light-colored clothes. It is like Cary telling Ron how he should make the mill a home for the inevitable woman who will enter his life, imagining her as someone other than herself even as she is probing to see whether she could fit the part, probing to see whether she can remake him as she wants him to be — susceptible to her. When Emmi and Ali marry, they dress identically in gray suits — their outfit for their last dance together as well.

As the film starts, Emmi comes into the Asphalt Bar out of an inhospitable nature; it is raining heavily; Emmi is out of place. At first, in fact, it looks as if there is no place for anyone in this place. The bar appears empty and dark; the camera catches her in the doorway, looking past empty tables, then it looks at what she sees down the corridor: a group of men and women staring at her. She does not look like the others. This framing suggests a stark opposition; the shots are held: one against many, the individual versus the social. However, the "social" here is a group that has no real social standing, and it is not all there is to see. Barbara, behind the counter, is closer to Emmi than any of the customers. She moves to wait on Emmi, who explains how she comes to be there: it's raining. "And I said to myself, 'Emmi,' I said to myself," she tells her, "'you had better go into that bar'" ("Und da hab ich mir gedacht . . . Emmi, hab ich gedacht, geh doch einfach in die Wirtschaft," 54). Barbara, whose name doubles her real name, speaks to Emmi, who, in order to make herself understandable, recounts her own thought processes as if they were being told by someone else. She also explains why she has come in out of the storm; she has often walked by the bar before and has been struck by the music. In fact, its music plays through the opening titles, drawing us in: the "Arab music" of the bar emanates from the extradiegetic world of the film. Emmi is drawn to something without knowing what calls her.

It is to a different music that the first scene between Emmi and Ali unfolds. The young woman that Ali rejects (his penis is broken, he says) puts on a German song about a black Gypsy and eggs him on to dance with the old woman. A joke? A dare? At whose expense? It is to this music that this black man dances with Emmi. At the end of the film, Emmi will ask for it to be played when they dance together again, but in the middle of the film, celebrating their marriage, when she asks for "our song" it is Arab music that is played and which presumably answers her desire. As always in this film, nothing stays singular.

Emmi responds to Ali's first invitation to dance as if the word "dance" were not in her vocabulary, or as if he were not speaking German. A bit later, however, she compliments his German; later in the film, when the shopkeeper pretends not to understand Ali's German, Emmi retaliates by telling him that Ali speaks better German than he does. Indeed, a variety of "Germans" are spoken in the film. It is not one language, no more than all foreign workers are "Arabs" or "Turks," with whom they are interchanged. Ali's German is punctuated with sentences of negative affirmation. Sitting alone is not good, and she is sitting alone ("Du allein sitzen. Macht viel traurig. Allein sitzen nicht gut," 55). Not that she is not good, he goes on to say. She is good, he says, although, he also insists, relations between Arabs and Germans are not good. To Germans, only Germans are human, and Arabs are dogs. Is Emmi an exception to this generalization? Or is it only a truth about men, not about women? Ali is forever pronouncing on what is and is not good. As Fujiwara says, these gnomic utterances seem to encapsulate timeless truths in a film that is always stopping, framing shots as if on something timeless, images of irrecuperable difference. Putting such truths in Ali's mouth, they are also being orientalized, racialized, perhaps in something akin to the way that Rock Hudson's acting style emerged playing Taza, the Apache. Although Fassbinder aims to show something — human hatefulness — whose causes are not just immediate and historical, he knows how dubious attempts to formulate this might be as the timeless wisdom of the Other. Ali's generalization about Germans is contradicted as his first conversation with Emmi ends: "You were good to speak with Ali" ("Du gut sprechen mit Ali," 56). It is when he says this that Emmi learns his name. Like her, he refers to himself in the third person. When she asks if that is his name, he explains it is the name Germans use for all "Arabs" and tells her his real name, which is the actor's real name.

Throughout the film, Emmi will go on calling him Ali except at the moment she acquires his name when they marry. Despite the visible prejudice against this "unnatural" and "unseemly" union, there is no law against it (unlike in Nazi Germany or in parts of the United States before the 1967 Supreme Court ruling in *Loving v. Virginia* made state antimiscegenation laws illegal). Fassbinder is not suggesting some form of oppression that stems from the state down: when the police are called by her neighbors because Emmi is entertaining Arabs in her apartment, they simply ask her to lower the music; the women in the building disparage the policemen even before then: they have long hair, so how could they be the law? Nor is Fassbinder suggesting some uniform economic motive: the landlord's son comes to intervene (Emmi is breaking her lease by having a tenant). When she claims that Ali is her fiancé (her made-up claim in fact sparks their engagement), he has no objection to Ali remaining in the apartment. Everything in Fassbinder cuts at least two ways. Emmi can even act as though Ali is her special name for him: telling her children his real name, she says to them, "I call him Ali." In fact everyone does.

However benign the relationship between Ali and Emmi looks as the film begins, it is not shielded from understated disagreements as Emmi gropes for common ground and common language, even in the Asphalt Bar. The morning after Emmi and Ali have sex, she awakens and looks appalled at the man in bed with her. He is wearing her dead husband's pajamas. Her husband was also a foreign worker—a Pole, she has told Ali; her parents didn't want her to marry him, and her fellow workers have treated her as a foreigner because her surname, Kurowski, is Polish. Her father was a Nazi, she continues, and hated all foreigners; she, too, was a Nazi—everyone was. Is Emmi appalled at having slept with Ali because she still is a Nazi or because she has repeated her initial rebellious union? Is there a difference between these impulses? She rushes to the bathroom to look in the mirror, much as Cary kept looking for herself in the mirror. But Emmi's face looking at this face registers misrecognition.

Before he ever entered her apartment, Ali had wanted to leave; or, rather, he says he would like to go in, but . . . Emmi rejects the "but."

If every yes is also a no, nothing ever changes, she says. But there is no way out of this bind of yes and no. In the kitchen together, the morning after, she is so happy she is crying because she is afraid, and Ali says to her, "Angst essen Seele auf," the phrase that titles the film. Emmi finds his laconic statement poetic and asks if it is an Arabic saying. The film also begins with a phrase in green letters across the opening shot: "Happiness isn't always fun" ("Das Glück ist nimmer lustig"). The supposed Arabic saying is part of Ali's arsenal of Arabic sententiae that includes his idealization of his father as a man roaming free and his declaration that mothers are never abandoned. These two conflicting claims are presented as if they speak the single truth of how good life is in Morocco. Of course, it is not so good that it keeps him there; there is no work in Morocco, and becoming a foreign worker seems like the route to survival. Emmi works hard, too; they begin to pool their resources in the hope of buying a little piece of heaven. Ali questions the phrase; Fassbinder winks at Sirk's title. The song that plays in the background, "A Little Love," does too. Self-contradiction is crossed by cross-racial desire.

In the first scene in Emmi's bedroom she reflects on the meaning of life; Ali is sitting on her bed, unable to sleep, stroking her arm because he needs consolation. She reflects on how quickly life can go by: "What should we do with our time?" ("Wass soll man den tun mit seiner Zeit?," 62). Ali tells her that lying in bed alone and thinking has made him think that maybe Germans are right about Arabs. Nonsense, Emmi replies, reminding Ali of his earlier statement, that thinking isn't good, it just makes you unhappy ("Viel denken — viel weinen," 56). But coupling, sex, relationship, talking together, does not overcome aloneness. Happiness isn't always happy. We should be nice to each other when we are together, Emmi says toward the end of the film, in the Asphalt Bar, acknowledging that he won't be faithful to her; he insists he will be and that he loves her. Just previously he has stood in front of the mirror in the bar's bathroom, smacking himself in the face repeatedly. Killing himself? Waking himself up? "Kif-kif," Ali says about his living situation, six men in one room, talking to Emmi at her kitchen table the night they meet (60); "Kif-kif" he says again toward the end to Barbara, who is trying to stop him from gambling away all his money, from destroying himself (94). "Kif-kif," he tells Emmi, means "It's all the same," and she admires the sentiment or perhaps simply the sound of the Arabic phrase. "That's funny," she says ("Das ist lustig," 61). He translates the phrase again for Barbara: "It's all the same! Do you understand?" ("Mir alles egal! Kif-kif! Verstehen? Kif-kif!," 94).

Thinking may not make for happiness, but it can liberate one from unthinking happiness, the kind that Hollywood films exist to provide and that Sirk showed Fassbinder could be deformed but not so completely as to guarantee them no audience — a point that Thomas Elsaesser has emphasized in work on Fassbinder since the 1970s.[91] *Fear Eats the Soul* was one of the first of Fassbinder's films to show the influence of Sirk. (In the stunning essay he wrote to accompany the 2013 Criterion Collection DVD of *The Merchant of Four Seasons* [1971], Elsaesser designates it as the first in a Sirk-inspired "cycle of films centered on the impossibility of love or trust within (homo- and heterosexual) couples.") Besides the shared elements of mise-en-scène that Fassbinder brought to his melodramas — mirrors, stairways, framed doorways, screens — the camera's relentless, fixated eye, as Elsaesser stresses, continually breaks and makes self-conscious the watching of Fassbinder's films, denaturalizing them. Staring onscreen, with gazes that mix hostility and desire (envy, jealousy), reflects our own relationship to films that invite identifications with their pathos, but also disidentification. Emmi may appear to be victimized, but she has strong desires to identify with those who victimize her. This is true of Ali as well, as is particularly evident when Emmi comes looking for him in the garage where he works. She is taunted by Ali's fellow workers as his mother from Morocco. Ali first joins in the laughter, but when the taunt is repeated, he doesn't laugh: the laugh is also on him. (This scene, with its repetition, repeats the structure of the film, with its replay and reversal of relationships.)

Emmi's complexity could be summed up or exemplified by her relationship to Nazism; Ali's, in his relationship to a Morocco he at once idealizes and yet has fled. Hence Elsaesser's *Fassbinder's Germany* takes national identity as the ultimate destination of the double binds and vicious circles in which characters and their desires are located: "The ironic discrepancies of expectation and tragic incompatibilities between the partners suggest that something beyond the difficulties of domestic bonding is at issue" (265). Certainly this is an arguable thesis for the trilogy of *The Marriage of Maria Braun* (1978), *Lola* (1981), and *Veronika Voss* (1981) or for *Berlin Alexanderplatz* (1980). Yet, as Elsaesser also suggests, this final point of reference builds on the dynamics of the impossible couple, on the fact that "love has the structure of a response to a demand that it can never fill" (69). That point, a basic Freudian/Lacanian insight, could more aptly lead to a notion that what exceeds the couple lies within them, not outside. Moreover, as Elsaesser forcefully puts it, and in a way that throws historicization into question as an ultimate explanatory principle, "radical exteriorization" (246) is precisely Fassbinder's goal.

Elsaesser suggests that the impossible situation in Fassbinder can be located in the space between titles of two of his films: *Love Is Colder Than Death* (1969) and *I Only Want You to Love Me* (1975–76, 241). "Fassbinder's was a both-and world. . . . He not only saw two sides at once, he was in two sides at once" (246). *Fear Eats the Soul* takes its occasion from the impossible coupling of a Moroccan foreign worker and a German cleaning woman, but their story might be the same if they shared a nationality. For even if they shared that, there would be no guarantee they shared much else, or that how they had a nationality was any more singular than how they had an identity or a sexuality: Emmi is alienated from her fellow Germans, including her family members.[92] Ali apparently has sexual relations only with German women, perhaps looking for the mother he says Moroccans never leave behind (this would make his fellow workers' taunt more painful). Between and within any two people there is the same divided situation. Traversing boundaries, as Elsaesser puts it (247), is the task of relationality—in the film and in our crossed relationship to it. It is as easy to love Emmi and Ali as it is to hate them.

That, too, is the case with Fassbinder, even with Fassbinder in his role of Eugen, insofar as it is a role and therefore impossible simply to collapse into his identity. If Fassbinder identifies with the part, he is the hateful human he hates. As Elsaesser suggests in the concluding chapter of his book, the fact that the personal and the artistic seem inseparable in Fassbinder is precisely a key to his success. The enormous productivity of the filmmaker has everything to do with the ways in which Fassbinder was embroiled with others, making films out of relationships that were themselves being acted out in intense, condensed periods of work, with marathon schedules often enabled by drugs and alcohol, and overheated personal relations. Elsaesser notes how Fassbinder's choice of melodrama allowed him a form whose operative temporality is that of "if only" (248), a time for possibility bounded by impossibility, for productivity that stares negation in the face. As Elsaesser puts it, Fassbinder's characters are not victims of the social so much as they are outsiders desiring to be outside, desiring not to be part of what they are a part. This means that the negative charge of social being is also what they desire; the desire not to belong is built into their desire.

In that respect, social existence exemplifies desire itself with its negative and positive pulls. Fassbinder makes El Hedi ben Salem "immortal"—he made him a star—as a way of getting rid of him. Abandoned by Fassbinder, the actor turned criminal, hoping his crimes would disgrace Fassbinder. But the police didn't connect him to the filmmaker: Salem alone was caught and jailed. He committed suicide in a prison cell in Nimes. Fassbinder heard of it some time later and dedicated *Querelle* (1982), another study in desired abasement—in desire as abasement—to Salem. It turned out to be his own last film. Productivity involves living off others, living off a part of oneself that is other than oneself, connecting with others through that part of oneself that enables transportation out of oneself. Identification thus involves the negation of a self-evident, self-confirming self. Self-negation seeks out the negation of the other. Destruction of self and other is involved in the making of work that exceeds oneself. Call it the couple. Call it the work of art. This is how one makes something outside oneself from oneself, along the lines of the fact that the self is not one. Eve Kosofsky Sedgwick remarks in *Epistemology of the Closet* on "the long, painful realization, *not* that all oppressions are congruent, but that they are *differently* structured."[93] This realization seems not yet real to critics who assume that categories of identity are self-explanatory, often by ignoring how the various categories—gender, race, nationality, sexuality—that intersect in anyone rob persons of singular self-identity. Try these categories out on Ali and Emmi; add to that their other identities, as Brigitte Mira and El Hedi ben Salem. Add Fassbinder. To identify with the work is to identify with something not living. It is to exist in the "if only" of the melodramatic mode of fictional existence. It is to identify with a life that is not life: with impossibility.

In an essay on impossibility as the melodramatic temporality of *Fear Eats the Soul*, Elena Gorfinkel argues that Fassbinder's film offers "a political supplement of 'bad feeling.'" She wrenches this supplement from earlier negative arguments about his films (*Fear Eats the Soul* among them), mentioning Richard Dyer's complaint that Fassbinder voids possibilities of political agency in work that specularizes the sufferings of marginal groups along with Kaja Silverman's embrace of a masochistic ecstasy that reduces gender difference to a feminized castration. Gorfinkel nudges their critiques in the direction of a productive negativity. "Negative affects . . . are here put to work," she writes, and precisely in their service of a precarious, asynchronous relationality.[94] (I noted something akin to this in the relationship between Ron and Cary in *All That Heaven Allows*.) The work performed is queer work, to follow John David Rhodes, who attaches Fassbinder's style to D. A. Miller's remark that style is "an exasperating materiality that won't disappear into social meanings."[95] This work is utopic in the sense of delineating a no-place within the social and the positive desire for this place. As Gorfinkel suggests, this place becomes available momentarily in precarious relationality, in the dance that Ali and Emmi perform at the film's beginning — a dance that is initiated as a joke and an expression of hostility, and that ends at the film's end when Ali collapses. Recovery and relapse is what lies ahead, momentary possibilities within the impossible situation.

Queer Relations: *Far from Heaven*

To review the trajectory of this chapter, I turn to an interview with Todd Haynes from 2003, included on the 2003 Criterion Collection DVD of *Ali: Fear Eats the Soul*.[96] Haynes begins with his first encounter with Fassbinder as an undergraduate in the semiotics program at Brown. He locates Fassbinder in relation to his contemporary filmmakers but in opposition to their desire to make directly political movies that tell you what to think. Haynes ends the first section of the interview by quoting, as I have done, the sentences in which Fassbinder articulated the notion that revolution belongs not on the screen, but in the capacity to think and feel that the viewer is given by what is shown. "Direct tenderness" is Haynes's phrase for this ability. Fassbinder learned it from Sirk; Haynes also learned it from Sirk by way of Fassbinder. As indicated in the title of the interview ("Todd Haynes: From Fassbinder to Sirk and Back"), directness is, in fact, a kind of indirection, requiring the breaking of automatic identifications as the way of making a connection.

To show what he means (it is a version of what Elsaesser calls a vicious circle and double bind), Haynes turns to the relationship between *All*

That Heaven Allows, Fear Eats the Soul, and his own *Far from Heaven*. He focuses first on the ambiguous title of Sirk's film, recalling what Sirk told Halliday: whereas the studio assumed the title meant that heaven allows everything (the promise of liberal society, assuring its subjects that they have or could have all they want), Sirk knew that heaven is stingy: we don't get what we want, especially not in the cruel optimism of the happy ending. Sirk shows what heaven won't allow; Fassbinder exacerbated the problems the impossible couple faces. In fact, Haynes claims, Fassbinder not only intensified but also reversed the dynamics of the couple: Wyman's Cary is divided between her desire for Ron and the tug of social and familial demand while Hudson's Ron is a rock, whereas Emmi, solid in her goodness, is in Ron's position and Ali is ambivalent and corruptible. As Ali finds a degree of acceptance in German society, he is unmoored, but for Haynes, that does not happen to Emmi. For him this shows what Fassbinder admired in Sirk: the woman who thinks. Haynes's feminism may explain his reading of Emmi, although it seems to me that one can be a feminist and still see that both Ali and Emmi are pulled in the two directions that Haynes divides between them. Indeed, when he turns to his own film, he acknowledges this about Cathy and Frank. Haynes's reading of Emmi, that Fassbinder crosses her gender position, instances Haynes's homoaesthetics.

In the next section of the interview, Haynes engages terms from feminist film criticism distinguishing the gaze from the look (the burden of Kaja Silverman's essay on *Fear Eats the Soul* in *Male Subjectivity at the Margins*).[97] Haynes focuses on the fact that Fassbinder's film thematically and technically is structured by the look freezing people into oppositional positions. The way Haynes plumbs the full force of opposition resonates with what I have been showing in this chapter. On the one hand, the look conveys desire. On the other hand, the look means to make distinctions, most crucially between us and them: it means to police desire. The look makes Ali and Emmi experience themselves as pariahs for loving each other, makes them feel themselves as outsiders rejected by society. But, as Haynes goes on to say, society needs also to incorporate and appropriate its outsiders, to use them, to take them in. In the exact visual replacement of Emmi by Yolanda in the scenes on the stairs, the film shows this process (of inclusion/exclusion) as the process by which society is made and made to continue. For someone to be let in, someone else must be shut out. Haynes sees this, too, in the scene where Ali is accepted by Emmi's fellow workers, who circle around him, feeling his muscles. He notes how Fassbinder shoots the scene, at a distance that allows us to identify with Ali but not because we are offered his point of view or a close-up that would convey a sympathetic connection directly from his face to our eyes. We can imagine what Ali must be feeling as he experiences the humiliating terms of his acceptance as an exotic. Acceptance that is also at the same time alienation, a violation of a being that is always already violated, even if he had stayed at home. This point is conveyed by the role El Hedi ben Salem played, again using his own name, in Fassbinder's *Fox and His Friends* (*Faustrecht der Freiheit*, 1975). In Morocco, Fox attempts to pick him up and bring him back to his hotel; an Arab man who works there prevents Salem's admittance, telling him that Arabs are not permitted in the hotel.

Haynes suggests that the scene in the art gallery in *Far from Heaven* (to which I will turn shortly) is most indebted to this regime of the crossings of a look that no one owns. There Cathy and Raymond begin to bond over the notion of being "the only one in the room," as Haynes puts it. The paradox of the "only one" is that mechanisms of social incorporation and exclusion constantly redescribe who is in and who is out. Under one or another social regime, anyone could be the only one — or one with everyone else. So, in the final section of the interview, Haynes notes that Fassbinder's mature oeuvre fastens on the victims, those whom society would exclude — women, racial minorities, gays — to show that victims are also perpetrators. He takes his example from *Fox and His Friends*, in which Fassbinder plays Fox (his real name is Franz Biberkopf, the name of the protagonist of *Berlin Alexanderplatz*), the gay man victimized by a group of predatory gay men who seem to accept him into their company. These men are well heeled, well connected, not some beleaguered minority, and Fox wants in (the scene in Morocco is one where he seems to have reached that goal). Although Haynes does not cite Sedgwick, he might have had in mind the passage from *Epistemology of the Closet* that I quoted earlier, or a sentence proximate to it: "A person who is disabled through one set of oppressions may *by the same positioning* be enabled through others."[98] Fox and Eugen (both parts Fassbinder acted) are two sides — victim and oppressor — of the double aspect of human desire. Haynes locates this dilemma in sociality, a result of the dynamic of exclusion/inclusion by which society operates. More fundamentally, it has to do with the fact that people can't be alone and can't be with others either.

Beside Fox Haynes puts an example from *Far from Heaven*: Frank's dilemma in suffering for his desire for men but being able nonetheless to hold on to his male privilege. Haynes will not claim Frank for gay liberation, will not simply celebrate Frank's version of coming out; he is still able to call the shots in a way that neither Raymond nor Cathy can. This is not, I hasten to add, to cast them as victims either: Raymond, for instance, can get on a train and leave, while Cathy cannot; she, however, can still return to her middle-class home, where presumably alimony will allow her to have Sybil to minister to her every need.

Haynes says that for him as a gay filmmaker, Fassbinder's refusal to privilege anyone is inspiring. Contradiction is the abiding condition of human being. The fragile, precarious attempt to affirm a connection is countered by the fact that making a connection is to become social and therefore involves a violation of one's antisocial solitariness. Desire for another does not dispel this antisocial impulse, as becomes especially clear when the object of desire is someone who is socially proscribed—a person of a different race or class, a person of the same gender. However, even within the most socially accepted of desires (say, that embodied in the exemplary couple of Haynes's film, Mr. and Mrs. Magnatech), there is, to start, the elementary division of gender. These differences are social constructs, to be sure (but just as surely internalized and incorporated); recognizing that difference need not be antipathy does not forestall some other division replacing one difference with another. If Frank were straight he still might never be home much. And, as the women confess over their daiquiri lunch, many of them would be happier if their husbands didn't want sex. Haynes insistently shows divisions within the same, within categories of identity that are assumed to be singular. It is not just a white man who shouts "Boy" at Raymond: a black man calls him that when Raymond brings Cathy to the café where she is the only one.

Haynes ends his interview with a final citation, a passage that I referred to earlier in this chapter. His last word is Sirk's, the notion that no one can be eindeutig, singular. So despite or, perhaps, in addition to the crossing of rocklike solidarity from the man to the woman that for Haynes described the relationship of gender-crossing from Sirk to Fassbinder, there is this more elementary first principle. It is a principle of original division as the source of the impossibility and possibility of the relationality desired that moves human desire along its antinomic paths: desire for another and to be alone; desire not to be the only one; desire to be the only one. As Sirk says further in the interview with Halliday (which Haynes also quotes), the principle of not being singular means that we cannot have full purchase on our own being. Characters in Sirk films — or in those of Haynes or Fassbinder — cannot be fully self-aware. Indeed, self-awareness requires the split between knowing and being. The camera may show us this, with a godlike look that is uncomfortably like the policing gaze of the social. It is what we are looking for when we look in the mirror — for that other self that inhabits us, or controls us, as we put on the face society desires or the face we hope will find a response to a desire society will not countenance. The movie theater where Frank attempts to pick up a man is showing *The Three Faces of Eve*. Since it is the 1950s, it is on a double bill with *Miracle in the Rain*, a Jane Wyman vehicle about a lost lover. The miracle of the title is a token from the dead lover that somehow finds its way back into the hands of the woman who has barely survived his loss. A material object makes a connection beyond mortal limitation. The double bill of two women's stories (of self-finding and self-losing) is Frank's story, too. More than that, it is also the story of transmission I have been pursuing from Haynes to Fassbinder to Sirk and back again, the circuits that are at once a closing of a loop and a Mobius strip of continuous replacement fueled by contradictions. At each moment in Haynes's interview, the possibility of going forward is rooted in impossibility; fittingly, Haynes ends with Fassbinder's identification with Sirk — his identification, that is, of hatred of humans with Sirk's love of them.

The place where that love and hate meet is their films. Haynes quotes Fassbinder quoting Sirk on the fact that films are made with things (mirrors, to take the most prominent of them) and people (made in a mirror stage that binds the alienation of self-discovery with social loss as social being). People and things are not different, and most certainly are the same on the screen, where we are not seeing anything but images moving with a life that is a mechanism: it is not in them (not in the person shot, not in each individual frame of the film, a still made to move only because it is followed faster than the eye can see by another one). Nothing ever changes on a film — the performances are unlike living performance; they are invariably the same, but because frames go too fast for us to see, we can never really see what is there at any moment. There is another life in films, but it is invisible. Yet it is that other life that we keep trying to see, and especially in these melodramas that go on extending and baffling our relationships to them.

....

To conclude, I turn now to the scene at the art show in *Far from Heaven*, which Haynes compares to the one he finds most beautiful in *Fear Eats the Soul*, Emmi and Ali in the garden café. Haynes's scene has a similar structure. Raymond and Cathy meet, and as they stand together talking and looking at a Joan Miró painting, the camera moves quickly and restlessly, catching others looking at them, staring away from what should be holding their gaze, the pictures on the wall, and looking instead with hostility at the picture Cathy and Raymond make for them. As Haynes mentions in the directorial commentary on the Universal DVD of his film, the space in which the scene takes place has been organized as a color field—the main characters are all in drab, olive-green attire; the walls are a greenish blue; the windows have been covered with gels, making the art space some kind of church, Haynes says (they also turn its windows into a kind of Mondrian).[99]

The art show scene catches Cathy in motion. It opens with a shot of her hurrying in, not looking at anything, looking for Eleanor (Patricia Clarkson), to whom she immediately apologizes. It ends, too, with her talking to Eleanor as she rushes off: "Jeepers, would you look at the time!" This is her refrain throughout the film; Cathy is on a schedule not of her own making, driven by her role as wife and mother, planning a party for her husband, picking up the children. In *All That Heaven Allows*, it appears that Ron and Cary are in different time zones, unable to synchronize; in *Fear Eats the Soul*, Emmi remarks on how precarious and short our time is. Cathy fills her time with the meaningless activities that define her social existence. She has no time for anything and is on the run until the moment late in the film when she has lost everything—her husband, her would-be lover—and collapses in exhaustion on the bed. Haynes takes the shot of her from Max Ophüls's *The Reckless Moment* (1949), in which Lucia Harper (Joan Bennett), the protagonist, finally crumbles for a second. Lucia's relentless activity in the film has been to stave off disaster, to make sure that home life is not disturbed. She is allowed a moment of release before the phone rings and she is back on duty. The phone also punctuates Cathy's life; often it is Frank calling, demanding a change in the routines she attempts to maintain. Haynes brings Cathy, weeping on her bed, to the zero point of the ironies of that earlier film, where it is the happy ending that secures the trap around these women.

When Cathy arrives at the show and hurries to join Eleanor, apologizing for being late, she is immediately included in the group that will at the end of the sequence become those who exclude her. Haynes says that Cathy begins to understand or experience in this scene what it would be like to be "the only one." This is Raymond's condition as the only black adult in the room; a guest at Cathy's party later says, with black servants in the room listening, that there are no Negroes in Hartford. The "only one" is the one who is, whenever possible, rendered invisible. Being seen together, Cathy and Raymond violate a divide. To inhabit the forbidden zone volatilizes the specter of forbidden desire. This is the locale of melodrama, as Christine Gledhill reminds us in "Rethinking Genre."

Raymond may be the "only one" in the room, but there is another "only one" there, too: Mona's uncle, Morris Farnsworth (J. B. Adams). Eleanor has alerted Cathy to the fact that he's "one of *those*." Indeed, much to Cathy's discomfort, Eleanor spells out what she means after using various euphemisms ("flowery," "light on his feet"), when she wonders whether Cathy, who has already been proclaimed in the town newspaper as being "as devoted to her family as she is kind to Negroes" might now be touted for her "kindness to homosexuals." "Oh—that word," Cathy says in reply to Eleanor's teasing. She would have it remain unsaid. Eleanor knows and yet would as soon not know.

Farnsworth is the only gay in the room, and evidently so (in his knowledge of the art world, his being from the wicked big city, his sporting a cravat and matching pocket handkerchief, his effeminate gestures and voice and neat little Poirot-like mustache). But he is not seen thanks to his urbane credentials and to Mona's (Celia Weston) power over her social group. Mona, Glyn Davis has suggested, might well be queer, too, a single woman filled with venom (to Davis, she is not the only queer woman: Sybil [Viola Davis] also fills that part).[100] These are possible outsiders who make their way in by operating or being situated in relation to the inside/outside distinction that allows them the benefit of marshaling the policing look, deflecting it from themselves.

Everyone knows (at least about Farnsworth), and no one says. This performance of the closet is not confined there; it is a structure that functions in multiple ways across and through many divides. In this scene Farnsworth opposes Cathy and Raymond; same-sex against cross-race, his knowingness about fakes against Raymond's knowledge of art, performed in front of a copy.

The opening encounter with Farnsworth and Mona is punctuated with the word "darling"—Cathy says it to Eleanor, Mona to Cathy, Mona to Farnsworth as she makes the introductions, Eleanor to Cathy as she saves her from the venomous group (she won't be doing this by the end of the film). The kind of seeing that is going on at the show is seeing to be seen. After the camera scans the wall, it turns a corner to find Cathy paused before a Picasso (the script indicates it is a "beautiful 'crying woman'").[101] We don't see what she sees, but when a camera bulb flashes we are reminded of Haynes and his camera work. It is the local reporter, Mrs. Leacock (Bette Henritze), who earlier caught Cathy as Mrs. Magnatech and noticed her noticing a black man in her backyard—and not calling the police about it. "Wife of Hartford Executive Communing with Picasso" is the byline Mrs. Leacock attaches to the photo she has just snapped. Cathy is a living picture, encapsulated, labeled, ready for hanging, if not on a wall, at least as a picture in the newspaper, which will mirror her social existence back to her.

Yet artificial life may point the way to the real. As Cathy approaches Raymond and his daughter, Sarah (Jordan Puryear), the camera catches them from various angles. Haynes is making pictures of them, shooting back and forth, as he puts them in relationship to the spaces of the art that frames them or which they frame in his shots. The scene in this makeshift art gallery (a confection of the ladies auxiliary carved out of a local school) is just about the only space in the film that is not fully occupied territory, though when it is claimed for the social dynamic of exclusion/inclusion it is the equivocal group around Farnsworth that does so.

As Cathy and Raymond come together, they register the awkwardness of their encounter. "How on earth" did Raymond know about the show, Cathy asks; he tries to turn her surprise that their worlds might meet on equal footing into a joke. Of course, she is still Mrs. Whitaker to him, while he is Raymond to her—her gardener, as Eleanor will label him when she rescues Cathy from this scene of socially humiliating contact. And then, coming as close as she can to recognizing what this social awkwardness is about, and yet voicing it in a non sequitur, Cathy assures Raymond that she and her husband believe in equal rights for Negroes and support the NAACP. Raymond sardonically responds by thanking her, presumably for her words of kindness to Negroes, and Cathy completes the social ritual by answering, "Not at all." Not at all: what thanks does he owe her for this "support"? It echoes the line Cathy uses again and again in her encounters with Sybil, from the opening of the film—"Oh Sybil, thank heavens"—and then her enjoining the children to help Sybil, the help without whom Cathy is helpless. The black woman who appears to live in her house, takes care of her children, answers the phone, keeps track of her schedule, and also knows what goes on outside her world and in a world of her own.[102] The potential brutality in these kind encounters is played outside the window between Sarah and Hutch and his friends (the character fetches her name from Sarah Jane, who is brutally beaten by her white boyfriend, as Sarah will be later in the film). The (im)possibility of something other than these hostile encounters—overt or masked—occurs as Raymond and Cathy start communing over the artwork before which they stand, the Miró between them, *The Nightingale's Song at Midnight and the Morning Rain*.[103]

The camera opens and then punctuates their conversation with close-ups of the reproduction of this painting from Miró's 1940s Constellation series. Cathy says she is having difficulty putting into words what she sees and how she feels. This is true in the excruciating conversations she and Frank have about his "problem," as it is in her conversation with Raymond, the first they have had in full view of others. There are no adequate words to discuss what is going on with Frank because there are either the euphemisms that attempt to say it without saying it or the clinical term that makes it an identity ready for treatment. But not-saying need not only mean a refusal to claim and own and affirm; the discussion about painting suggests the difficulty of turning what is seen or what is felt into words. It instances the aesthetic of impossibility. It is also about the difficulty of having an experience that has not already been prepackaged in language inadequate to and yet a crucial means to express the complexity of experience. "I don't know why, but I just adore it." Loving art and loving other people might not readily be seen as the same thing, yet "adore" suggests that connection even as it anticipates a language of spiritual adoration. "Heavens" is the most frequent term Cathy uses throughout the film, usually in the phrase "for heaven's sake"—always thereby signaling the film's title and its relation through that word to Sirk's film. Eleanor asks, "Who on earth was that *man*," and Cathy responds by asking, "For heaven's sake, *why*," then contextualizing her response by way of "that ridiculous story," the newspaper column that had equated her family feeling with her feeling for Negroes. Eleanor responds by noting how "familiar" she and Raymond appear, and Cathy counters, "Oh what does that *mean*? Familiar terms." Terms that draw strangers into the family. That make them the same as us?

Raymond accedes to Cathy's inarticulate feelings; along the lines of her adoration for the painting he offers his translation of her feeling into his own scene of translation. For him, it is hard to put modern art into words because it attempts to pick up where religion lets off. He posits a continuity, a divinity on the wall, that also involves perhaps some version of Peter Brooks's thesis about melodrama and its materialization of the moral occult. At best, Brooks glimpses what I think Haynes also shows here: the possibility that aesthetic experience holds a key to ways of thinking and seeing, that precisely because the life of art is not simply a human life it may exceed the constraints of the social. In this scene in the film, no different in its exacting camera work from others (Haynes, in fact, insists on closely following the camera procedures of Sirk and Fassbinder), Raymond articulates the route to this transformative knowledge: "The modern artist just pares it down to the most basic elements of form and color." Melodrama, we are often told, rather than paring it down, exaggerates and intensifies, magnifies, makes much of little. But it is, especially in the three films I have been contemplating, always also trying to find thereby a means to express something else, trying through them to draw us to some core experience of meaning difficult to come by otherwise. Cathy acknowledges what Raymond has just said as if it were itself an aesthetic experience: "Why that's lovely." She has complimented Sarah in similar terms earlier ("She's lovely"), and later in the film, in her last conversation with Raymond, she pronounces him beautiful.

Before and while they speak, the camera holds on to what they are seeing, a painting of shapes that evoke a scene of night and day, of the song and rain in its title, although the canvas is what Raymond says,

76 CHAPTER TWO

shape and color that do not illustrate the title. The first time the camera looks at the painting whole; the second time it focuses on its right side, where one of the forms looks a bit like an eye looking back at the viewer. There are recognizable shapes in the image — the moon in particular, while the red circles and black lines of the image look like some circulatory system, inside the body, or like a map of the cosmos. Heaven and earth are the phrases that keep bounding Cathy's world or, rather, keep suggesting intrusions on it — "What on earth?"; "For heaven's sake" — as if there were something else that explains the world, something in it and yet apart from it. Something that could refuse the ways in which difference works in the world to make divisions that replicate themselves and reinforce difference, to suggest some other regime of different colors and shapes whose difference does not make that kind of difference: shapes in the painting are sometimes recognizable, mostly not; connections are drawn by lines that seem to remap and reintegrate along lines difficult to put into words, lines that can make one world out of these disparate forms, and that do so by acknowledging formal identities between the nonidentical. These unrecognizable things nonetheless call forth feelings and thought; in the space of their attempted articulation they produce connections of thought and feeling that attach us to others by way of something outside us that also is inside us. The attachment here comes by means of a reproduction of an object that somehow came from someone but is no longer attached to its maker; it is exerting its gravitational pull on us, the pull of a life in dead things, in things that have a life that exceeds our own, that exceeds, indeed, our very categories of life and death. This is Haynes's diagrammatic method in his film. Reading this scene is a matter of doing what we do looking at this painting: connecting the dots to see another world in this one.

To see that other world entails negating this one. As Wilde wrote in "The Ballad of Reading Gaol," "each man kills the thing he loves," a refrain repeated early and late in that poem.[104] Fassbinder set Wilde's lines to music in his last film, *Querelle*, dedicated "to my friend El Hedi ben Salem M'Barek Mohamed Mustafa"; Haynes began theorizing what was to become his film practice by writing about Fassbinder's film and a homoaesthetics that required identifications that surpass identity: identification in that case across gender and toward a submission to something beyond oneself.[105] As Wilde's poem intimates, the killing of the beloved is only one of the possible meanings of his refrain; killing one-

IDENTITY AND IDENTIFICATION   77

self—whether in consummating or in refusing love—is another. "The artistic life is a long and lovely suicide," Wilde wrote to H. C. Marillier in 1886, years before his trial and condemnation literalized the point.[106] Wilde's love was "the love that dare not speak its name," to cite the words of Lord Alfred Douglas, the lover who embodied the suicidal, murderous relationship that Wilde articulated before ever meeting him. "The love that dare not speak its name" is a profound antisociality, an unnameable impossible that nonetheless coexists with the possible; it coexists precisely to show how impossible the possible (the conventional, the socially mandated) is even as it glimpses the possibilities in the impossible. The name of this love has no proper, singular name.

What is possible is the fragility of a connection unlikely to survive in this world. Haynes made *Far from Heaven* after *Velvet Goldmine*, a melodrama/musical about the persistence in glam rock of a Wildean legacy of a performance that forsakes identity. The film opens with the birth of Wilde, delivered from outer space, and pins together its performative world through a brooch that descends from Wilde, stitching together, wounding, and bejeweling those who follow Wilde in the wake of his spectacular performance of shamed celebrity that we might call, after Sedgwick and Michael Moon, "divinity." This is a divinity far from heaven and materialized in bodies that reach for something else. In the art gallery scene, we see Cathy and Raymond groping their way toward it and each other by attempting to articulate the inarticulable meaning of the painting they contemplate and which, with its eye, may be contemplating them and, if so, transporting them to the constellation that Miró is inventing. The reason to pin this to Wilde lies first in his notion that the love that dare not speak its name is what has been spoken in philosophy since Plato and in literature and art in its wake, in religion even before Jesus became the sacrificial embodiment celebrated and identified with in "The Ballad of Reading Gaol."[107]

I pin Wilde to the films I have been discussing in recognition of the Wildean impulse that Haynes makes explicit. That impulse is not Wilde's alone, of course, and it comes to Haynes as well from Fassbinder, his importation of Wilde into the recirculation of Genet in *Querelle*. Haynes likewise reimagines Genet in *Poison*, although not in the same way, since he pits the Genet plot against two others and mixes genres as well. Doing it likewise does not mean doing it in the same way except insofar as it entails a refusal of boundaries: sameness in difference. If people are not singular, eindeutig, relationality occurs along the tracks of this principle of nonsingularity. It was on the track of this kind of queer relationality that I opened this chapter by contemplating how Sirk and Fassbinder and Haynes are connected to each other, and why I have argued that they each seek to reimagine what the other has done in a shared enterprise of representing the impossible as what ruins possibility even as it intimates something beyond the possible (intimates it in forbidden intimacy, the familiarity of the unfamiliar, having feelings not one's own). Film embodies this in bodies onscreen who have been immobilized as images and then set to work, given life thanks to the movement of the camera. Writing does this, too, as the writer becomes the words written—words for the most part that precede the writer's existence and survive the writer's death. Dying as the artistic life is dying into the strange life that the artwork has. The author we read is always dead. The film actor is not alive. We give life to these things by attempting to find the life that is in them already.

Wilde called this life "personality"; he sought it in his love life and his artistic life, which were the same life. "It is Art, and Art only that reveals us to ourselves"; music or actors or images "have given form and substance to what was within us; they have enabled us to realize our personality."[108] Wilde's use of "personality" is as odd here as the claim that Sirk made his films personal and this enabled Fassbinder to connect to them on the basis of his personality—odd because the personal each claims is not personal to either, as Fassbinder discovered when he read a novel in which he found himself. What is personal to each is something they share to their undoing. Everyone is different from everyone else, and yet everyone is the same. The same because, materially, we are all made of the same stuff. The same because some extraordinary things— whether written, painted, sculpted, filmed—are capable of transporting us into a life that moves alongside the worn grooves in which we spend our wasted lives. Melodrama keeps opening what lies beyond these closures, creating an aesthetics of impossibility not to reclaim the truth of identity or the possibility of individual agency supposedly tied to self-discovery and self-realization, but by offering the (im)possibilities of identification with "personality," which is to say, with something impersonal, not living and not dead. I'm not there.

PART II · *MELOS + DRAMA*

THREE

THE ART OF MURDER

Hitchcock and Highsmith

Even before film had sound, when it was "silent," it was accompanied by live music coincident with images onscreen that also are live, but not in the same way. Film has always been the mixed-media, remediated phenomenon that melodrama names in its etymology. What does the + in *melos* + drama add up to? "Melo-drama," Hitchcock early affirmed, was a preferred term for his practice precisely because it was hard to define: "Try to define it for yourself and see how difficult it is," he opens his essay "Why I Make Melodramas" (1936). For Hitchcock, the word intimates a way of getting at what is real precisely through situations that seem un-real, exaggerated, impossible. "I use melodrama be-cause I have a tremendous desire for understatement in film," he writes.[1] "Understatement" suggests the torsion between the impossible plot situation and the underplaying of characters who negotiate the worlds that the film creates for them as if they were ordinary. It suggests verbal taciturnity; there is something silent in films even when they have sound. Alongside what we hear or see there is something unheard and unseen. The relationship between what is palpably there and what isn't is far from evident. Music in film is such an understatement, moreover, because it is an under-scoring that "speaks" a different language than words or image offer; it thereby further opens the disparities that define film, a counterpoint where meaning may reside beyond our ability to capture it in words.

What happens when we add melos to drama? "Understatement" (Hitchcock's word), "underscoring," "counterpoint" (mine)—these are some initial attempts to formulate what arises from the plus, the addition that opens the possibility in the impossible. In this chapter, I add Hitchcock to Highsmith (following in the wake of their conjunction in *Strangers on a Train*, her 1950 novel and his 1951 film) to contemplate the sound world heard in two Hitchcock films—*Strangers on a Train* and *Rope* (1948)—and the music in Highsmith; the second half of this chapter looks especially at her five Ripley novels. Hitchcock and Highsmith come together since murder and sexual identity, their shared theme, is a matter of melodramatic understatement.

In the discussion that follows, my focus is not the "impossible situation" engaged in the previous chapters, and it might seem that in leaving that plot behind, melodrama no longer is the subject. The union of melos and drama, however, *is* melodrama (I cling to the literal precisely to show that it is more than that). That union is itself an impossible couple. Finding terms for what can be made of this union is as much a question here as in chapter 2. In shifting the focus to music and to what could be seen as a merely formal problem, I hope to allow to surface something that I engaged in chapter 2: the moments when aesthetic experience is thematized; for example, when Ron makes the mill beautiful and habitable in *All That Heaven Allows*, or when Fassbinder appears onscreen, forcing us to consider the director's role in his films, or when Cathy and Raymond bond over a Miró in *Far from Heaven*.

What also surfaces in the films and texts in this chapter is something underlying the previous one: the saliency of male-male erotics. Rock Hudson's sexuality can be imagined to underscore the impossibility of Ron's relation to Cary (complicated further through her relation to Agnes Moorehead's Sara); likewise, Fassbinder's sexual relationship to El Hedi ben Salem M'Barek Mohamed Mustafa inflects the role of Ali in *Fear Eats the Soul*. These offscreen relations affect those onscreen only to underscore the impossibility in all relations, most poignantly in the ones we most desire (sex, or the unbearable, in a word). The geometries of relationality in *Far from Heaven* allow Todd Haynes to make Frank's homosexuality explicit but in a matrix that crosses it with the greater impossibility of Cathy and Raymond's relation.

The unsaid behind the palpably impossible manifests itself in the coupling of Philip and Brandon in *Rope*, or of Bruno and Guy (the couple that joins Hitchcock and Highsmith); it is a crime inseparable from murder. Philip and Brandon turn murder into a social occasion, and although they are not allowed to get away with it, the triumph of the social order is a "happy ending" as equivocal as the ones in the melodramas we have already considered. The examples in this chapter even more palpably affront the social order: in their evident male couples, in their murders. Highsmith's Tom Ripley gets away with it and even achieves something like a continuous happy ending in the defeat of the social as his murders go unpunished (increasingly they become thought experiments that ally him to his author), and in his successful simulations (the character who first seems to be a homosexual psychopath winds up as the happiest of married men in the four subsequent novels). Brandon and Philip are consummate hosts. These realizations, the impossible made possible, solicit us: Hitchcock's technical mastery in *Rope* is always on display; his cameo appearances draw our attention to his relation to his films. Our response cannot be separated from him, much as Highsmith locates herself in Tom and draws us in by way of him. That transgender plot of identification is played out in Tom's aesthetic projects—his self-making, his painting, or the harpsichord that both he and his wife, Heloise, play. Hitchcock and Highsmith draw us to them through their arts of murder. How Hitchcock gets away with it is what we can never get too much of, as D. A. Miller has suggested, most recently in "Hitchcock's Understyle: A Too-Close View of *Rope*."

I will get to Ripley at the end of this chapter, but to open the path to the aesthetics of impossibility I start with a publicity photo of Farley Granger shown with his record collection, *Call Me Madam* quite visible.[2] "Broadway show tunes fill his record shelves," the accompanying label reads; "Farley usually has a stack of them on the machine playing day and night." Other shots show Granger in what is described as his new bachelor pad in Laurel Canyon; he is bare-chested in one, carrying logs in another. The photos presumably mean to offer an image of a sensitive but masculine figure to the teens who would be reading *Modern Screen*, where the story ran in March 1951. But of course the picture signals something else. "Is he musical," Philip Brett reminds us, was for a time a way of asking obliquely about someone's—some man's—sexuality when more direct utterance was felt to be impossible;[3] having

THE ART OF MURDER 85

Granger posed with Ethel Merman's picture visible, D. A. Miller would be quick to tell us, all but gives the answer that the question prompts. "Is he musical?" "Call me madam."

In the following discussion I pursue this musical path of identification and its equivocations in a direction not taken by most musicologists—at least judging by the example of the commentary on Bernard Herrmann's score for *Vertigo* (1958; for many, the apex of his accomplishment), where analysis of the music is far less oblique, offering the notion that musical language can be translated thematically, that discrete musical motifs (often referred to as if they were Wagnerian leitmotifs) can be attached to a feeling, a place, a character, or a theme.[4] The recurrence of a motif, musicologists seem to suppose, produces a kind of immediate identificatory effect. There is much to discuss and to dispute in such an approach, not least the danger of banality, cliché, and redundancy that Theodor Adorno and Hanns Eisler deplore in their book on film music.[5] If image, text, and sound in a film add up to something, can that something be captured in reductive labels and clear-cut concepts, proper names, or two-word phrases?

Thomas Elsaesser, in "Tales of Sound and Fury," his crucial essay on family melodrama, talks suggestively about music as "punctuation" in the drama. Is punctuation part of a linguistic system? In a brief excursus on punctuation marks, Adorno writes: "There is no element in which language resembles music more than in the punctuation marks."[6] Adorno contemplates punctuation marks as images, seeing them as forms of bodily expression, as body parts—fingers and eyebrows, for instance. Punctuation, for him, alludes to something in language not captured by words: rhythm, musicality, breath, life. Can music be translated into words? Adorno answers by positing a complex dialectical relationship that refuses language as the repository of full meaning. Film theory, in the wake of Eisenstein, also would not endorse a linguistic model for the translation of drama to film, but would instead insist on the primacy of the visual, although Eisenstein, too, could imagine a dialectical function for sound in film, one that allies it to and makes it another form of montage.[7]

Elsaesser follows Adorno and Eisenstein in his analysis of melodrama, underscoring the role of music. His essay offers several complexly intertwined if also disparate historical genealogies for the role

86 CHAPTER THREE

of music in film, and for the kinds of punctuation effected. One example he briefly mentions is the carousel scene in *Strangers on a Train* where "The Band Played On" plays in the background; rather than the underlining of stark difference that Elsaesser associates with the main current of melodrama, music here offers instead an "ironic parallelism" that runs in counterpoint to overt thematics.[8] This is a kind of montage effect in line with the dialectical use of music that Adorno and Eisler promoted. By looking at Hitchcock and Highsmith under the rubric of "melodrama," I follow Elsaesser to what he calls the "dictionary sense" of the term: "a dramatic narrative in which musical accompaniment marks the emotional effects."[9] In unfolding the implications of this definition, Elsaesser names music as one of the "elements" in a "system of punctuation" that lends "expressive colour and chromatic contrast" to the story, providing an emotional "orchestration." Elsaesser's "dictionary sense" stretches precisely what it proffers, the literal; it offers music as language, "a system of punctuation," but also as an "element"—which could mean a "letter" (in Latin *elementum* is a letter of the alphabet), or could be one of the basic material substances on the chemical table. Sound is figured by Elsaesser as something visual, a color—a usage completely idiomatic since musicologists use the word "chromatic" to describe the tones that augment those in the diatonic scale on which modern Western music is based. Accompaniment becomes amplification—"orchestration," Elsaesser writes. It could lead one to wonder whether music brings out something that is primary (emotion) or adds emotion as a secondary effect. Elsaesser favors this dictionary sense because it points the way to locating the "problems" of melodrama as "problems of style and articulation."[10] In following the dictionary definition that Elsaesser proffers I aim to be alert to the "problems" of identification and singular meaning entailed. When Elsaesser's sentence articulates the "problems" of defining melodrama as "problems of style and articulation," one set of problems answers another: when "problems" echo and mean to answer "problems," tautology falls short of identification precisely by a reiteration that says the same thing twice, not once. This doubly problematic definition of melodrama leaves unsaid what melodrama is.

Mouvements Perpétuels

Was Farley Granger musical? According to *Include Me Out*, his autobiography, music was a welcome but belated discovery. He wasn't born musical. Having begun his movie career at age seventeen, Granger interrupted it to serve in the army during World War II. The "barracks were filled with music all the time," he reports; there, for the first time, he heard Mozart, Dinah Shore, and Benny Goodman. And also, he notes, in an afterthought that is more than that, this was "the first time I heard a recording of a Broadway show." He recalls, "I was so caught up by its lyrical beauty and emotional power that I didn't know whether to laugh or cry." He felt no need to hide either feeling from the "musicians" he was with: "Even the most hard-boiled of them understood that kind of reaction to a terrific piece of music."[11] His barracks mates, with their record collections, metamorphose into "musicians" (listeners and collectors become performers) who empathize as he weeps and laughs to *Carousel*. Yet they remain, or at least some of them do, hard-boiled.

Granger's musicality is wide ranging yet focuses especially on the Broadway musical. Granger had his first musical experiences on base in Hawaii. That also is where he had sex for the first time, with a woman named Liana (whom he continued to see), and, the same night, with a handsome lieutenant named Archie, whom he never saw again, but about whom he never stopped thinking. "I never felt the need to belong to any exclusive, self-defining, or special group. . . . I have loved men. I have loved women," he affirms. So, what should we make of that Ethel Merman publicity shot? Granger doesn't include it in the book, but Merman does appear. She starred in the first Broadway musical he saw: "She was extraordinary! She was magnificent! I was transported! I was blown away! I was in love!" Later he got to know her and found "she was a knockout off the stage as well, with a vocabulary that could make the Army, Navy, and Marines blush." When his ten-year exclusive contract with Samuel Goldwyn had ended, he pursued a stage career. Granger ends his life story with winning an Obie, "proof that the world I fell in love with when I saw Ethel Merman hold an audience in the palm of her hand during my first trip to New York was where I belonged."[12]

What world did he fall in love with? Where did he belong? D. A. Miller's *Place for Us*, an analysis of his love affair with the Broadway

88 CHAPTER THREE

musical, suggests an answer, not least when he analyzes his own relationship to Ethel Merman and parses her name for its mixed message of maternity and masculinity.[13] For Granger, too, she is a potential barracks mate so out in her musical performance that she and her male audience seem to change places: she's the hard-boiled one, they are covered in shame, blushing. Merman seems to occupy that galvanizing locus of identification that Zarah Leander provided for Douglas Sirk. She indicates, in Miller's terms, the place not literally provided for us in musicals whose plots assume impossibility as the fate of women or of straight couples, a place for us inhabitable only as a subtext "which is never given literal expression," except perhaps when we sing along.[14]

Was Farley Granger musical? Here's another answer to the question: he certainly is as Philip in his first Hitchcock film, *Rope*. It is not until almost twenty minutes in to that eighty-minute film that we learn the piano that sits in Brandon's (John Dall) well-appointed Manhattan living room (its walls covered in artworks) is Philip's instrument. Brandon mentions he has been able to arrange a debut for him to perform at Town Hall, and the party he's hosting, he tells Kenneth (Douglas Dick), is a farewell party. Philip is being taken off to the country, "locked up," Brandon says, so that he can practice six hours a day in preparation for his recital. We know, of course, another reason Philip might be locked up; we saw him drawing the noose around David Kentley's neck when the film began. And we know that this is a farewell party for David, too, his body snugly located in the cassone off which the guests are fed. "I hope you knock 'em dead," Kenneth responds, keeping up the unknowing double entendres, as does Janet (Joan Chandler) a minute later, when she wonders if the debut will make him "horribly famous." "These hands will bring you great fame," Mrs. Atwater (Constance Collier) predicts, as Philip sits down to play the piano, resounding the music/murder double entendre. Whatever being musical means, it means more than one thing. In this film whose language is double entendre (as Miller demonstrated so persuasively in "Anal *Rope*"), perhaps there is no surprise in finding Philip's musicality nudged in the direction of a murder that itself refuses to be a murder mystery. Hitchcock dispenses with such straightforwardness by having the first shot inside the apartment be the disposal of the body. This film's plot, like that of a Highsmith novel, is not one that hinges on our not knowing who did it.

As Rupert Cadell (James Stewart) observes, Philip is very fond of the tune he plays every time he sits at the piano. It is the first of the three movements of Francis Poulenc's *Mouvements Perpétuels*, a composition from 1918 revised in 1939, which is also the basis for the orchestrated music heard as the film opens and closes. Jack Sullivan, in his exhaustive survey *Hitchcock's Music*, devotes four pages to *Rope*. For him, the Poulenc piece plays into the double entendres that characterize the script Arthur Laurents wrote. For Sullivan, as for Elisabeth Weis before him, Philip's playing keeps showing his guilty hand: "This is a superb example of a Hitchcockian musical performance acting as a barometer of guilt and anxiety," Sullivan comments. Poulenc's music is a perfect choice, he opines, since his "early piano music is all about charm turning sour." Philip's "botched performance" of the piece, we are to understand, parallels the murder he does not get away with.[15]

Kevin Clifton follows Sullivan's lead, taking up Philip's guilty unraveling in Granger's "strange" piano performance, his "strange musical behavior" in playing music that Clifton quotes Laurents as also describing as "strange."[16] Clifton's essay offers a "pure" musical analysis of Poulenc's piece. It also mentions something that Sullivan does not, that "Poulenc was a known homosexual," and ties this to the analysis: Philip's playing betrays his strangling of David "as well as other connotative meanings of depravity associated with homosexuality."[17] Clifton credits Miller for reaching this conclusion; however, Miller's essay, precisely by pursuing connotation, refuses the simple denotations at which Clifton arrives. Miller's essay is an inquiry into how one can describe the two main figures in *Rope* as "homosexuals" absent any literal evidence that that is what they are. If Miller's essay affirms that Brandon and Philip "are" homosexuals, it does so by asking what it would mean to say that.

David Schroeder's *Hitchcock's Ear* turns from literal music to thinking about Hitchcock as a kind of composer and his films as a score. Nonetheless, his analysis proves as reductive as Clifton's: Poulenc is in *Rope* because he was "openly homosexual"; Hitchcock wanted his piano music for the film because the piano has feminine associations, thereby sliding into a homosexual register; the music goes awry, and Hitchcock's film moves into new territories of "disarray and imbalance." We might be reading Robin Wood in 1965 and the numerous Hitchcock critics since then who are sure that his films ward off a shadow world in order to affirm law and order.[18] In this framework, the translation of music into homosexuality has to be homophobic. Although Sullivan never says "homosexual" in his analysis of the music in *Rope*, his insistence that the music is there for the double entendre in which music really means murder can't arrest the double entendre, as is clear, for instance, when he alludes to "the nervous piano performance of Farley Granger's Philip" ("nervous" is not a neutral adjective) or in his characterization of a "convoluted, Jamesian interaction between two characters who imply more than they say."[19] Double entendre means "two meanings" yet usually means one thing. But what does that one thing mean?

Poulenc was, we are told, an "openly homosexual" composer. Meaning what? Philip Brett and Elizabeth Wood, in an essay written as a follow-up to Brett's ground-breaking inquiry in "Musicality, Essentialism, and the Closet," pause over the numerous ways in which homosexuality finds its way into music. They suppose that under the regimes of the closet a connection between music and homosexuality must be "difficult to decipher." This could imply that if composers were out they would all write the same kind of homosexual music (whatever that would be), a questionable assumption, as Brett and Wood acknowledge. Is it really closet evasion that explains the multiple ways of being gay in music? They provide a list (it fills a page) ranging from "high modernist withdrawal" to flamboyant "eccentricity," thematic codings (e.g., Benjamin Britten's pacifism) to the Pet Shop Boys' lack of affect. Poulenc appears thanks to his "musical camp on the one hand and his religiosity on the other." He does not seem openly gay to them.[20] No single mode of connection can be found in this list of artists presumed by Brett and Wood to be gay. They depend on Miller's "open secret" to give terms to what they are saying, that any form of musicality can be associated with — or dissociated from — homosexuality, could prove it, or not.[21] This at least leaves double entendre double.

In his "pure" musicological analysis of the first movement of *Mouvements Perpétuels*, Clifton reads the left-hand part as an example of a lack of linearity and the right hand as linear. The left hand, in this account, circles around on itself; until the final measure of the movement, every measure is identical, an alternation of two notes (B-flat and F) that interrupt a line that rises two notes and returns halfway back. What Clifton calls a lack of linearity matches Sullivan's description of Philip's "guilt-ridden mind . . . traveling in futile circles, falling back on itself."[22] Clifton describes the left hand as "unchanging, an evocation of a mechanistic stasis in the absence of musical growth and development." Is he really talking about music, or is this pop Freudianism? The sinister left is countered (you guessed it) with a normative right hand, "more goal-oriented."[23] It's a lovely just-so story belied by the fact that the music in the right hand, as it noodles its way down scales whose tonality is indeterminate, is composed of longer but similarly repetitive units. (The initial four measures are made of the first two measures played twice. These are then reiterated twice again, interrupted by a four-measure unit in a somewhat jolting tonality full of a chromaticism otherwise absent from the piece; it also is played twice.) The final measure breaks this pattern; both hands are working together to produce a chord that defies any key signature and that fails to provide the kind of conventional harmonic closure that Leo F. Forbstein (credited with the music for *Rope*) gave the Poulenc piece (uncredited) when he orchestrated it for the film.

Poulenc's music can be said to be "queering the pitch" (to cite the title of the collection edited by Brett and Wood in which their essay appears). Clifton works hard to make it normative and "musical"—that is to say, harmonic. What is wrong with the piece, for him, lies in how it is played; its playing reveals that Philip is a murderer and a depraved homosexual. "Philip is not a very good pianist." His "performance is full of unmusical stops and starts."[24] Was Farley Granger musical? Is he playing the piano? Sullivan says so: "Hitchcock required Farley Granger to learn the musical piece his character performs." Schroeder repeats the claim: "Granger actually does the playing himself."[25] In Laurent Bouzerau's documentary "*Rope* Unleashed" (2000), Granger recalls that he had to learn the piece as best he could, at least simulating the fingering. "It was recorded of course," he adds; we are not hearing him play even if it appears that he is.[26]

Arthur Laurents (Granger's lover at the time *Rope* was shot) confirms this in his interview in the documentary: "He practiced it like mad, Farley. He couldn't really play it, but at least the fingers looked right." Hitchcock does not give us much opportunity to see Granger's hands at the keyboard; when he does show them, most often it is his right hand moving over the keys, simulating the part, out of synch with the music heard; when we see both hands, the left is barely moving,

92 CHAPTER THREE

not even attempting the unproductive round that Clifton saw there. In his autobiography Laurents offers a vignette of Granger practicing "a piece by Poulenc he was going to pretend to play in *Rope*, finger-synching." "Finger-synching" seems congruent with how the film intimates what it never says directly. In the Bouzerau interview Laurents says that during rehearsal homosexuality always was referred to as "it." He savors the deliciousness of the situation in his written account (delicious for Hitchcock, he claims): "It was very Hitchcock: it tickled him that Farley was playing a homosexual in a movie written by me, another homosexual; that we were lovers; that we had a secret he knew; that I knew he knew—the permutations were endless, all titillating to him, not out of malice or a feeling of power, but because they added a slightly kinky touch and kink was a quality devoutly to be desired."[27] Laurents turns Hamlet's consummation, the devoutly wished absolute ending, into the perpetual music of double entendre without end that provides the underscore of melodrama.

"You're awfully fond of that tune," Rupert quips as Granger sits at the piano for another go at it. Hitchcock may be fond of the Poulenc because it offers a musical version of the much commented on and disavowed technical "trick" of the film: making it seem as if the camera is in perpetual movement, its stops and starts hidden by what is nonetheless there to be seen, blackouts on the male backside one recurring feature of a punctuation alternated with a few more-usual cuts.[28] Granger is not literally playing. The film is not literally a single uninterrupted take. Music is not to be taken literally, and nor is murder (not on film, that is, or in a novel): it is an art, Brandon and Philip aver; Rupert agrees, though it might not qualify as one of the seven lively arts, he adds. Hitchcock gets away with murder to the degree we believe there is a corpse in the chest, or that Philip's hands are responsible for it—or for the tune he murders—or to the degree we are roped into seeing the film as one long perpetual movement. Poulenc's music is in the film not to tell us the truth about the murder or about sexuality but as a token of the life that art proffers, not least in the strange union of melos and drama, a counterpoint that does not resolve into unity or identity.

Rupert, the figure in the film for the desire to know the literal truth, is an instigator unwilling to recognize his own desire in the mystery he is so intent on solving: there is no getting out of the perpetual motion machine. In token of this he winds up with a bloody hand that mirrors the cut Philip's hand suffers when he recoils from Mrs. Atwater's mistaking Kenneth for David, the living for the dead, one of Janet's lovers for another. The bloody hand identifies Rupert and Philip, just as Mrs. Atwater's error highlights the round of substitute lovers that Janet has assumed in a heterosexual roundelay that she intimates only Freud could comprehend. Rupert attempts to exonerate himself and to place himself outside of the machine he has set in motion. "Your touch has improved," he first responds to Philip's playing, but he cannot escape the film's many "touches" as it moves toward its conclusion. Philip reproves Brandon for his "touches," that rope that ties everything together, inescapably, and which, so doing, unravels the normative distinctions Rupert hollowly expounds as he holds up the rope that might as well be around his neck.

In "Hitchcock's Hidden Pictures," an essay on *Strangers on a Train*, D. A. Miller fastens on "touch" (including its use in *Rope*) to find a term for the way in which Hitchcock grabs his viewers and makes us his own. He attaches touch to the picture of Hitchcock (fingers on his lips) found on the back of the book in Farley Granger's hand early in *Strangers on a Train*. In the contemporaneous *New York Times* review of the film, Bosley Crowther complained about Hitchcock's "touches," registering his resistance to Hitchcock in precisely the term that Miller endorses as the source of our pleasure and discomfort in his films.[29] Touch metaphorizes the experience in which we become the instrument on which Hitchcock performs, Miller affirms, complicating our delight in finding him in his films. In *Rope*, Hitchcock's hidden picture (his cameo appearance) is a neon sign seen most insistently as Janet and Kenneth reconcile; he's between them, interrupting the heterosexual roundelay that constitutes Janet's sexual history, a compulsory heterosexuality in which Brandon played a part, and which he is now directing over the body of her most recent partner; this marriage plot is thrown further into question by David's mother, absent, bedridden, longing for her son, and by his father, her addled husband, devoted to books—yet another impossible couple. Hitchcock's cameo is a sign made of flashing lights, an electric recording, going on and off, like his (un)interrupted film, like Philip's simulated piano playing, perpetually a round of endless double entendres.

D. A. Miller begins "Hitchcock's Hidden Pictures" with an inquiry into the ontological status of Hitchcock's cameo appearance: What is the nature of the experience we have when we recognize Hitchcock as Hitchcock in his film yet not in its fiction? Hitchcock ups the ante of his cameo appearance in *Strangers on a Train* through the hidden pictures that Miller has noticed, starting with his photo on the book jacket. When we see Hitchcock's photo it does not give us the pleasure we usually get from his cameos, Miller suggests; rather, we experience the humiliation of being on the outside of something we thought we were in on when we spot him easily, as we can't help but do when he crosses paths with Guy Haines, carrying a double bass as big and round as he is. He is doubled by a musical instrument. That visual/musical doubling gives us terms for the place for us that these visible/invisible pictures intimate, the place marked by the plus of melos and drama, the addition that takes us somewhere other than we would be if all we had were the words of the drama or the images onscreen, the place where impossible and possible meet.

Although Miller offers "touch" as the term for the phenomenon he investigates, music seems to me closer to what he seeks to describe, something neither linguistic nor visual. "Touch" bears a meaning it dares us to find and refuses to say. This is territory Miller has explored so productively throughout his career, from his investigation of the open secret on, the nonreductive relations between the literal and the connotative, the explicit and the implicit. His analysis of the strange touches that, once found, are both mesmerizing and disquieting, and that connect us to Hitchcock by disconnecting us from the fiction onscreen, could be compared to Adorno on punctuation marks, those "friendly spirits whose bodiless presence nourishes the body of language." This nourishment, as Adorno continues, also takes its vampiric pleasure in undoing the pretense of language to control meaning. Punctuation marks are described as bodiless, yet to Adorno they look like body parts. Hitchcock is in *Strangers on a Train* as himself and in his pictures (and if there, visibly/invisibly, Miller continues, perhaps he is among numerous barely perceived shadowy bodies in the background; perhaps he is everywhere, "in" his characters). "Inconspicuousness," Adorno writes, "is what punctuation lives by. . . . In every punctuation mark thoughtfully avoided, writing pays homage to the sound it suppresses."[30] The sign appears only not to be seen as such but to indicate the sonorous life of language invisible in writing; the disappearance of all punctuation marks from writing would mean only that somehow writing had managed without them to nonetheless make present what it cannot visibly make present by any sign, its sonority. Touch comes close to music — so close that Miller ends with Hitchcock's simile in which he likened his audience to an organ on which he played, yet Miller prefers to think that the best analogy for what Hitchcock does is a game of charades, where words are translated into visual gestures, literalized in bodies that make nonsense of literalization and of the words they translate. It is this deliteralization of the literal that, for Miller, epitomizes the perverse pleasure of being touched by Hitchcock.

Film music, when most successful, is invisible, inaudible; that, at least, is what Adorno claimed. Following him, Claudia Gorbman titled her book on film music *Unheard Melodies* (Elisabeth Weis called hers *The Silent Scream*). The heard signals the unheard. For Adorno and Gorbman, this can make music insidious. Likewise, for Gorbman, classical Hollywood film is by definition melodrama because it manipulates the viewer's emotions, producing a "trance-like spectatorial immersion" that reeks of ideology, enforcing conventional meaning, conventional pleasures.[31] Music is invisible and virtually inaudible since it is the soundtrack of the real (that is to say, it mystifies the real so that it can be swallowed whole), commodification, reification, mechanization, standardization. Yet this must be one side of the story — although perhaps the entire truth in the kinds of films that Fassbinder and Haynes deplore for telling us what to think and feel, not the goal of the kinds of melodramas they learned to make from Sirk. Music resonates with the unsaid and the unspeakable. Gorbman and Adorno, dialectical thinkers, know this; Miller does, too, in his "touches."

Music in film usually is analyzed as either diegetic or nondiegetic, music justified by being part of the mise-en-scène or music that has no source in what is being shown. But, as Gorbman observes, music easily transgresses this distinction, as at the opening of *Fear Eats the Soul*; it refuses to hold in place the line separating the real and the fictive. Music that starts in an onscreen radio or piano in *Rope* can be amplified and orchestrated. The Poulenc piece is either simulated/played at the piano or orchestrated over the credits. The two functions are kept discrete, yet there is also a unity of a sound world rooted in Poulenc that is distorted and inverted when orchestrated and "properly" harmonized. The film music as film music plays against itself if by "itself" we mean the piece played on the piano; however, no performance of the piece actually is offered, just fragments of it. In the play of diegetic against nondiegetic use of the "same" music, the very regime of identity is played against itself. Such dialectical deployment of music is something that Adorno and Eisler enjoin. At times, what they propose is rather formulaic — music cutting across the grain of a film, operating as ideological critique, enforcing a countermeaning as true meaning. This use of film music, it seems to me, ties it firmly to the making of preconceived meaning (even if that meaning is oppositional). Such a use is far too like what Adorno and Eisler mean it to oppose and is incapable of doing the work musical punctuation can perform as an indeterminate opening beyond the categorical. Like Miller, Adorno and Eisler think that film music finds its best model for such a function in incidental music in drama, or in musical comedy numbers — in melodrama as the dictionary defines it: "They have never served to create the illusion of a unity of the two media [drama and music] or to camouflage the illusionary character of the whole, but functioned as stimulants because they were foreign elements, which interrupted the dramatic context, or tended to raise this context from the realm of literal immediacy into that of meaning."[32] What is called "meaning" here is placed in opposition to the literal. It, presumably, is dialectical, an effect of montage. For Miller it is so elusive that "meaning" misnames its effect; meaninglessness comes closer to the truth: "touches" name the unnamable.

Music is literally elusive. Unlike what the camera invites us to see, music cannot be located. Once we see something we can only not see it if it is withdrawn from view or if we shut our eyes, but we cannot not hear music if it is audible; once it is close enough to be heard, we cannot shut our ears. We don't need to see the piano to hear it being played, and the sound we hear does not stay in the instrument that produces it. It fills the air. It enters us. This is the effect that Miller describes as touch. Gorbman has recourse to the notion of a "sonic envelope" to explain the effect of the film score, a psychoanalytic trope for the phenomenon. Adorno and Eisler state, "Motion picture music, being at the mercy of this relationship [between the objective and the subjective], should attempt to make it productive, rather than to negate it in confused identifications." "Confused identifications" are those that make equations between what we see and what we hear. Identification is confusion. Identity is the confusion of identification. To be identical in the regime of the culture industry, Horkheimer and Adorno insist, is to be a copy.[33]

Music exceeds this regime, or it can. "Pure" musical analysis attempts to tie music to meaningful structures of harmony, rhythm, or the rules of the tone-row; any attempt to translate these terms must involve the realization of the impossibility of translation. So recourse is had to the unconscious, to emotion, to an "aura," to some premodern mode of being-together as a form of sociality not dominated by the commodity (but then the danger of a ritualistic conformism arises, and with it the specter of totalitarianism). What is it that we listen to in music? For Jean-Luc Nancy it is for something unheard, the possibility of what holds us together in a world, something that resonates beyond and yet is in us; music is something we make that remakes us, a "sonorous matter" in which we play a part.[34] What music does is not singular; nor is "touch": it is a multivalent word in Nancy's vocabulary (*se sentir* means to touch, to hear, to feel, to think, to sense). Nancy's Heideggerian parsing of listening for what is not simply heard is not easily translated into the perverse terms of a relationality that shatters our sense of how the world works, or furthers the despairing sense that it works despite us, against us. It is the perverse accomplishment of *Rope* that its music attaches us to an incessant vibration, the life *in* art that exceeds our own.

And the Band Played On

To consider now the music in *Strangers on a Train* and its relation to the melodrama of the impossible relationship between Guy (Farley Granger) and Bruno (Robert Walker) there, I turn to the ironic, indifferent refrain of "The Band Played On" included in Dimitri Tiomkin's score for the film and found in Highsmith's novel as well. "The Band Played On" is a popular tune from 1895 that was still popular in the 1950s.[35] Hitchcock's attachment to music is palpable in his most evident cameo in the film, doubled by a double bass that "makes him out

98 CHAPTER THREE

to be musical," as Miller says. Miller lists other such appearances in a footnote—Hitchcock carries a violin case in *Spellbound* (1945), a cello in *The Paradine Case* (1947), a horn case in *Vertigo*—and concludes with a striking formulation: "It's as if his direction were being imaged as a performing art, the rendering of a preexisting score."[36]

"A preexisting score": the notion is key to the way in which melodrama remediates the impossible situation by musical means. In a literal sense, a preexisting score is on several counts a feature of the fairground scene in *Strangers on a Train* in which Bruno murders Miriam (Laura Elliott). This is a scene in which the impossible sexuality of women, so central to melodramas like those considered in chapter 2, is played for keeps—and yet to a musical accompaniment. "The Band Played On" preexists its manifestations in Hitchcock and Highsmith, just as the fairground scene, with its stark juxtaposition of pleasure and murder, comes to them as a familiar German expressionist film trope, as Elsaesser noted when he nudged *Strangers on a Train* in the direction of melodrama by way of this musical mise-en-scène.[37] Bruno arrives at the Metcalf amusement park just behind Miriam and her companions after one of the many stretches of the film in which no music is heard; the sound level is amplified to include the calliope music of a merry-go-round in the background; "Carolina in the Morning" is heard faintly beneath the ringing bells and loud voices of barkers hawking their wares, enticing the crowd to try their hand at games or to get on a ride. As the scene proceeds, music becomes more prominent. "The Band Played On" is heard distinctly at the moment Miriam and her male companions buy tickets to board the merry-go-round; it sounds as she looks back at Bruno (not for the first time: they have been exchanging glances throughout the preceding shot/reverse shots, and once they are mounted she will be in front of him, again looking back). Miriam enjoins her companions to sing along, and she picks up the refrain, "Casey would waltz with the strawberry blond." They all join in, Bruno's voice heard most clearly at the lines about Casey's head exploding; his lips are closed as the refrain concludes, with Miriam and her companions singing about Casey's marriage to the girl with the curls.

This music might seem to be used simply for literal predictive value ("But his brain was so loaded it nearly exploded") or for ironic juxtaposition ("The poor girl would shake with alarm; / He'd ne'er leave the girl with the strawberry curls, / And the band played on"), since Miriam doesn't shake when Bruno approaches; she invites his attention. Sullivan notes that this is the only time Laura Elliott ever sang in a film. For him, the song is hers before "it becomes Bruno's leitmotif."[38] Although Bruno seems averse to singing the line about marrying, it's not the case that disposing Miriam disposes of her. She never leaves him because he can't get her — or, at least, her glasses — out of his head, nor the tune that was playing when he put his hands around her neck; it gets reactivated when Bruno sees Barbara. In the fairground scene, the tune is heard loudest and most fully when Bruno has squeezed the life out of Miriam, after some faint noises from her throat, when she falls silent and her glasses and Guy's incriminating cigarette lighter lie beside each other. This is one of the most intense visual sequences in the film, and it is also insistently musical. To the melody line and its relentless oompah-pah waltz accompaniment, a third line is added, a running arpeggiated figure. The mechanical insistence of the calliope is intensified. Sullivan finds here what he calls "the film's most unsettling crisscross," as Miriam's song becomes Bruno's motto.[39] But something more primordial, and not simply a transfer of property from one character to another, is involved.

Bruno and Miriam singing together; Bruno strangling Miriam: this way of "necking" in the lover's paradise (the pun appears in the novel) literally enacts a song that is itself about a dance that is alarmingly out of control and yet is at the same time a courting ritual ending in marriage. It is, in fact, difficult to say exactly, literally, what the song is about: Is it an ironic warning about or a celebration of romance? In the fairground scene, all the music heard is played in the organ-grinder sound of a simulated calliope. Whatever affective charge the various numbers might have in some other performance, this treatment levels them all to a sound that signals the preexisting and fully routinized pleasure of mass entertainment in which romance or violence has been turned into "fun." Amusement park terror is not supposed to end in murder or crashing explosions. Miriam's scream in the Tunnel of Love, which is visualized as though the dark shadow of Bruno had overtaken her, is in fact the chortle of pleasure as she pushes off the boy she perhaps wants to have on top of her.

Hitchcock took the tune from Highsmith's novel; there, Dick, Miriam's date (what's in a name?), sings the refrain "with vehemence" before Bruno joins in. Highsmith assigns Bruno the line, "His brain was so loaded, it nearly exploded," as does Hitchcock after her, while, in the novel, Miriam addresses Dick as Casey, opening her mouth wide so that he can throw popcorn in. Bruno is revolted: "Miriam looked ugly and stupid with her mouth open, as if she were being strangled."[40] In the novel, as in the film, Miriam is satisfying her oral cravings; in the film popcorn is what Bruno consumes in the Tunnel of Love, while Miriam's double dates won't let her have any since her eating would get in the way of their necking. Highsmith and Hitchcock each work the valences of oral pleasure. In the novel it is her open mouth from which song pours, into which she puts food insatiably, that, without his knowing it, determines Bruno's path to strangulation, shutting the mouth through which food and song go in and out, fulfilling thereby the desire to extinguish "life" in both its biological meaning and the aesthetic meaning conveyed by song.

At the fair, Highsmith's Bruno also is having a good time; he's dazzled by the lights, tingles to the music. He is in an amusement park, and although he's sure he will murder Miriam, he has no plan and is incapable of forming one: "He felt he was about to experience again some ancient, delicious childhood moment that the steam calliope's sour hollowness, the stitching hurdy-gurdy accompaniment, and the drum-and-cymbal brought almost to the margin of his grasp" (76). Highsmith's words refuse to say exactly what is just beyond Bruno's grasp; they move into some form of preexistence to which Bruno seems to be submitting. The music described by Highsmith sounds much the way it does at the end of Miriam's strangulation in Hitchcock's film. In a song that occurs only in the novel, the background tune "A Pretty Girl Is Like a Melody" plays while Bruno is on the merry-go-round, mounted behind Miriam; "Bruno loved the song and so did his mother" (77). It is a Ziegfeld tune, and Bruno's mother, in the novel, was a Ziegfeld girl. It's not hard to imagine that the loathing and desire he feels for Miriam are oedipal. Yet, even if this is so, his feelings are more than (or less than) Bruno's particular pathology. He is tuned into a tune that is being played through a mechanism calculated to bring to the edge of consciousness some confluence of unspeakable desires.

A strange corollary to this mode of preexistence can be found in D. A. Miller's reveries occasioned by his recognition of Hitchcock as "musical." He wonders whether Hitchcock, tubby double in his arms, has come to the train station from Miller's Music Store, where Guy is headed when their paths cross and where Miriam works as a clerk. Hitchcock provides this musical association for Miriam; it is not in Highsmith's novel. In the window of the store where Miriam works, and which sells records and instruments, and which bears his surname, Miller sees the album of a favorite musical, *Carousel*. (Since we are pursuing preexistence, we might recall that it also was *Carousel* that set Farley Granger on his musical path.) In the mood to sing along, as he often did in piano bars, as he tells us in *Place for Us*, Miller is ready to join Miriam and Bruno when they begin their duet; he does, and then continues, perhaps still under the sway of "Bosswoman Miriam" (perhaps a recall of the call of Merman), especially tickled when Hitchcock obliges him and the music changes to "Baby Face" for the boat ride in the Tunnel of Love:

> I now began mouthing the words to the new song, which I knew quite well:
>
> > Baby face
> > I'm up in heaven when I'm in your fond embrace
> > I didn't need a shove
> > 'Cause I fell in love
> > With the cutest baby face!
>
> But just as I sang to myself, "I didn't need a shove," the boatman on screen took up a long pole and—*gave Bruno's boat a shove with it*. I did not believe my eyes.[41]

Miller sees the boatman "literalizing the words of the song"; this, for him, is like the hidden pictures he has found in the film, another invitation to derailing. It takes us away from the literal, since the boatman's shove is a literalization of words not meant literally; indeed, it is a literalization of words not heard in the film—Miller is singing them. But they are not *his* words either. Miller credits the film for setting this chain of events in motion.

I am not at all sure that the synchrony of shove for shove that Miller discovers actually occurs; but if they are nonsynchronous (but remembered as synchronous) this may be even more in keeping with Miller's proposal about his experience, which is not only a personal one, even if that's how it feels: a chain of associations gets started that has a life of its own and that turns the act of critical attention and interpretation in unexpected directions, creating a temporality hard to hold on to or to recall exactly. The tune finds Miller and confounds him. This is the aesthetic effect of melodrama, its relocation of the impossible situation. "The visual literalization of a verbal figure" that Miller claims for "too close reading" began with hearing a tune. I don't know how this particular song got written, whether the words or music came first. All the musical prompts in the fairground scene are wordless; in the telling moment when the scene of the murder concludes, music and image are not accompanied by any words, except the words we might sing to the music or the ones we provide when we try to account for what we see and hear. Just before he turns music into words, Miller sums up the effect of the "shove" as having "its own independent raison d'être; thus self-bracketed, it stems the narrative flow, suspending suspense itself."[42] Something preexisting, and with its own reason for being, exists as a kind of strange pocket in time and yet out of a narrative sequence. Even in a song, a story may be told, but often to a melodic structure based in repetition and variation; the harmonic "home" to which pop music aspires does not necessarily coincide with the resolution of the plot provided by the lyrics. Is "Baby Face" about romance or obsession? It is certainly about something that, however it got into one's head, it seems impossible to get out. Lacanians would perhaps say "mirror stage" and find some mother-child relation here not unlike the one Highsmith hints at in her account of the pleasure Bruno experiences in the surround sound of the fair. These tunes are catchy.

Miller's derailing train of associations come from the asynchronous synchronicity of the confluence, but nonidentity, of visual, verbal, and aural. We can more easily say that music is playing in the fairground scene than identify exactly which moment in any tune is to be heard, and especially which moment in the lyrics might pop into our heads given that pop songs use the same music for different words at different points. This is not so different from the Poulenc piece that plays in *Rope*, which not only exposes the repetitive at the expense of harmonic resolution but also aspires to sound like a popular tune even if it is not one. It seeks a form of preexistence (as if we might already know the tune Poulenc has composed) that also is a form of coexistence, a perpetual motion that is at once self-contained and yet seems to come from a sound world that it taps.

In Hitchcock's film and in Highsmith's novel, that form of existence

THE ART OF MURDER 103

resides in the transfer of identity. Highsmith literally makes the exchange — Guy goes through with the plot Bruno proposed; they double each other. Hitchcock transfers guilt without literalizing the deed. Bruno does not strangle Mrs. Cunningham, but, looking at Barbara, he is strangling her, hearing the music that played when he strangled Miriam. Or, rather, as Sullivan notes about the moment after, when Barbara realizes that he was looking at her and really imagining he was strangling her, "at this chilling moment 'The Band Plays On' crisscrosses from carousel organ to Tiomkin's full orchestra, now part of the underscore."[43] Diegetic becomes nondiegetic. Describing Dimitri Tiomkin's contribution to *Strangers on a Train*, Sullivan underscores its "musical crisscross," noticing how musical themes refuse to stay put. We've seen this as he describes the disquieting movement of Miriam's song to Bruno's head. But, as I've said before, there is reason to question to what degree the song belongs to either of them; if music has a kind of independent preexistence, this challenges Sullivan's conventional musicological habit of treating musical motifs as emblems of character.[44] It also poses a question to the notion that music in *Strangers on a Train* not written by Tiomkin was chosen by him. That certainly is not the case with "The Band Played On," which Highsmith chose, although in the light of the kind of transfer to which Miller testifies, it is probably not quite right to say that either. Music perhaps chooses us.

As part of the crisscrossing by which one character's leitmotif becomes another, Sullivan considers that the particular success of this Tiomkin score for Hitchcock lies in its use of "crisscrossing motifs organized into nine medleys, some packed with as many as six ideas."[45] The first of these dense medleys is heard in Miller's Music Store, and, like the fairground sequence, it involves diegetic sounds. Other medleys intersperse Tiomkin's "own" music with preexisting tunes. Throughout the film, a remarkably small number of motifs, whether composed by or supposedly chosen by Tiomkin, recur. They build up a sound world for the film that throws into question the notion of musical belonging, and which ushers us into that other world that Miller calls "too close reading." Too close for comfort, it reconstitutes ourselves, our identities, beside ourselves, a location that derails us but that also indicates the promise of such an unsettling state. Musical crisscrossing and medleys are central to the queerness of changing places in this Hitchcock film. As much as in Poulenc, if not quite so literally, the score for *Strangers on a Train* involves a perpetual motion, a round that may start in one person's mouth and wind up in another's, that may lodge in someone's head and then encompass others as well. Adorno and Eisler note that although film music necessarily is tied to a script, it is most effective when it creates another unity, that is, not when it simply underscores or ironizes, but when the necessarily fragmented music fulfills "a tendency to vanish as soon as it appears."[46] Tiomkin's music is treated by Sullivan to the banalizing thematics of situation or character ownership; however, it has the ability to continually metamorphose. The medley sequences move from the glassy high violins that signal the eerie un-canniness of Bruno (and his mother) to the romantic violin sound that occasionally pours over Guy and his fiancée, Anne; the music accompanying Bruno's stretched arm down the drain can become Guy's drive to win the tennis match. This principle of theme and variation, without ownership, characterizes the film from its opening in which the music Tiomkin wrote to accompany the opening credits refuses to attach to either character or to suggest the movement of the plot. It is only at the very last second of the film that the music, for the first and only time, reaches a harmonic resolution. This musical path does not coincide with plot ironies or moments of heightened emotional tension in any kind of regular identificatory manner. Indeed, mostly the music is heard at low volume, providing a kind of continuity that often is at odds with the melodramatic twists and turns of the plot. In that respect, too, the music can be termed queer; it lies aslant any question of identity. The final momentary conclusion/resolution does not efface the stronger sense of an underlying current of transformation whose beginning preexists any beginning and whose ending likewise only can be cut short artificially. The valence of that musical world cannot be captured in a single word description; nor can it be tied to individual psychology. Sullivan briefly suggests some "paranormal" explanation for the ways in which music travels, and then retreats to insist that it is psychological.[47] But the uncanny doubling that is central to Hitchcock and Highsmith refuses this distinction. (These effects could be compared to the inventiveness of Beethoven's Melodram as it seeks a way beyond the impasse of the impossible situation.)

This is the moment to consider a very odd musical interlude in the film: Guy's encounter with Professor Collins, which occurs after his meeting with Miriam in Miller's Music Store and immediately after

Bruno's fatal embrace. The scene begins with the synchrony of Bruno consulting his watch and Guy his. Then a voice is heard singing—the only other time this has happened in the film is just before, when Bruno sang along with Miriam and her companions. This voice sings a song about a man who had a goat that he loved just like a kid. The script reads "Close Shot: The feet opposite Guy stretch out and touch Guy's feet," but in the film Guy and Professor Collins do not repeat the game of footsy Guy played with Bruno (it stops Tiomkin's music), nor is this encounter like the foot tap that Guy witnesses on his last train trip as he hurries to Metcalf, or the one he runs away from in the final moments of the film.[48] Guy preserves ironic distance from Collins, assuring him that he will not make it to the Metropolitan Opera with "The Goat" as his audition piece. But then, it turns out, Collins is his alibi, and Collins has no recollection of their meeting. Miller notes this failure of recognition and treats it as akin to the unseen manifestations on which he is intent. What has happened in this exchange with Professor Collins involves the substitution of the physical touch of foot to foot with the strange little tune that Collins can't get out of his head and which he then uncannily cannot remember, just as he cannot remember seeing or speaking to Guy. The strange tune is in the public domain, the only bit of music in the film that Warner Bros. did not need to pay rights to use. It epitomizes the independent existence of music.

Professor Collins's excuse also seems to epitomize something, an all-too-familiar story. He was too drunk; he blacked out, as Bruno does in his trance, absorbed by Barbara–Miriam–eyeglasses–"The Band Played On." This moment of forgetting may uncannily not be all that different from a moment of remembering if both depend on something preexistent that can be recalled or that recalls you and that can't be gotten out of your head even if it can't exactly be consciously recalled either. Professor Collins perhaps does not want to make conscious his devotion to a song about a man who loves a goat as if it were his "kid," a punning confluence that may itself be an evasion of a more palpable range of erotic attractions in the film and especially in the current that flows between Guy and Bruno.

Like so much other quoted, heard music in this film, the emotional valence of "The Goat" is difficult to put into singular terms. This odd little song, which found its way late into the film—at whose instigation?—allowed a cameo appearance for an actor best known as a radio voice, an identity that tallies with the invisibility of a persistent music difficult to put a face or name to. In fact this actor had the almost anonymous name of John Brown (a name that anglicizes Bruno; he was in fact English—and Jewish, a fact his real name does not make immediately legible). Passing from his screen name to his real name we move from the diegetic to the nondiegetic, from the proper name to its always being improper. But ending with a word belies my own investments in language, which will always lag behind the music that plays on and on indifferent to any attempt to turn it into words. So doing, I may be responding the way Miller does when he spots Hitchcock on the back cover of a book and buys it and makes it his own. Too close reading may attempt to make aesthetic captivation one's own, but it is the experience rather of being found out. This unsettling experience is nonetheless the way in which the impasse of the impossible situation is not the last word.[49] Relevant to the disquieting affective charge of music might be an anecdote Tiomkin offers in *Please Don't Hate Me*, his autobiography. At a preview screening of Hitchcock's *Shadow of a Doubt* (1943), for which he wrote the music, "they giggled through my sinister harmonies and laughed loudly in moments of terror"; he was sure his music had failed. Tiomkin condoles with Hitchcock, only to be told he has misunderstood. The music worked: "That was tension, Dimi. The laughs were a sign the picture had them on edge."[50]

....

The fairground scene where Miriam is killed is a singular event in Highsmith's novel. There is no return to the fairground, no final ride on the whirligig with "The Band Played On" playing again. Music in the novel is pretty much confined to the scene it shares with the film. There is, however, something like a sound track in the novel. It starts with the ring of the telephone: "The telephone . . . Bruno had been staring at it. Every telephone suggested Guy . . . the one thing needed to make his happiness complete . . . to hear Guy's voice" (107). Bruno knows he must defer this immediate satisfaction, and he resorts to letters—many of them—to communicate with Guy. Sounds become words: a novel is being written. Alongside the melodrama of human relations—Bruno's pursuit of Guy by way of killing Miriam—there are these continual signals of authorial self-reflexiveness.[51] Much as phones suggest Guy to Bruno, if Guy's phone rings, he is sure Bruno will be on the line, certain, too, that despite whatever resolve he manages to muster, he will be incapable of resisting his voice: "Guy picked up the telephone, knowing it was Bruno, knowing he would agree to Bruno's seeing him sometime today" (204). Guy knows this because what starts on the phone extends beyond it.

Telephonic manifestation is part of the way Bruno appears to Guy "out of nowhere," as he always does. And when he does, it's as if he is in Guy's head: "Guy felt his inner voice had asked him the question in the same way" (121). If there is some noise in the bushes, it must be Bruno. "He tried to feel rather than see. It was still there, faint and evasive, where the darkness deepened at the baseline of the woods"; a nameless "it," nothing; something "his own thoughts had created" has a name and a body. Guy recognizes its breathing: "Bruno's breath hissed in and out between his drawn-back lips. Guy hit the mouth again with his right fist. . . . The bleeding mouth spread wider" (128–29). Bruno's presence is not confined to his body or to the technologies that make it proximate to Guy. He is a mouth that cannot be closed, a life that extends on his breath beyond the limits of his body. The telepathic relation of Guy and Bruno—their doubling—may begin in "the period when Bruno had been haunting him by telephone" (190), but it extends beyond any boundary. It is the life of the novel, exceeding its plot, the melos that accompanies the drama.

The telepathic bond of these secret brothers points to a likeness beyond recognizable identity and difference that demonstrates the principle Bruno enunciates on the train: "Any kind of person can murder" (204). A murderer is not a particular kind of person, not an identity. As with film music, this can be viewed, as it is by Mark Seltzer, as some insidious mechanism that robs one of individuality and rationality, dissolving identity into a self-reflexiveness that violates the boundaries of human being, feeding life into an inhuman mechanism; but this can also serve as a revelation of what lies beyond the limits of the human: "Guy and I are supermen!" Bruno declares (261). Guy is a murderer and an uncompromising architect. At the end of the novel he is designing a bridge: "The murder that had seemed an outrageous departure, a sin against himself, he believed now might have been a part of his destiny too" (211). To murder is to create.

Guy may wince at a press release that describes the quality of his buildings as their "singingness" (217), but in a letter to Anne he de-

108 CHAPTER THREE

scribes being an architect as "like directing a symphony" (100); the idea for the house he will build for her "sang in Guy's head" (86). The soundtrack of Highsmith's novel plays in Guy's mind. It is a transcription of Highsmith's aesthetic, voiced/ventriloquized when Guy recalls his own belief in the "unity of all the arts" (178), which surpasses any art form or any artist. It proves the simultaneity of opposites that he and Bruno embody. "Who are you?" Guy asks a shadowy presence in his bedroom. Bruno answers, "You" (181). "Who knew whether the electron was matter or energy?" Guy wonders, fastening on an elementary component of the world that exceeds a basic material distinction. "Perhaps God and the Devil danced hand in hand around every single electron" (181), he speculates, in concluding the thought. This dance refuses the Peter Brooks melodrama of good and evil opposition to move beyond the categorical to the melodrama of an elementary particle incapable of further definition. What it is remains unnamable, not captured by any further linguistic equivalent.

Where do works of art take place? What is their form of existence? What does melodrama as a remediated form (melos + drama) make possible for us to grasp about the impossibility of human relations? "Each man kills the thing he loves," Wilde wrote; it becomes a poetic refrain. Fassbinder turned it into a cabaret number. Highsmith spins out a fantasia about an antisocial existence that looks uncannily like its opposite. Her Ripley novels—believe it or not—are as much a meditation on murder as they are on a range of aesthetic forms that extend her melodrama of impossible existence beyond the written word.

Ripley's Sound Track

Like most characters in melodrama, and with more justification given his crimes against society, Tom Ripley fears being caught, hemmed in, his life made impossible. *The Talented Mr. Ripley* begins with Tom sure he is being followed, half-sure his pursuer is a policeman or some other agent of the law. (It is also possible he is being cruised; it turns out that it is Herbert Greenleaf, a respectable businessman wanting to find a friend of his wastrel son Dickie's in the hope of getting him to return home.)[52] When the phone rings, Tom thinks it must be the police and wonders if its ring is "the theme song of his existence."[53] Really, the theme of Tom's existence as a character is his telepathic power, Highsmith's means of authorial transport, not a mode of capture. Tom thinks ahead, and his thoughts become what will happen. This thinking is an escape from social impossibility, the policing of the social; by always being ahead of those who would stop him, Tom survives, holding on to an achieved social existence that breaks all the rules without seeming to. It is an aesthetic existence.

Tom's theme song is not the telephone's promised social cohesion and social conformity ("Reach out and touch someone," Bell Telephone ads used to say; our world of cell phones and hypermediation may be closer to the virtuality of the aesthetic existence on which Tom—and Highsmith—bank). At several instances in the first three Ripley novels, the same tune pops into his head, identified in *Ripley's Game* as "a Neopolitan tune"; "Tom seemed fresh as a daisy, singing now in Italian a tune he'd been whistling before: '. . . papa ne meno / Como faremo fare l'amor . . .'" (828). The verse cited is somewhat truncated and garbled ("como" may simply be a typo for "come"). The first time "he burst[s] out singing" this song in *The Talented Mr. Ripley*, a fuller text is given: "Papa non vuole, Mama ne meno, / Come faremo far' l'amor?" (179). "Papa doesn't want, Mama neither, / How will we be able to make love?" Even this more complete text seems truncated. In the lyrics that precede this refrain (the only part of the song quoted by Highsmith), the singer is in love with a lovely girl ("Bella ragazza," the song opens); the refrain explains why she remains unattainable, the parental prohibition (or is it disinclination?) reiterated. Tom never sings the verse; the lilting refrain is, for him, "a happy song . . . associated with good luck," as we are told when it occurs to him in the shower in *Ripley Under Ground* after he had "not sung the song in a long time" (345). Although the song is about unfulfilled love, its melody registers no pain at all. The love made possible by prohibition perks him up: the tune suggests the sexuality that accompanies Tom's aesthetic life.

The text of the song may be about a frustrated romance, but its tune is, as Tom claims, "joyful," cheery. Just before the song first pops into his head he thinks he will write a letter to Dickie Greenleaf's girlfriend Marge and confirm her suspicion that Dickie "was running away from her and that he wanted to be with Tom, alone." For Tom, it is true; now that he has killed Dickie and Tom has assumed his identity, "he and Dickie were very happy together." The thought sets off Tom's giggles, and he starts singing the song: "He sang in Dickie's loud baritone that he had never heard" (179).

Tom's theme song is attached to a having that also is not one, a coupling in the singular. He has, by this musical means, by this feat of impersonation and incorporation, solved the problem Fassbinder identified as Sirk's and as his own, of having a relationship and yet being alone. It is clearly Highsmith's problem too. Extraordinary about the way in which Tom has Dickie by becoming Dickie is his ability to sing in a voice he never heard sing, and yet which the sentence seems to affirm really is "Dickie's loud baritone." He has managed the happy impossible situation of the song: If Daddy and Mommy don't want to do it, don't want *him* to do it, how will love-making occur? Indeed, if they didn't want to do it, how did they ever become Mommy and Daddy? Out of context, the refrain seems to ask: Is there reproductive coupling outside the usual system of sexual reproduction? Do children necessarily have parents? The answer is intimated the moment that Dickie emerges from Tom's mouth, in this uncanny vocalization, reproduction located somewhere in the vicinity of vampiristic incorporation and imitative cloning. This is the life aesthetic objects have.

This is not at all like Anthony Minghella's 1999 film of *The Talented Mr. Ripley*, whose explicit aim is the transformation of the novel into musical terms. As Minghella says in a documentary directed by Toby Reisz, *Inside The Talented Mr. Ripley* (1999), his film is as much a musical as it is a thriller.[54] In other words, it is formally a melodrama. Even before the film has begun, music is heard while the production company logo is onscreen, a lullaby written by Gabriel Jared. The song, from which much of Jared's film score derives, is titled "Cain's Mother, a Lullaby." Minghella wrote the words. At the moment the singer Sinead O'Connor arrives at the lines "Cast into the dark / branded with a mark, / of shame / of Cain," a speaking voice-over takes over, that of Matt Damon, who plays Ripley in the film, wishing none of it had ever happened: "If I could just go back. If I could rub everything out. Starting with myself."[55] While he speaks, we see hands at a keyboard; then, as the opening scene proper begins, we see Tom at the piano, wearing someone else's Princeton jacket (this impersonation sets the plot in motion). He is accompanying a blowsy-voiced classical mezzo-soprano singing words to the lullaby tune. In the documentary Damon claims that with two months' practice he learned to play the piano for the part, and it is presumably his hands we first see. Damon may be playing in the opening moment of the film, but he certainly is not when Tom tackles Bach's *Italian Concerto* in the emptied concert hall where he works as a men's room attendant, nor when he plays it again in his Rome apartment. His hands are visible later when he sits beside Peter Smith-Kingsley (Jack Davenport) to play the theme of Vivaldi's *Stabat Mater*.[56]

That instances of musical performance were faked, like Farley Granger's in *Rope*, is not remarkable; equally expected is the insistence in the supporting materials on the DVD that just as Damon worked to learn to play the piano so did Jude Law (who plays Dickie Greenleaf) to play the saxophone he never had touched before (the closing credits give at least one of his solos to James Talbot, however). In Highsmith's novel Dickie is a bad amateur painter (after he becomes Dickie, Tom produces "a painting in Dickie's manner" [138]). But in Minghella's musical translation, Dickie is a jazz enthusiast; to worm his way into his good graces, Tom has to become one, too. Minghella's film offers an argument between Dickie's jazz and Tom's classical proclivities. It makes Tom uptight and constrained, while Dickie is the freethinker who lives in the moment. Told this way, the story involves Tom coming under the spell of Dickie, a cautionary tale about how one should stay in one's place. As the sad lullaby conveys in words and in its late romantic harmonies, it is an archetypal story—of Cain and Abel—where good, free Dickie is killed by evil, envious Tom and suffers the consequences.

The construal of the novel in these moralistic/musical terms as articulated on the Paramount Pictures DVD promotional materials seems highly skewed and may belie the film as much as it does the novel. Dickie's free spirit amounts to little more than following the lead of his penis, getting Silvana, a village woman, pregnant. (Silvana [Stefania Rocca] was added by Minghella, as was Meredith Logue [Cate Blanchett], to serve as Tom's beard when he pretends to be Dickie.) Silvana kills herself. Minghella seems to think he has made a feminist film by adding victimized women to the plot, or by endowing Marge with what he terms her "unerring radar for the truth" even as she is powerless before the "collusion of men."[57]

Marge condemns Tom as a murderer but not Dickie for his responsibility for Silvana's death, making her complicit with her own victimization. Tom also is willing to excuse Dickie, assuming his womanizing is a cover for his desire for him, that he is pretending to be straight as much as he pretends to be a jazz musician. Minghella's film offers a lonely, desperate, closeted Tom whose salvation lies in finding a partner. Dickie isn't it, but Peter Kingsley-Smith, expanded from a brief appearance in Highsmith's novel, is. When Tom kills him at the end of the film, it is clearly a moment of *liebestod*, Cain's lullaby sounds, hardly the happy song that burbles its way through Highsmith's novels ("Papa non vuole . . .").

Minghella makes much of Tom's brief encounter with Peter in Highsmith's *The Talented Mr. Ripley*. Catching himself after he begins making up to Peter in the way he had to Dickie, Tom stops himself from accepting Peter's invitation to live with him, momentarily regretting that he didn't let things with Dickie take their own time: "He *could* have lived with Dickie for the rest of his life, travelled and lived and enjoyed living for the rest of his life. If he only hadn't put on Dickie's clothes that day—" (274). Minghella's film seizes on this as Tom's truth (it is voiced in Damon's initial voice-over). Minghella lets Tom replace Dickie with Peter, only to have him kill him because of his flirtation with Meredith. (She happens to be on the ship to Greece on which Tom and Peter are sailing at the end of the film. She spots Tom and thinks he is Dickie; in order for Tom to continue his impersonation, Peter needs to be eliminated.) Minghella's "moral" here involves his sympathy not only for a victimized woman he has added to the story, but for closeted Tom, too, who, pretending to be straight, has to kill the man the director has given him to kill. There is no way out for Tom. He is in the throes of a compulsory heterosexuality imposed on him by the film and its notion that this reflects the impossibility of being gay in the late 1950s, the period in which it sets Highsmith's slightly earlier novel.

That time change moves the plot into the era of la dolce vita, which Dickie and Marge and Meredith and Freddie Miles (Philip Seymour Hoffman) all exemplify, a world of money and pleasure. For the males it is connected to the cool, sexy sound of jazz. Dickie disparages Marge's sense of jazz (she is accused of equating jazz and Glenn Miller). Freddie Miles is killed in this film, but not because he suspects that Tom and Dickie are lovers, the suspicion for which he dies in the novel—funny and macabre, since the couple Tom and Dickie have become is Tom's solitary double state. In the film he sees that Tom has replaced Dickie as he does in the novel; there Freddie notices that Tom is wearing a bracelet of Dickie's that Tom never saw Dickie wear (141). This moment of intimate knowledge between Freddie and Dickie opens a queer possibility also intimated in Minghella's film after Dickie breaks his date to go sightseeing with Tom in Rome. He prefers to hang out with Freddie. They are in a booth listening to jazz—the scene might come from Miller's Music Store in Hitchcock's *Strangers on a Train*, where couples preview albums. Freddie and Dickie are head-to-head, sharing earphones, grooving to the music that supposedly secures free straight masculinity. Freddie sends Tom a look that is the amalgam of class disdain and queenly triumph. Philip Seymour Hoffman plays perfectly the ambiguous amalgamation of class and sexuality that he breathes not a word of in his DVD interview, where he insists on class alone as the explanation for Freddie's dislike of moocher Tom.

Indeed, the DVD extras talk authenticity yet never intimate that there might be questions, even in the film, about Dickie's or Freddie's sexuality. The word "homosexuality" is never uttered. "Ripley's pathology is not explained by his sexuality," Minghella writes in the introduction to his screenplay, and the proof lies with Peter, whom Minghella describes as "the most centered character in the film."[58] It is not clear in the film, however, whether either Marge or Meredith knows that Peter is gay. Perhaps they are supposed to know, as we are, by the fact that he is firmly set on the classical music side of Minghella's dichotomy: he directs a boys' choir. Minghella develops the character into the mold of a determinate identity; he then makes him another victim of the world the director has created, surrounding that final death in the film with the pathos attaching to inauthenticity and unachieved coupledom.[59]

Minghella's musical plot of difference is belied over and again in the novel's representation of sexual identity. Marge suspects that Tom is queer, and Tom insists that he isn't. Such insistence is not necessarily a denial of desire; it certainly is a refusal to attach desire to an identity. (Tom's New York friends have tired of him saying, "I can't make up my mind whether I like men or women, so I'm thinking of giving them *both* up" [81].) Normative notions of having a singular identity and being true to oneself are nonsense when the desire to be and have are conflated and a single person can constitute a couple. Tom's main talent lies in impersonation: he is himself when he isn't. He can look like Dickie not so much because they look alike as because neither is so unique as to be distinctive. In Dickie's closet, trying on his clothes, Tom also tries on his voice. In Minghella's melodrama, on the way to the scene in the closet, a song starts playing on the sound track as Tom boards the train from Rome, abandoned by Dickie, who has chosen Freddie. It is Bing Crosby singing about wooing a girl; Tom, sporting Dickie's jacket, is suddenly in front of a mirror singing to himself, singing along with Bing. "May I," he croons, until Dickie appears, replacing the image in the mirror and stopping the show.

But what show is this? In a film that claims to be an argument between jazz and the classics, why this pop number? Tom is only wearing Dickie's shoes, tie, and coat; when Dickie appears, Tom is revealed in his undershorts, his ass raised. This moment when singing along with Bing becomes singing to himself—to Dickie—replays Matt Damon's most consummate act of impersonation in the film, when he delivers "My Funny Valentine" in the style of Chet Baker. Early in the film, hearing Baker, Tom can't tell if the singer is a man or a woman. (Dickie has named his boat "Bird," after Charlie Parker, not with the usual woman's name. Marge points out this anomaly with her usual "radar" skill; it doesn't seem to make her suspect Dickie's sexuality.) Dickie tells Tom about his boat when the Chet Baker album tumbles from his briefcase as Tom stages the revelation for Dickie that he is a jazz aficionado. Is music tied to identity? Music refuses to stay put, facilitating identification because identity is not a matter of singularity. In his introduction to the screenplay, even Minghella opines that Bach's inventions lie behind jazz improvisation. And the big concerted jazz number in the film is the pop song "Tu vuò fa l'Americano"; the song epitomizing the dolce vita moment is one in which Italians wish nothing more than to be Americans.

Slavoj Žižek has rightly deplored Minghella's film for turning Highsmith's novel into a story about the closet.[60] For him, the truth about Tom's sexuality is that he has none. He quotes from a letter that Marge sends Dickie and that Tom receives: "All right, he may not be queer. He's just a nothing, which is worse. He isn't normal enough to have *any* kind of sex life, if you know what I mean" (123). Žižek cites her unerring radar approvingly, but he takes this truth in a disappointingly conventional Freudian direction in which Tom's confusion of having and being means a short-circuiting of the normative oedipal structures of desire. Another way Žižek puts this is to suggest that Tom is "a male lesbian."[61] The suggestion is apt insofar as Tom stands in for Highsmith. But if he means to intimate that lesbians really don't have sex (lacking a Dickie, presumably), desire is misconstrued along lines akin to the heterosexual reproductive imperative that subtends Minghella's model of the relation of persons (male and female, gay and straight) and music as an inevitable opposition operating under the imperative of identity.

What gets lost in this translation is what Minghella's film, when it succeeds, shares with Highsmith's novel: the sheer pleasure of impersonation, the inhabitation of an identity not one's own—precisely because the notion of one's own identity is a misnomer. This is the triumph of Damon's performance of Tom/Dickie, and key to Highsmith's inhabitation of Tom. Take, for example, a moment of recognition Tom has late in *The Talented Mr. Ripley* when he imagines what would follow if he killed Marge (Highsmith is playing out a plot possibility). The scenario unfolds in his head: "His stories were good because he imagined them so intensely, so intensely that he came to believe them" (253), a kind of prescription for making acting believable that sounds a bit later like a version of method acting as he begins to hear in his head exactly what he would say about how Marge came to be dead.[62] "It was like a phonograph playing in his head, a little drama taking place right in the living-room that he was unable to stop" (253). Once the needle finds its grooves, it plays itself. Tom may be inventing a scene, but the scene is already there, in him and outside him, mechanical and yet human. This phonography is, most immediately, Highsmith's writing; when her script burrows into Minghella's melodrama, it deforms its intentional musical patterns of true identity and the moral occult into something more interesting—and truer, too, to the energies of melodrama's transgressive remediation of the relationship of music and words to arrive at another way to inhabit the impossible situation and make it habitable. As Highsmith herself reported about writing *The Talented Mr. Ripley* in *Plotting and Writing Suspense Fiction*, "No book was easier for me to write, and I often had the feeling Ripley was writing it and I was merely typing."[63]

This way of being singular plural—of living a life not one's own in aesthetic experience—is glimpsed as well in *The Talented Mr. Ripley* in how Tom inhabits his Venetian palazzo. He is Tom and he is Dickie, still (always) inventing himself anew, and surrounded by beautiful objects: "furniture that did not resemble furniture at all but an embodiment of cinquecento music played on hautboys, recorders, and violas da gamba" (214). Things embody sounds, become musical instruments.

116 CHAPTER THREE

Collecting art, perfecting his French, Tom cuddles up in furniture that envelops him the way sound surrounds and holds one: "The curve of the sofa fitted his shoulders like somebody's arm, or rather fitted it better than somebody's arm" (250). Beyond the distinction of persons, far from Minghella's distorting pathos and humanism, Highsmith's Tom luxuriates in a "fit" that has unseated categorical difference between persons and things. He is in the surround of art. As are we, too, reading the novel.

Minghella's Tom has as his mantra "I thought it would be better to be a fake somebody than a real nobody" (130), a sentence he needs to unlearn. Highsmith has supplied the prompt for the line, but the feeling lasts for only a page. At first, when Tom realizes he can no longer claim to be Dickie, "he hate[s] becoming Thomas Ripley again, hate[s] being nobody" (192). Then Tom seizes on the reality of acting to pass immediately from the sense that his own existence is "unreal" and "beg[ins] to feel happy even in his dreary role as Thomas Ripley." He is so happy he starts overplaying the part: "After all, would anyone, *anyone*, believe that such a character had done a murder" (194). In *Strangers on a Train*, there is no such thing as a kind of person who murders. Anyone can because there is no such thing as kinds of people in the first place. Tom exchanges being one nobody for being another. Being nothing means one can be anything. Tom decides to play himself; not many pages earlier in the novel, when he became Dickie (which means, came to sound like Dickie), he found that "it was strangely easy to forget the exact timbre of Tom Ripley's voice" (122). For a while, Tom has to practice playing both. Neither is truer to himself, though "mostly he was Dickie. . . . Sometimes, if the song on the radio was one that Tom liked, he merely danced by himself, but he danced as Dickie would have with a girl" (122).

At the close of the introduction to his screenplay, Minghella regrets that Highsmith died before he could meet her, since "if I were to have pleased anybody with this adaptation I would have liked it to have been her." He continues, "She imagined Ripley sitting at the typewriter"; likewise, writing his script, Minghella had her in mind. He cites a few sentences from *Plotting and Writing Suspense Fiction* that describe the stance of the writer that he takes as his own, concluding with this statement: "*In a word his invented people must seem real.*" As Žižek comments, real for Minghella means humanly comprehensible, whereas what is real about Highsmith's Ripley is some inhuman core that does not answer to the moral categories Minghella wrestles to make sense of Highsmith's world and make it the kind of melodrama of the moral occult that the directors who have been the focus in this book eschew.[64] Against his own moral and musical designs, Minghella virtually concedes his error. "Ripley . . . proves to be the more genuine improviser," he writes, outdoing the great initiators, Bach and Mozart, as well as the jazz greats—Bird, Miles Davis, Sonny Rollins, Dizzy Gillespie—who are the sites of Dickie's most fervid identifications.[65] Highsmith might have approved of Minghella's film—after all, she claimed to like the first film version of *The Talented Mr. Ripley*, René Clément's *Plein Soleil* (1960), in which Tom's fear of the police is realized. What she most admired there was the performance of Alain Delon as Ripley. His poker face never betrays a trace of the play of human identity that Matt Damon wears as his mask.

One of Us

Ripley's Game perhaps comes closest to giving readers (or film adapters) a guide to how Highsmith would have her aesthetic project be apprehended. As the novel starts, Tom has been approached to murder someone for Reeves, the fence for whom he does odd jobs in exchange for favors like fake passports he may need. Tom refuses but then thinks how he can maneuver Jonathan Trevanny into doing it. He is retaliating for the slight he received when Trevanny said dismissively to him, "I've heard of you" (601), I know who you are, and I am nothing like you. Ripley's game—Highsmith's game—is to show up that difference. By circulating a rumor that Jonathan's leukemia has significantly worsened and that his death is imminent, Tom wagers that with nothing to lose, moralistic, judgmental Jonathan will become a murderer. The rumor takes hold; a friend writes to Jonathan, telling him he knows the secret of his immanent death: "I was told you knew, but weren't telling" (613). Tom puts Jonathan in the place of the open secret and the unsaid; he becomes unrecognizable to himself, becoming Tom. By the end of the novel, when Jonathan dies, having proved along the way that anyone can murder, he takes a bullet meant for Tom.

Like Tom, Jonathan began life imagining he would be an actor; he is married to a French woman, like Tom, from the second novel in the series onward. Jonathan's wife, Simone, inherits her husband's moral stance (Tom's Heloise shares *his* amorality); Simone regards Tom as a monster, a Svengali (835), and Jonathan's "horrible connection" to Tom is something too "disgusting" for her to name (846; her vocabulary points to unspeakable sexuality). By the end of the novel, her morality is shown up: she spits at Tom but takes the money Tom offers her.

Money, however, is not ultimately why Trevanny agrees to play Ripley's game; rather, he becomes one with Tom because "he didn't care much about his own life" (779). Is Jonathan "one of *us*," Ripley wonders; "but us to Tom was only Tom Ripley" (690). In this novel, unlike any of the other Ripley novels, Highsmith allows readers to be in someone else's mind beside Tom's: Jonathan's. He has the consciousness afforded by free indirect discourse that Tom has. Indeed, he has the same consciousness as Tom does; his mind reading echoes Tom's. His dying thought fastens on Tom's aliveness: "Tom was driving the car, Jonathan thought, like God himself" (865). As the novel ends, Tom goes from being unable to believe his double is dead to accepting Jonathan's death with the equanimity of living once again untouched by the inevitability of death. Ripley's game is a game for the living, a life that exceeds the ordinary boundaries of life and death. It is the life of the artwork, Tom's transformation of the impossible.

In *Ripley's Game*, that other life lived alongside one's own is attached to music. Once Jonathan has killed the first time, Tom lends him a hand for a second murder. It takes place on a train aptly named *The Mozart Express*. After Tom and Jonathan have bonded (Tom does Jonathan's murder, crisscross, on the train) and Tom has told him how his disdainful knowingness set him up to become Tom's double, Tom worries about revenge for the murder just committed. An apparent non sequitur follows: "Tom decided to acquire a harpsichord" (744). A harpsichord, Tom thinks, would fit "in the category of cultural acquisitions," and within a page, he has bought one. "This purchase gave Tom a heady lift; it made him feel invincible" (745). A few pages later, Heloise is playing the treble of a Bach chaconne (764), and Tom hears its "pure" notes as "a message from another century"; soon he is "playing the base of a Goldberg variation," knowing how it should sound because he knows "Landowska's recording" (771).[66] For Tom, Bach is "instantly civilizing" (828), so he tells Jonathan after they have killed and incinerated the mafiosi who attempt to kill them. This remark about Bach comes a page after he has broken into his theme song, *"papa ne meno / Como faremo fare l'amor."* When Jonathan awakes the next morning in Belle Ombre, Tom is playing the harpsichord, and Jonathan thinks Tom's thought: "As Tom had said, *instantly civilizing*" (830). At the end of the novel, after Jonathan is dead, Reeves visits, to get filled in on how Tom played his game. Reeves instantly spots the harpsichord, and Tom says he and Heloise plan to take lessons. As the novel draws to a close and, once again, Tom expects the police might come (but they have not yet — and they don't), he practices the harpsichord. As Walter Benjamin writes, "There is no document of civilization which is not at the same time a document of barbarism."[67] The simultaneity that Benjamin avers needs to be grasped as such, not taken as a license for a moralism in the name of the political condemnation of art. "Art is not required to explain itself, neither to politics nor to morality," Jacques Rancière writes at the opening of an essay on Vincente Minnelli's films — his musicals and melodramas. Rancière argues for the possibilities — for politics and ethics — in artistic autonomy from the stranglehold of the categorical and the social. As he says, melodrama may show characters caught in the "'real' fiction known as society," but that real is in question, as his scare quotes indicate; melodrama is capable of opening a queer interval where everything does not add up to one thing.[68] Music plays there, invincible.

In *The Boy Who Followed Ripley*, the novel that follows *Ripley's Game*, music plays this central role. Frank Pierson, the boy who follows Ripley, seeking him out as his chosen mentor, has killed his father. Tom attempts to get him to exorcize his guilt and adopt a Tom-like relationship to the murder by having him write up an account of what he did (the boy becomes another authorial surrogate). Frank ends with a brief paragraph: "Music is good, any kind of music, classic or whatever it is. Not to be in any kind of prison, that is good. Not to manipulate people, that is good."[69] Musical distinctions, and their attachments to achieved identity on which Minghella's *Talented Mr. Ripley* banks, are explicitly refused.

Tom echoes the boy a few pages later when his neighbor Antoine, making a late night appearance, is surprised to hear rock on the record player. "Ah, no more harpsichord music," he remarks. Tom replies: "What's the matter with rock? . . . My tastes are catholic, I hope" (74–75). The record that Antoine hears is not identified, but we know Frank put it on. Tom takes Antoine to be voicing suspicions about Tom's mode of living: "He seemed to be sniffing the air as if in hopes of picking up a scent of perfume" (73). Antoine confirms Tom's thoughts (as usual, Ripley's thoughts anticipate the plot, giving him preternatural powers of telepathy), asking whether Tom is entertaining someone. "Male or female," he inquires.

We are not told what piece of music surprised Antoine, but it's easy to guess. Earlier, when Heloise had put on a Lou Reed album, Frank responded: "The music had really struck a chord" (65). Frank puts "on the Lou Reed record again" (70) after he finishes writing his confession for Tom. (He and Teresa, the girl at home with whom he is in love, both own copies.) Lou Reed's celebrations of transgression ("Take a Walk on the Wild Side") are one significant musical strain in the novel. Classical music also abounds: Tom practices Scarlatti on the harpsichord; *Swan Lake* plays on the Belle Ombre turntable; Mendelssohn is heard frequently, as is opera. When the scene changes to Berlin nightlife, a steady disco beat gets associated with the pulse of life.

Frank is drawn to Lou Reed's music. Nonetheless, on his second visit to Belle Ombre he brings Tom a Dietrich Fischer-Dieskau recording of Schubert lieder. "Just what I wanted," Tom says (19). How could Frank have known, Tom wonders, and he asks, "From the harpsichord?" (21). This non sequitur makes sense because Tom's harpsichord teacher looks, to him, like a "French Schubert" (18; not quite a Franz Schubert, although France and Franz are homophones). Tom's association of the harpsichord and Schubert is a thought that occurs a page before Frank arrives with his gift, his choice of a Schubert lieder album inevitable given the kind of musical mental telepathy that moves through Highsmith as its underscore; inevitable that Frank (whose name chimes here) would bring Tom a record that reads his mind (in a literalization of this, in the final Ripley novel, *Ripley Under Water*, Heloise plays Schubert on the harpsichord). Indeed, Tom had guessed Frank's identity before he told him who he was when he spotted his name in a *Herald Tribune* story about the runaway son of a millionaire, an apparent suicide who threw himself over a cliff. He notices his name next to an article about Frank Sinatra "making another final appearance" (14). One Frank leads to another. Identity glides into identification.

"Is he musical," we know, can be an oblique question about sexual identity. Heloise asks it directly. "Is he a *tapette*?" she asks about Frank;

THE ART OF MURDER 121

"That meant homosexual" (88). "Not that I can see," Tom replies, an answer that tells us as little about the boy as it does about Tom or about Heloise's understanding of Tom's sexuality—or how their relationship works. When Tom imagines what life at Belle Ombre would be like without Heloise, he thinks there would be "no one to switch on the gramophone and fill the house suddenly with rock music or sometimes Ralph Kirkpatrick on the harpsichord" (119). Heloise provides the sound track for his life: "She had become a part of his existence, almost of his flesh." Being one with him means "the infrequency of their making love" (119). It embodies the line from his song: "Papa non vuole . . . Mamma ne meno." Music is sex by another means, or, better, another way to get at what sex can seem to offer.

"Heloise existed," Tom muses in *Ripley Under Ground* (458), the first novel in which she appears, much to the surprise of any reader who might think that Tom's attachment to Dickie proves that he is gay. She is incomprehensible to him (Highsmith gives us no access to her thoughts beyond those she shares with Tom), embodying a contentment a bit at odds with Tom's restlessness, although he admits to himself that it is not much of a difference—neither of them has much purpose in life. "Tom felt odd sometimes making love with her," the passage continues, "because he felt detached half the time, and as if he derived pleasure from something inanimate, unreal, from a body without an identity" (458). A body without identity also defines Tom. Heloise exists the same way the sofa did in Tom's Venetian palazzo, to wrap its arm around him. Her material existence is made for him because she is made of what he is, too. "She was a partner," his thought continues, "though a passive one. With a boy or man, Tom would have laughed more—maybe that was the main difference" (459). With someone of the same sex, perhaps, the relationship would have been more risible because freer of the constraints that burden marriage when the heterosexual couple is saddled with the mystery of otherness. Marriage to Heloise is not like that: her material existence and the catholicity of the music she provides intimates another form of relationality.

In *The Boy Who Followed Ripley* Heloise's association with music points to what flows between them and what holds the relationship together freely. This current joins Tom and Heloise and Frank when they listen to Lou Reed. It also is associated for Tom with Berlin, despite its political situation, divided by the wall, occupied by foreign troops, not really located in a country, a place apart. Tom takes Frank to Berlin, where he is kidnapped, finally to be rescued by Tom. Once Tom found out that Frank was a millionaire's son, he assumed he would be kidnapped; thinking it makes it happen. Tom is inordinately upset when his thought is realized and no wonder, since he translates kidnap into "rape, in the sense that he had been snatched away. Tom had never felt thus shaken by something that he himself had done" (130), precisely because he has done it by thinking it. These worries about identification are tied to the life that fictions have when they invade our minds, the reality we confer on them and recognize in them; they play like a tune we can't get out of our heads and that happily goes on indifferent to us.[70]

Tom rescues Frank first by killing one of the kidnappers (it is the only murder Tom commits in this novel), then by scaring off the other two, trailing them from an assignation in a gay bar he made with them. Tom is in drag for this second escapade. Before Frank is taken from him, Tom's Berlin bar tour features gay bars populated with transvestites. In one, they sing from *Madama Butterfly* in a drag show routine that also includes the operetta number "Das ist die Berliner Luft" (111). Transvestites have catholic tastes. Frank loves the shows. "I'll never forget this day—my last with you," he says to Tom; "the words of a lover," thinks Tom, who believes Frank is not a tapette (123).

Despite all the "evidence" that might lead one to suppose that Frank is a tapette (Tom, too, for that matter), this story of the boy's adoration for Tom, and Tom's solicitude for him, is an identification that does not add up to a recognizable identity. Tom has been reading Christopher Isherwood's *Christopher and His Kind* while Frank is in a trance listening to Lou Reed. The freedom Tom associates with Cold War Berlin comes to him from Isherwood's depiction of Weimar Germany. Perhaps Frank's trance state is akin to what music conveys wordlessly, taking one to another place, a place of likeness, but not of identity. Tom and Frank share a bed several times in the novel, but there is no way of knowing whether they have sex. Nor is it clear that Tom and Heloise do the one time they sleep together in this novel. Frank has slept with Teresa, the girl he loves, but he lost his erection. His misadventure in heterosex parallels what happened to Tom on his honeymoon, as he recalls in *Ripley Under Ground*; the sound of a parrot singing something from *Carmen* interrupted coitus. "It is impossible to make love while laughing," Tom comments (335). In conjunction with his thought that he might laugh more with a boy than he does with Heloise, this could suggest that same-sex partnership for Tom would be a laughing matter in which no sex would be involved. But recalling that when Tom goes to rescue Frank he asks the drag queen making him up to take *Carmen* off the record player and to sing "that song about the slick little girl" (177; "Make Up," from Lou Reed's *Transformer*), it may be that music from *Carmen* inhibits Tom's assuming drag because of the risibility of compulsory heterosexuality, especially when it is tinged with the melodramatic doom of impossible romance. Tom's jolly song about unfulfilled desire counters this music.

Tom, Highsmith claimed, wrote the first novel about him. He also shares her musicality (she *was* musical). According to Joan Schenkar in her biography, Highsmith played the piano, if not all that well. Like D. A. Miller, "Pat loved piano bars and musical comedy." Judy Holliday was an early, lifelong friend. So, too, was the gay classical composer David Diamond (he helped Highsmith find a psychiatrist); Diamond claims that Highsmith was obsessed with music, Ravel in particular. When she appeared on the BBC radio show *Desert Island Discs* in 1979, her choice of music, as Schenkar notes, included musical comedy and a classical selection (a piece by Albeniz that Tom substitutes for Heloise's Lou Reed at the end of *The Boy Who Followed Ripley*). Andrew Wilson, in his biography of Highsmith, gives the full list of her choices, which includes a number of classical items (by Bach, Mozart, Mahler, and Rachmaninov), as well as George Shearing's "Lullaby of Birdland," extending the range from Broadway to jazz. "Her choice of music was varied," Wilson notes. Or, we could say, catholic.[71]

This catholicity can be contrasted with a musical translation akin to Minghella's in Liliana Cavani's *Ripley's Game* (2002), this time following the prompt of the novel's harpsichord. Tom (John Malkovich) lives in a Palladian villa with Luisa Harari (Chiara Caselli), a harpsichordist (the film ends with her in recital in Palladio's Teatro Olimpico in Vicenza). We first see her playing on the lower keyboard of a harpsichord while Tom plays jazzy riffs on top to her more classical bottom. What their hands do is a version of their relationship, a bit of tamely kinky S/M. Luisa gets off on Tom's evildoing. Unlike Highsmith's Heloise, she knows he murders; she also wants to hear all the details of his relations with Jonathan's wife, which he agrees to provide only if he can sodomize her. Homosex gets played out in their heterosexual relationship (Luisa tells him he would make a perfect wife—he cooks and sews—perhaps she will marry him). Tom's relationship to Jonathan Trevanny (Dougray Scott) continues this mild S/M scene, Cavani following the novel faithfully enough but draining their relationship of sexual tension and pleasure (Wim Wenders does a much better job of representing it in his *The American Friend* [*Der amerikanische freund*, 1977]). As Jonathan comes to be like Tom, he becomes, like him, colder and harder. In this adaptation, Tom chooses Jonathan simply because it's the game, meaninglessness, joyless kink. To the degree that Cavani captures something in Highsmith, it lies in a lifelessness that represents freedom from human social identity. But here it is something that bored straight couples do to make sex more interesting.

Tom and Luisa in the film are like a parody of Highsmith's Tom and Heloise, a gambit Highsmith tried out in the final Ripley novel, *Ripley Under Water*, through Pritchard and his abused accomplice wife. They have decided for no reason to expose Tom. One or the other of them plays Dickie on the phone. Pritchard finds a corpse (of the art collector Thomas Murchison, whose corpse Tom throws in a river in *Ripley Under Ground*), and he leaves it on Tom's doorstep. Tom responds in kind, dropping it in the pond in the backyard of the house the Pritchards have bought in his Villeperce neighborhood. Trying to fish it out, they fall in. Tom sees it happen. His desire to kill them has been fulfilled by doing nothing. That desire is not just a game he plays for the sake of the game; it is also played for the possibility of infusing meaninglessness with meaning. The universe squares his antisocial desire to go on living a life filled with good meals and music. The Pritchards' S/M game is an end in itself. They act like the police, suspecting Tom, yet they do not turn him in either. They are a hinge that parodies both the law and its transgression. Tom is where the music is and where our pleasure lies.

The Artistic Life

In conversation with Reeves (Ray Winstone), Cavani's Tom proposes himself as master of a finishing school; the double entendre points to the aesthetic project Highsmith shares with Hitchcock. Tom is trying, with those worth the effort, to make his own remodeling project one to emulate. *Transformer,* the Lou Reed album title, provides one name for this project, thematized by music in *The Boy Who Followed Ripley.* In *Ripley Under Ground,* where the attempt to replicate himself is most intense, Highsmith conveys her cross-media, transpersonal project through painting. Through these efforts beyond words—to reach out and touch someone (by telephone, telepathy, hidden pictures, and unheard melodies)—we glimpse a material existence into which human existence is to be—*is*—folded. The journey of self-transformation is one of undoing, not a place for a knowledge that can be claimed as one's own; not a place of identity, but of identification. It is where we are homos, as Leo Bersani might put it, recognizing our material sameness. Although Highsmith novels tend to represent access to this place through intense male-male bonds, Heloise, for Tom, also is a locus for this kind of relationality. When Tom reflects on his relationship to her, Heloise's material opacity as an object of his desire and bafflement is summed up this way: "She was like a picture on the wall" (458), an apt comparison for the ekphrasis of *Ripley Under Ground.* Since Tom is recognizably a vehicle for Highsmith, this relationship also could be seen to convey lesbian desire.

In *Ripley Under Ground* Tom impersonates the painter Derwatt, appearing as him in the London gallery that represents him (representation is also a version of impersonation), which has just hung a show of his new paintings. Tom has built an entire enterprise around Derwatt, including a company (Derwatt Ltd.) that sells art supplies under his signature. "Derwatt" is a brand, not a name; it has the artificial life of the corporation. Tom has extended his artistic life (the real Derwatt committed suicide). Forged paintings by Bernard Tufts, chosen by Tom for the job, are being sold as Derwatts. Bernard duplicates the artist who lives on in his work; Tom doubles his body in order to authenticate the forged paintings that have come under suspicion by Derwatt collector Thomas Murchison. Tom tries to persuade this other American Tom that there are no fake Derwatts. For Tom, there is no difference between real and fake. At Belle Ombre a Tufts Derwatt hangs in the place of honor over the mantelpiece while a real Derwatt occupies another wall; "Tom loved both pictures. By now he had almost forgotten to remember, when he looked at them, that one was a forgery and the other genuine" (307).

Tom fails to persuade Murchison that the fakes are real and tries instead to convince him to stop pursuing the charge of forgery by telling him the truth, wanting him to recognize Bernard Tufts as a genius who has found his "second nature" (310) as his "real" nature in his forgeries. This argument fails, and Tom realizes why: *"Murchison was not artistic"* (362). Tom serves the other Tom a wonderful lunch: "It was the kind of lunch that under other circumstances would have given contentment, even happiness, would have inspired lovers to go to bed . . . and make love and then sleep. The beauty of the lunch was today wasted on Tom" (362) and on the other Tom he wishes to make like him. Tom fails here, as he does with the boy who followed him, and who finally commits suicide, making true the false report about his father's death. Tom kills Murchison.

Artistic life is Bernard's; he lives in paintings that do not bear his name or identity. Although agonized by this life, since he cannot be himself, and blaming Tom for setting him up as a forger, he also believes that Derwatt appeared to him after his death and told him to "carry on" his work (476). This haunting destabilization of personal identity intimates the life of art beyond the artist. (This was the current I followed from Sirk to Fassbinder and Haynes.) In an impassioned moment, Bernard reads aloud from Derwatt's diary (I imagine it is a passage from one of Highsmith's notebooks): "There is no depression for the artist except that caused by a return to the Self. . . . The Self is that shy, vainglorious, egocentric, conscious magnifying glass which should never be looked at or through" (444). The "Self" is not the source of painting. Nor is it what a painting reflects. Nor does a painting, even one with representational aims, reproduce "reality." "The Derwatt over the fireplace . . . was a pinkish picture of a man in a chair, a man with several outlines, so it seemed one was looking at the picture through someone else's distorting eyeglasses," an effect that makes Derwatts hard to see, Tom notes; neither the object nor the viewing position is singular (306). This Derwatt is not a Derwatt, although the description begins as if it is, and the generalizations about it are said to apply to other Derwatts. In the real one in Belle Ombre, two little girls are difficult to locate in the visual color field of a painting that at first does not appear to be representational; when its background is seen as flames, "the emotional effect [is] shattering" (307). The real subject is destroyed before one's eyes when color is apprehended as a fire that will destroy the represented figures. The experience described involves finding the girls only then to see them being destroyed. The eye flickers between abstraction and representation. This visual double take enacts the difficulty in translating the visual (or the musical) into words even as it also suggests the disquieting literary effects of Highsmith's writing.

Heady exchanges of life and death that usher one into artistic life are played out in *Ripley Under Ground*, starting with the title of the novel. Bernard hangs himself in effigy in Tom's wine cellar (where Tom bashed Murchison to death, as Bernard knows). He attempts to kill Tom by burying him in a grave that Murchison once occupied. Tom survives this attempted live burial; what he represents can't be killed. He follows Bernard to Salzburg, where Bernard, seeing him, thinks he is seeing a ghost (Tom does not disabuse him) and commits suicide. Tom makes use of Bernard's remains — once he has burned the body, removing any signs of identification from the corpse — finally to put to rest the supposed alive really dead Derwatt, noting that it is "appropriate that Bernard should give his remains to be thought of as Derwatt" (585). The appropriateness of the misappropriation of one corpse for another lies in the fact that materially, bodily difference makes no difference. The dizzying substitution of living and dead, of one body for another, is this novel's way of apprehending the limitations of human life from which artistic meaning is made, dissolving the impossible melodrama of "real" life for the real possibility of artificial aesthetic life.[72] Bernard has, as it were, murdered himself to be Derwatt, and his suicide is simply the literalization of his artistic process. But that process also was Derwatt's own, as his diary intimates; Tom prolonged his posthumous life.

Tom's relationship with Bernard is a site for intense identification, for another reclamation project of making his likeness (Tom succeeds best with readers of Highsmith). Bernard, in being so perfectly Derwatt and so miserably himself, is halfway to the position that Tom occupies being Tom. It is an imitation that began with Dickie, although the Dickie who appears in *The Talented Mr. Ripley* largely comes from Tom's imagination of him. Tom paints like Dickie does, indeed better and more seriously, quite seriously by *Ripley Under Water*, where, rather than turning to music for equanimity and inspiration, he sketches. He is cultivated, as Dickie was not. He lives a life of elegance and comfort, on Dickie's money, on his Derwatt scam, and on the allowance Heloise has from her wealthy father. His mode of life, which everyone questions — he appears to do nothing — is a life anyone might want to have, a picture of bourgeois domesticity that verges on an atavistic aristocratic existence. The value of that life, however, does not lie in a subscription to the values it appears to reflect, as critics sometimes claim; it hollows them out in simulation, knowingly.[73] Passing by toney London hotels, Tom thinks: "Behind the genteel respectability of those narrow lobbies some of the best murderers of the present day took refuge for a night or so, looking equally respectable themselves" (315). This insight reflects Tom's "underground" existence. In the literal London Underground, Tom rides an escalator into those depths. (He's on a shopping trip: Tom never returns home without gifts for Heloise, which always fit perfectly and please her exceedingly, for a moment, at any rate. Like Tom, she lives in the present, and we never see her wearing anything he buys her; not a shred of sentimentality attaches to these objects of attachment.) Along the Underground wall Tom is amused by a sign printed in small capitals: "I LOVE BEING HERMAPHRODITE" (348). "How did they do it?" Tom wonders — not, as we might suppose, about being a hermaphrodite, but how someone wrote this in one direction while going in another, a sexual figure of speech for Highsmith's accomplishment as a writer.

Tom's attraction to Bernard lies precisely in how fully he lives in work that exceeds himself and that will survive him: "In Bernard there was a mystery, and it was mystery that made people attractive, Tom thought, that caused people to fall in love" (386). Is Tom in love with Bernard? In love therefore wanting to be him, to kill him? Or in love with Bernard because he has already killed himself? Because he could therefore "really" live the afterlife that is Tom's life? "It was strange, and exceedingly pleasant, to daydream about Bernard's drives, fears, shames, and possible loves" (386). No doubt this is authorial transportation through the mind of Tom. And, in fact, it is through telepathy that Tom is able to follow Bernard. He recalls a conversation that he and Bernard had about the relationship between artistic life and the artist's literal life span. "Can anybody imagine Mozart living to be eighty?" Bernard asks. "Can you imagine Bach dying at twenty-six . . . ? Which proves a man is his work, nothing more or less" (487). Tom disproves this thesis by extending Derwatt's life through Bernard: a person's work may outlive him because it was not his to begin with. In the midst of their discussion about composers, Bernard mentions he would like to visit Salzburg again. That later prompts Tom to the telepathic certainty he will find him there. He does. Thinking to visit the Mozart Museum, he finds Bernard there, too (another ride on *The Mozart Express*). Tom follows Bernard into the museum and sees him "leaning over the keyboard of Mozart's clavichord" (549). It's the first time Bernard sees the ghost of the Ripley he buried in Murchison's temporary grave. He sees Tom while Tom is lost in thought, "awed as always by Mozart" (549).

What is artistic life? What is the life we live that art intimates as it goes beyond the sayable? Tom muses how, in French, "forge" means to make, while in English it means to fake (477). In this linguistic translation, the same word crosses a line of supposed difference in language which is not one. Tom glimpses the non-self-identity of the word on the page, even when, in context (whether we are reading a book in French or in English) we may think we know where we are, what meaning is at hand. This doubleness moots the difference between real and fake Derwatts in *Ripley Under Ground*; it is palpable in the lively art of impersonation, the theater of Tom's performances. It is evident in painting, too, especially when it flickers between representation and abstraction and lets us know we are only seeing paint. In music what is on the page can be realized only in performances, no two of which ever are the same, and none of which can be said simply to deliver the musical notation.

In *Ripley Under Ground*, the faked Derwatts make Derwatt's career, grant him posthumous fame. At least in the United States, where Highsmith was not a successful author in her lifetime, posthumous fame (publication of all her writing, including previously unpublished stories) was undertaken by the publisher W. W. Norton once she was recognized—thanks, in large measure, to the success of Minghella's *Talented Mr. Ripley*. That history uncannily repeats the story Highsmith tells in *Ripley Under Ground*, a double story about what survives the writer—the work can be misapprehended through all the lenses of ordinary misapprehension that pass for an "understanding" of how things are, what people are, what normative difference is. In opposition to this, the work abides in a dialectical coincidence with its opposite. Tom, the embodiment of happy marriage, success, comfort; Tom, the murderer, the aesthete, queer.

These are the double lives Highsmith shared with her alter ego, and that we do, too, reading her. According to the autobiographical statement quoted in Anna von Platta's biographical sketch in a volume of drawings by Highsmith published in the year of her death, in adolescence she was drawing and carving, following in the footsteps of her mother, a fashion designer, and her father and stepfather, both graphic artists.[74] Somehow, unaccountably she became a writer. Maybe not so unaccountably. As material practices the graphic arts include writing and painting. In her preface to this volume of her drawings, Highsmith claims not to have been trained to draw. She thinks, as Guy does in *Strangers on a Train*, that all the arts are one, first formulating this in a way that gives precedence to writing: all the arts are said to share the goal of storytelling and communication. In typical Highsmith fashion, this formulation survives for a paragraph and is revisited as she draws to a close on the second page. For the writer, she says, what a painter does is quite something else from the writer's practice; likewise for the composer. Theirs is a kind of immediacy and presence that the writer cannot achieve. Any painter or composer, Highsmith concludes, probably could write a short story. But not the reverse: "Painters and composers fill me with great awe." Their work exceeds the limits of plot that might bind a novel to melodrama, but not when we read the melos that accompanies the drama, an understanding that takes us, by way of too close reading, past or more deeply into the literal.

Highsmith draws her writing into the orbit of the awesome precincts of painting and music, especially through Tom as he pursues his own aesthetic path, in which plotting is his being, painting and listening to music the source of replenishment. Reading is, too. In *Ripley Under Water*, Tom is moved by Richard Ellmann's life of Oscar Wilde, his story of Wilde's end as a kind of Christlike martyrdom. It is a fitting relationship for Tom to have in that novel, haunted as he is by a persecuting double who is far gone in a sadomasochism that looks like a version of the police and the norms of social control even as it echoes Tom's derailment of those norms. A more uplifting version of Wilde provides the epigraph for *Ripley Under Ground*: "*I think I would more readily die for what I do not believe in than for what I hold to be true . . . Sometimes I think that the artistic life is a long and lovely suicide, and I am not sorry that it is so.*" This is from an 1886 Wilde letter. The sentences describe a kind of aesthetic practice that also is an ascetic practice, the renunciation of truth, which is likely to be a lie that is socially accepted as truth. This is a form of dying to the world in order to be true to artistic life, something not true to life when truth to life is understood conventionally and ideologically.

Highsmith's aesthetics were Wildean; so, too, were Hitchcock's. I began this chapter recalling Thomas Elsaesser's essay on melodrama, his suggestion that having music punctuate text brings both to another place at which both seek to arrive. I close by recalling Elsaesser's essay on Hitchcock as a dandy.[75] As Elsaesser stresses, Hitchcock's dandyism took the most improbable form—he dressed as a quintessential respectable English businessman. With a costume of controlled bearing and unexceptional deportment, he made films that can be misapprehended as exercises in control, as endorsements of law and order; or— but this is more difficult—they can be seen for what they are. To do that involves seeing hidden pictures, hearing unheard melodies, and exploring a terrain that departs musically from the strict rules of narrative into a world where murder and untoward sexuality are the means to aesthetic life. We live there in aesthetic pleasure.

FOUR

WILDEAN AESTHETICS

From "Paul's Case" to Lucy Gayheart

I have previously mentioned Oscar Wilde as a name to attach to the aesthetic aims of melodrama. Wilde's notion of the enhancement of personality is not about individualization and identity but identifications best arrived at by their multiplication, a process that Wilde describes as "theatricalization"; he epitomizes this, for example, in Shakespeare's boy actors, who, by assuming women's parts, arrive somewhere beyond normative definitions of gender and sexuality.[1] He exemplifies it, too, in Thomas Griffith Wainewright, the writer, forger, and murderer, whose "disguises intensified his personality."[2] It is thus no surprise that Patricia Highsmith's Tom Ripley began life as an actor who gives consummate performances of a being that seems detached from the usual trammels of identity; Highsmith makes explicit her Wildean aesthetic, as I have noted, in an epigraph to *Ripley Under Ground*. There, exceeding the usual limits of being oneself is couched in terms of self-sacrifice and suicide. There is a cost to aesthetic existence. Wilde's life, of course, exemplifies this in the excruciation of his trial with its combination of a wit meant to deflect any possibility of conviction — meant to keep the play of signifiers from ever arriving at the word that would nail Wilde — and its frequently earnest defense of a love that cannot be named. Wilde's trial, which hinged on the cusp of being and acting, is familiar melodramatic territory, named succinctly in the title of Douglas Sirk's final Hollywood film, *Imitation of Life* (1959). The trial is reenacted in Todd Haynes's *Velvet Goldmine* (1998) and, more obliquely, in his *I'm Not There* (2007), especially when Cate Blanchett, playing Bob Dylan, gives celebrity interviews whose disavowals and refusals define where "stars" exist—eating shit and being divine, to recall Eve Kosofsky Sedgwick and Michael Moon on this.[3] Asked to say a word for his/her fans, Blanchett/Dylan says, "astronaut." Haynes opens *Velvet Goldmine* intimating the extraterrestrial origin of Wilde, an origin that, of course, replays the persona of glam rock a hundred years later. Artistic life shapes "real life," a thoroughly Wildean point.

Willa Cather has been attached to Wilde, most forcefully in an essay by Sedgwick that first appeared in 1989.[4] There she explores possibilities of cross-identifications, first in ten dense theoretical-historical pages that subsequently were included in the axiomatics of *Epistemology of the Closet* and then in a section that begins with a reading of Cather's story "Paul's Case" (1905) as the prelude to a glance at later Cather in relationship to Henry James and Marcel Proust. It is a dazzling essay intensely alert to the difficulty and promise of cross-identification, of affordances beyond identity, "unrecognized pockets of value and vitality that can hit out in unpredictable directions."[5] Demonstrating this, the essay ends with a breathtaking unpacking of multiple anagrammatic puns buried in the final words of Cather's *The Professor's House* (1925), a demonstration that in language that might be supposed limited to literal signification there are immense possibilities that coexist with denotative meaning. This linguistic demonstration points to a life that exceeds and yet inhabits life, not least when life seems a site of impossibility, loss, and limitation, as it does to Cather's protagonist.

One affordance of Cather's Paul: once placed in the genealogy of Wilde's Wainewright, he seems to lead to Highsmith's Ripley. Highsmith herself lived, in her adolescence, in an apartment house at 1 Bank Street, in a building erected on the Greenwich Village site where Cather and Edith Lewis had resided for many years in a townhouse at the same address; this is one of those coincidences that look overdetermined. It makes a material connection that seems to be the effect of the preexisting aesthetic link, or so Wilde might claim.

Wilde figures in Sedgwick's essay as a site for Cather of the difficulty and possibility of identification. "Paul's Case" offers a protagonist who

134   CHAPTER FOUR

is palpably Wildean, a dandy and an aesthete who, in the first half of the story, is treated to a brutalizing gaze akin to the one that broke Wilde. The kinship is not merely an analogy. Sedgwick focuses on and amalgamates two pieces of Cather's journalism from 1895, one written as Wilde's trial came to its inevitable conclusion, the other penned several months into his two-year sentence of hard labor.[6] These pieces of writing, a half dozen or so pages from Nebraska newspapers to which the twentysomething Cather was a regular contributor, are rearranged and condensed by Sedgwick into a few citations that crystallize how appalling Cather found Wilde. Sedgwick's question is what enabled Cather, ten years later, to draw back from the averseness rehearsed again in the opening Pittsburgh section of "Paul's Case," how she managed to turn the second half of the story in a direction unexpected at first: Paul escapes and has a week in New York that seems fulfilling and in which his first person, glorying in luxury financed by stealing, seems to be affirmed. Part of the answer to this question about the volte-face in the story lies in Sedgwick's analysis of Cather's journalism on Wilde, for even there, she notes, Cather moots condemnation of Wilde for the crime that sent him to prison. Although Cather's writing about Wilde is animated by the trope that names sodomy as the crime not to be named—Wilde "has made even his name impossible," Cather writes in the opening of her second 1895 piece—she also refuses to name his actual crime. "The sins of the body are very small," she continues, and Sedgwick quotes, compared to his true crime, which is the crime against art.[7] Cather transposes the sexual into the aesthetic, naming "the unspeakable crimes of artificiality and insincerity," as Sedgwick sums up this transposition from one place (the body, exonerated) to another (the writing, condemned). This transposition opens "a small shy gap of nonidentification," Sedgwick writes—a space of nonidentification of outlawed sexuality with outlaw writing; nonidentification of Cather and Wilde as writers in order to leave open the possibility of queer sexual identification with Wilde.[8] Or, better, Cather displaces that identification through the figure of Paul, the effeminate boy with whom the mannish lesbian identifies across gender toward a shared sexual identity itself based on another nonidentification, this time of gender identity with sexuality. As Sedgwick outlines in the opening section of her essay, one of the routes to homosexual identity in the late nineteenth century lay in the supposition that men who love men are not men, and likewise for women who love women. Shared liminality becomes the basis for an identification.

Paul was based on a student of Cather's, as she explained in a letter written in 1943, and the teacher in the story was based on her; but Paul also recalls Cather, most explicitly in the luxuriance of his New York life. In the Pittsburgh half, as Cather notes, "you will recognize one part of Paul" in the "nervous, jerky boy" in her Latin class; "the other part of Paul," she continues, "is simply the feeling I myself had about New York City and the *old* Waldorf Astoria."[9] However, this parsing of identifications is only part of the story, for Paul's initial aesthetic proclivities reflect Cather's staple journalistic assignments: reviews of plays, operas, art exhibits—the world in which Paul lives. Just as he hangs out in actors' dressing rooms in Pittsburgh, so, too, did Cather. That is where she met Isabelle McClung. Cather's nonidentifications are costly saving gestures, the protection of difference in a matrix that intimates sameness.

These are among the gestures that shape the melodramas of aesthetic life, as when Paul pauses for a moment in the picture gallery in Carnegie Hall before paintings of Paris by Jean-François Raffaëlli "that always exhilarated him," or a "blue Rico" before which he "lost himself."[10] These scenes of aesthetic absorption intensify when the concert starts. "It was not that symphonies, as such, meant anything in particular to Paul, but the first sigh of the instruments seemed to free some hilarious spirit within him" (471); the sentence continues by conjuring up *The Arabian Nights.* Commentators regularly pounce, along with the narrator, at the distinction drawn, condemning Paul for his limited musical knowledge and his passivity. However, what seems to be happening here also could be likened to the gap that Sedgwick notes in Cather's relationship to Wilde, the opening of a space of nonidentification that allows for possibilities that otherwise would be foreclosed. Paul's lack of knowledge is also a lack of mastery, a giving up of self and its claims in order to submit to something outside himself, outside the scope of knowing; this something nonetheless resonates within. Against the frozen smile on his face with which Paul masks and displays his aversion to his surroundings, giving in to the music also releases a "hilarious" spirit within, some form of joy (and of *jouissance*) that is self-shattering. It is further described when the soprano soloist arrives.

136 CHAPTER FOUR

With her there, Paul is able to forget that his teacher also attends this performance, and to put behind the excruciating scene of mutual embarrassment they played when he showed her to her seat. Cather, too, can put herself behind—this moment when Paul forgets her is the last of her pedagogic presence in the story; she is mentioned precisely to be replaced by the singer. Not that the singer really resembles Cather: she is "by no means in her first youth, and the mother of many children" (472). But when Paul sees her in her satin gown and tiara, cloaked in an "indefinite air of achievement," he succumbs. It is not the sounds that she makes but the "air" that she inhabits that exhilarates him with a life he thinks of as "the only thing that could be called living" (472). Cather describes her air as "world-shine," a word that seems to be translated from the German—the soprano is German—and perhaps is transposed from the nonce word that Isolde intones at the end of the "Liebestod" to describe the life that she shares with Tristan: "Weltatem," world-breath.[11]

Paul follows the soprano to her hotel (Pittsburgh's Schenley anticipates the Waldorf of the New York half of the story), and as she disappears behind "the swinging glass doors" (472) he imagines himself continuing through the revolving door with her. The second half of the story realizes this fantasy of transportation to another world. As Sedgwick points out, it is a fantasy of wealth and culture, of a place where Paul belongs.[12] And so, oddly, given the resources of minoritarian identity on which cross-identification is based (two marginalized, non-gender-conforming individuals bonding over the sameness of their difference from others), the aesthetic culture in which Paul is absorbed, and which seems to point to his nonconformity from the hardworking world of his father and the other lower-middle-class inhabitants of Cordelia Street, turns out to be culture itself. This is, of course, central to the painful paradox of Wilde: condemned to hard labor for his aberrant sexuality at the very moment that audiences were rushing to see *The Importance of Being Earnest* in London, he is cultural icon and pariah, beloved and the object of aversion, embraced through disidentification. The German soprano is an example of this dynamic but from the other direction; she is a married woman, a mother who cannot be confined to those marks of social conformity. The release from social identity into aesthetic identity, however, is not without cost. Cather marks the fact that the soprano is aging. Voices don't last.[13]

The defiant red carnation that Paul sports at first (perhaps "naturalizing" Wilde's signature green boutonniere) is, at the end of the story, a flower in the snow about to be a grave marker. "It was only one splendid breath they had," the narrator, now one with Paul's thoughts, comments (487); by labeling the brevity of this life as also "splendid," the "brave mockery" of the flowers' defiance of mortal limitation, and Paul's, is also affirmed. Flowers behind glass, brought indoors to live beyond their natural life, work the way music and art do in the first half of the story, toward defining a life within and yet apart from ordinary life that is the source of value. Paul's life ends thanks to the exigencies of "real" life — he runs out of money, money that he has stolen and thereby removed from its ordinary syntax of labor and exchange. But in using it this way, Paul may simply exacerbate the permitted crimes of the masters whom the inhabitants of Cordelia Street idealize; in this, too, he anticipates Highsmith's Ripley. Paul takes his life in the melodramatic gesture of Anna Karenina (or Carker in Dickens's *Dombey and Son*, Lopez in Trollope's *The Prime Minister*), throwing himself in front of a train in the final moment of the story. Cather continues her identification with him even here: Judith Butler has described as orgasmic release the moment when Paul's body is thrown up in the air and then "gently relaxed" as consciousness and imagination fade to black and Paul falls "back into the immense design of things" (488).[14] That design, which exceeds human life, is the life that aesthetic experience proffers, beyond oneself; turning oneself into a work of art — Wilde's life project (realized by Wainewright) — entails being shattered, atomized into the material particles that persist beyond oneself and that suggest a life beyond identity in the matter from which other possibilities beyond bounded life can be lived.

Cather glimpsed that ending again in *My Ántonia* in thoughts her alter ego, Jim Burden, has upon arriving in Nebraska and feeling at once wiped out and included in a depersonalizing immensity. Jim's beginning marks Cather's end — his words appear on her tomb in Jaffrey, New Hampshire: "That is happiness; to be dissolved into something complete and great."[15] But this transformation from life to death and from beginning to end also happens in artistic life. In her moving posthumous account, *Willa Cather Living*, Edith Lewis makes this her writing project. But as Lewis tells the story, it is one Cather glimpsed as she got to know the opera singer Olive Fremstad, upon whom, with a mix

138   CHAPTER FOUR

of aversiveness and identification akin to her identification with Wilde, she modeled the protagonist of *The Song of the Lark*, transposing herself into her. Lewis dates Cather's inveterate Metropolitan Opera attendance to 1905, the year of "Paul's Case" (he, too, attends an opera performance in New York). She tells, as well, the story of Cather going to interview Fremstad but finding her too worn out and exhausted to comply, and how, that same night, Fremstad performed when the scheduled singer was indisposed; she appeared, needless to say, not worn out by bodily fatigue, but, in Lewis's words, as "a vision of dazzling youth and beauty." Her vocal performance, Lewis continues, was so "opulent" and "effortless" that "it seemed as if she were dreaming the music, not singing it."[16] Her performance, that is, tallies with Paul's own abstraction in the concert hall. It is as if Fremstad has turned singing into something else even as she herself seems to have been transformed and relocated into another being, another place.

This is the world that Cather marks by way of *The Arabian Nights*, a fairy world, a troll garden that might also be located on the Mediterranean, or in Paris, or in the color blue on a canvas that might outdo whatever the sea or sky has on offer. Aesthetic transformation is nonetheless a material phenomenon — from one "real" (the sea, the sky) to another (the canvas). It is also what Fremstad embodies when Lewis records Cather's response to what she sees onstage: "'But it's impossible,' Willa Cather kept saying, 'It's impossible.'"[17] But it isn't. And it also is what Cather herself counted on in her own transformation into a diva in her novel, a transformation of her words into another medium. Such remediation is an aim, as I have been arguing, of melodrama as it moves from one impossibility — the fatigue in this instance of a body incapable even of speaking, the body of a star who also is refusing contact with the journalist who might want a word for her fans — to another impossibility, a performance that itself refuses the limits of its art to become something else, dreaming not singing. So doing, it enters the territory Cather claimed in "The Novel Démeublé," "the thing not named, . . . the overtone divined by the ear but not heard by it," reclaiming for aesthetic experience terms of an excoriated sexuality that cannot be named.[18]

This transposition of art and life is familiar Wildean territory — indeed, it is the plot of *The Picture of Dorian Gray*. This is not a piece of writing Cather respected in her early journalism, but in her preface to

WILDEAN AESTHETICS 139

a reissue of a revised *The Song of the Lark* in 1932 (Cather revised this novel more than any other, trying to whittle it away to fit her unfurnished aesthetic), Cather compares her novel to *Dorian Gray*. "The life of nearly every artist who succeeds in the true sense (succeeds in delivering himself completely to his art) is more or less like Wilde's story, *The Picture of Dorian Gray*," she writes. A page later, as she describes the Wagnerian soprano's arrival into artistic achievement, Wilde's novel is conjured up again, but this time to say that Cather's story "is the reverse of Wilde's," precisely because, unlike Dorian, who lives the way a picture can, the soprano suffers in her life, while "her artistic life is the only one in which she is happy, or free, or even very real."[19] This reversal reverses its terms. It reiterates what Cather wrote in a letter of 1916 about her novel when she was first at work on it, telling Dorothy Canfield Fisher that recounting the story of the triumph of any artist is difficult because "the order of their development is from the personal to the impersonal, when they cease to be proper material for a human story."[20] Ceasing to be materials for a human story, they don't cease being human. They become an impossible "real": what seems impossible—what *is* impossible within mortal limits—is exceeded in a life that persists beyond those limits and which is nonetheless coincident with lived life.

Perhaps inevitably, music is a privileged site for this realization because of its seeming to translate something palpable into a place beyond language. Cather's aesthetic—to write, but in a manner unnamable, to make what sounds nonetheless be heard beyond what the ear hears—is one in which writing aspires to the condition of music, an ideal in the work of Walter Pater rearticulated by Wilde. Cather herself finds words for this transformation in the preface she wrote for the 1925 republication of Gertrude Hall's 1907 book, *The Wagnerian Romances*. The value of Hall's book, Cather proclaims, lies in its ability to suggest Wagner's music. She reports herself "astonished" by Hall's chapter on *Parsifal* (as she was by Fremstad's transformations in her performance of Kundry): "I was astonished to find how vividly it recalled to me all the best renderings of that opera I had ever heard. Just the right word was said to start the music going in one's memory. . . . What Miss Hall does, it seems to me, is to reproduce the emotional effect of one art through the medium of another art."[21] Cather herself did that in *Song of the Lark* (the fact that the novel about a singer fetches its title from a painting by

Jules Breton further suggests its ekphrastic remediated ambition). She did it again in her late novel *Lucy Gayheart* (1935).

Cather's penultimate novel is named after a protagonist who has invariably reminded commentators of her predecessors among figures of the artist in Cather's oeuvre. Lucy comes from a small Nebraska town (here named Haverford, but a version of Red Cloud, where Cather grew up); she then spends three years in Chicago studying piano seriously. She shares this story line with the diva heroine of *Song of the Lark*, but whereas Thea Kronborg is catapulted into stardom, Lucy has no star career. In her final months in Chicago, she becomes the practice accompanist of Clement Sebastian, a world-famous singer. He dies in a boating accident, pulled down into Lake Como by his regular pianist, James Mockford. Lucy, shattered by his death, returns to her hometown. At the point of resolving to return to Chicago and continue her studies (and her piano teaching), she, too, drowns. The book is framed by present-day memories of Lucy, twenty-five years after her premature death, and a brief third book, also set in the present, in which Harry Gordon, the man who had hoped to marry Lucy, finally comes to terms with her death. Death by drowning, Fredric Jameson has observed, is a quintessential melodramatic plot device.[22] Cather uses it twice in a novel that seems anything but *The Song of the Lark*'s story of artistic triumph, though it shares with it the Wildean story of the personal becoming impersonal.

Commentary invariably thinks of this late Cather novel as "valedictory," in Janis Stout's word, reminiscent of early stories of Cather's of failed artists ("The Joy of Nelly Deane" [1911] is mentioned by Stout and James Woodress, for example), which can be seen as Cather's own worry that her belated career would never get started, or that if it did, it would go nowhere.[23] "Paul's Case" is not usually associated with this late novel, perhaps because to compare Lucy with Paul, as Blanche Gelfant remarks (in a note to her essay on the novel that goes some way in the direction that I pursue here), "seems particularly invidious in light of Richard Giannone's statement that 'Paul's attachment to art is false, subjective . . . insane.'"[24] Nonetheless, just such positions are taken, if without the invidious comparison of "cases," in noting *Lucy Gayheart* as a kind of falling off of Cather's powers. "Lucy Gayheart was not a character that Cather loved," Woodress opines, continuing, that she "had no patience with failures, especially sentimental artistic failures." Stout demurs from this position only by assuming that the character who begins "as an appreciator or absorber of beauty" is on the verge of being a "producer . . . , a serious artist" when she dies.[25] Lucy, these commentators suppose, is like Paul, if not quite the pathological case that Giannone makes him out to be on the basis of his relationship to art. What seems particularly baffling to me about these responses is the notion that Cather would have no interest in or appreciation of artistic responsiveness, as if, let's say, she only wanted readers who also were themselves painters, novelists, or composers. At the very least, it seems as if critics who are made uncomfortable by Paul or Lucy may be registering their discomfort in their own activity. People who can, do; those who can't, teach, seems the lesson they have absorbed and pass on.

Cather's melodramatic plot of drowning makes forever impossible a relationship between the accomplished artist and his accompanists. As Gelfant observes, to the degree that Cather seems to be identifying with her characters and their situation, the novel intimates "her welling doubts about the permanence of (her) writing."[26] Gelfant locates this in the way in which Cather bends what could be a set of narratives about thwarted love into a different kind of love story. Lucy and Clement Sebastian are the impossible couple in Gelfant's account; he is married and years older, and, of course, he dies at the end of the long first book of the novel. Gelfant notices the triangulation of this plot with Lucy's relationship to Harry Gordon, whom Lucy rejects in favor of Sebastian. Gordon, in turn, rejects Lucy, precipitating her own fateful plunge. As Gelfant sees well, it is less these impossible love stories that animate Cather's novel than another kind of love. At a crucial point late in the novel, after she has lost Sebastian and rejected Gordon, Lucy wonders whether "Life itself" is her lover.[27] As Gelfant says, life in this novel is associated with "breathing: of in-spiring and being inspired."[28] And breathing, inevitably, is associated with singing, with the intake of air that makes voice possible, with its release into song (arias, airs).

Lucy's decision to go on living immediately becomes for her a way to reclaim Sebastian. Thinking of returning to her musical life, she recalls the first piece he had sung when she became his accompanist, a tenor aria from Mendelssohn's *Elijah*. Sebastian is a baritone, but he likes to sing this selection even though it is too high for his voice. He titles the aria "If with all your heart you truly seek Him" (34), and this is the title Lucy recalls (155). The text of the aria in fact reads "me" instead of

"Him"; the singer is quoting Jesus, singing as him. Cather wrote a letter to a correspondent who caught the textual change, explaining that "the whole story verges dangerously upon the sentimental (since youthful hero worship is really the theme of the first two parts of the book), and if I had used the text of that aria as it actually stands, it would have been quite unbearable."[29] Unbearable, that is, would be the identification of art with divinity. "Oh, now she knew! She must have it, she couldn't run away from it. She must go back into the world and get all she could of everything that had made him what he was. Those splendours were still on earth, to be sought after and fought for. In them she would find him. *If with all your heart you truly seek Him, you shall ever surely find Him*" (155).

Through Lucy's decision to pursue the love of life, Cather poses the question of the relationship of the world — of earth — to something that although found there also is found within, something, moreover, that lasts beyond earthly life. Lucy's resolution is restated as she ends her meditation in a way that points to how difficult Cather makes her decision, how precarious it is: "Let it all come back to her again! Let it betray her and mock her and break her heart, she must have it" (156). To have him again is to lose him; or, rather, to have him is to have "it." This is not a translation from "him" to "Him," but from "him" to "it," something whose ability to last is not human. Another impossible love also is intimated at this moment; in the mockery Lucy braves, the word conjures up the choking embrace of James Mockford that kills Sebastian. (Woodress describes Mockford as a "sinister homosexual").[30] The betrayal and mockery that Lucy anticipates suggests how she will have him/it; by dying as he did, pulled down by and with Mockford. Lucy dies in a body of water that she thinks is only a shallow ford but which is in fact a bottomless river in which a tree below grabs hold of her inexorably.

The melodramatic plunge into another life is related to music in the novel. Aside from a reference to a waltz tune that plays as Lucy and Gordon skate early in the novel (flying over a surface that, later in the novel, will open to take Lucy), the effects of music are registered when Lucy hears Sebastian in recital. The first time occurs the night before she auditions for him to temporarily replace his ailing accompanist. Lucy's initial response to Sebastian's appearance onstage is comparable to Paul's response to the aging soprano. Immediately impressed by what is called his "personality," by which Cather seems to mean something like his personhood, his physical presence, Lucy registers his size, his age, "his tired eyes," and judges he looks the part: "'Yes, a great artist should look like that'" (24). Gordon also has something akin to Sebastian's physical solidity; art is anchored bodily even as it seeks something beyond and yet within. This is a realm one might call "personality," but perhaps not without recalling that the root of the word, *persona*, means a mask; it implies a being tantamount to looking "like that."

Questions of the relationship of life to artistic life arise in the song that opens Sebastian's lieder recital, Schubert's early "Lied eines Schiffers an die Dioskuren," "a Schubert song she had never heard or even seen" (24). The singer is a sailor (*ein Schiffer*), afloat, pledging a votive offering of his oar to the Dioscuri if he returns safely. (The Dioscuri are the protecting gods of sailors in Greco-Roman mythology. They were brothers, one of whom offered to die in the place of the other, and they were rewarded with the twin existence of stars.) Cather has Lucy summarize the text as if the singer has arrived safely thanks to "their mild protecting light," and quotes the phrase describing their power, *"eure Milde, eure Wachen,"* their gentle vigilance. Yet the summary recognizes no guarantee in the mode of address, registering the distance between the singer and the object of the song: "a noble salutation to beings so exalted that in the mariner's invocation there was no humbleness and no entreaty" (25). Cather further insists on this when she allows Lucy to paraphrase the song, providing words for it that are not its text, even though typographically they seem to be: *"In your light I stand without fear, O august stars! I salute your eternity.* That was the feeling." In turning the song into other words in order to capture its feeling, Cather registers that she is trying to capture not just the words of the song, but its music, as well as its manner of delivery, by way of a "feeling" that might be in the song, or in Lucy, or in Sebastian. And if it is "in" them all, it must not be a feeling that is exactly or solely theirs.

It matters for the melodramatic drowning plot that this initial song should be about safely crossing water; it matters, too, that the address to the heavens be made to the stars. Early in the novel, snug in Gordon's sleigh, "a tiny moving spot on that still white country" (9), Lucy has a kind of epiphany as the first star appears. "It brought her heart into her throat" (10). Lucy's "heart" is, of course, also in her family name, Gayheart, but this leap from inside to out is situated in her throat, as

144 CHAPTER FOUR

if she were about to speak or sing. The light releases something in her that is also palpably outside her. "That point of silver light spoke to her like a signal," and not surprisingly; Lucy's name means light. She may not be destined to be a star like Sebastian, but she is identified with the first star of the evening. This light speaks symbolically. It is itself and more than itself. The signal releases "another kind of life and feeling which did not belong here." It is related more to the whiteness of her surround than to the small dot she makes on the landscape. But even this surround is her: at the very opening of the novel Lucy is described as a "mere white figure" crossing the horizon (4). Identifications continue: "It overpowered her. With a mere thought she had reached that star and it had answered, recognition had flashed between" (10). If this recognition is related to where and who she is, it translates that into something almost unrecognizable. Whereas later in the novel, grasping life, Lucy will submit to an "it," here the word for what she is experiencing is "something": "Something knew, then, in the unknowing waste; something had always known, forever!" The world of white is now an unproductive blank that nonetheless is animated by something in it that knows and recognizes her. It is an eternity, yet lodged in matter.

Lucy's thoughts about the first star of the evening tend in the direction of the Schubert lied she first heard Sebastian sing addressing the twin stars. "The joy of saluting what is far above one was an eternal thing," she concludes (10). This thinking is like the salutation of Sebastian's song. But to call it his, or to call this thought hers, is to err. Lucy recognizes something she calls an "eternal thing," and it is important to hold both noun and adjective in mind. This she does, but just for a moment before she retreats from the understanding she has had about something larger than herself in which she exists but in which her existence as herself does not matter. She leans on Gordon's shoulder for support against the escape she has glimpsed: "It hurt, and made one feel small and lost."

Feeling called, found and lost: this also is the effect of Sebastian's singing on Lucy. The Schubert set ends with a late song, "Der Doppelgänger," the double. Cather's ekphrasis takes off as Lucy fills in the scene she imagines. Rather than describing the text of the song in which the speaker sees himself, separate from himself, a pale ghost standing bereft outside of the house where his beloved once lived, Lucy experiences the song as moonlight: "With every phrase that picture deepened—moonlight, intense and calm, sleeping on old human houses" (25). A black cloud crosses the sky, and Sebastian is no longer to be seen. What Lucy imagines as an effect of the song, not of its words, but of the combination of word and music, is translated from her feelings to the song. As the recital continues, Lucy herself plunges into a similar state of inattention and blank darkness: "She was struggling with something she had never felt before. A new conception of art? It came closer than that. A new kind of personality? But it was much more. It was a discovery about life" (26). Lucy's struggle with "something" may be the "something" of her earlier illumination, although since it is a "new feeling" it cannot be exactly that. Indeed, it resists further translation. It locates the vicinity of art and personality, close to one, yet far beyond the other. "Life" is the word for this "it," and yet, as Lucy continues, life means "love as a tragic force, . . . passion that drowns like black water." The cloud in the sky has become the depth of water. Fittingly, Sebastian's encore is a setting of the Byron lyric "When we two parted," and Lucy receives it as an omen. Yet it is not simply a signal of their twinned fates (that twinning has been signaled in the Schubert set, addressed first to the Dioscuri and finally to a ghostly double); it is also a way of summarizing the effect that music has had on Lucy: "Sebastian had already destroyed a great deal for her" (27).

Later in the novel, after he has drowned and Lucy has fallen into despair, she is revived by another performance. "As Lucy had been lost by a song, so she was very nearly saved by one," the narrator comments (150), laconically linking Lucy's experience with Sebastian to the one she has when an aging soprano sings in Balfe's *Bohemian Girl* in Haverford. Again, Paul's experience seems to be replicated. This soprano, too, is "far from young," and "her voice was worn," but her phrasing remains expressive (152). "This poor little singer had lost everything: youth, good looks, position, the high notes of her voice. And yet she sang so well! Lucy wanted to be up there on the stage with her, helping her to do it" (153). Unlike Sebastian, who has high notes that do not belong to his voice, this singer is almost without voice yet able to convey something that compels Lucy: "The wandering singer had struck something in her that went on vibrating" (153). Again the word for this wordless connection is "something," and now the mode of connection is by way of a vibration that can't be confined. This is, once again, the life that a few pages later Lucy will embrace, a love of a life that goes on without

146 CHAPTER FOUR

oneself, a love that acknowledges mortality, the world-breath of Isolde's Liebestod.

The life in music, the novel has been intimating, is itself not confined to one kind of music or another. An early, obscure Schubert song is coupled with a late one in a recital that ends with a piece whose composer is not mentioned (Byron's lyrics were set numerous times throughout the nineteenth century and were close to being popular songs). Balfe's opera was coming to the end of its popularity in the early twentieth century of Cather's novel setting, and it barely is grand opera. Schubert's early song is like a hymn or a folk tune, a simple ABA structure. It is by means of a change in the accompaniment when the block chords of the first section are replaced by moving arpeggios that the music conveys the possibility of safe arrival over moving waters. The singer's line never varies, but something does, suggesting at once uncontrollable movement—life—and harmonic arrival. "Der Doppelgänger" is quite a different kind of lied. Not strophic, and without a structure of assurance, it is more like a recitative, an imitation of voice accompanied by music. It is close to Melodram, except that the voice in this song, although never singing the kind of melody to be heard in the first lied, is nonetheless singing, not speaking. Singing approaches speaking. The accompaniment is only a sequence of chords, punctuation that does not resolve harmonically. Technically set in a minor key, the final chord is an unexpected major. The aging soprano's singing touches Lucy because of its phrasing: "she glided delicately over the too regular stresses, and subtly varied the rhythm" (152). She takes a hackneyed aria and finds its musicality precisely by violating the literal and stolid score and discovering where the life in the music resides. It is neither in the words, which go unmentioned, nor exactly in the score as written; nor is it in the voice. Schubert's late song, which seems to be dismantling the musical supports of harmony and melody, is also seeking thereby the kinds of effects that a singer without a voice might hope to find or to release.

Lucy hears Sebastian a second time in recital in an all-Schubert program, the song cycle *Die Winterreise*, the winter journey: "She kept feeling that this was not an interpretation, this was the thing itself. . . . The singing was not dramatic, in any way she knew. Sebastian did not identify himself with this melancholy youth; he presented him as if he were a memory" (32). The singer does not become the presumed protagonist of the cycle; he sings without identification with him in order to identify with the music itself. Yet, at the same time, that "thing itself" is a memory of the thing. Sebastian's singing mirrors the structure of Cather's novel, which opens and closes as a memory of a girl who died twenty-five years before, someone all but forgotten. The life she still has is the one being recalled, a kind of double life, or of living beyond oneself, which is the life of the work of art. Sebastian disappears into the darkness, the cloud Lucy conjures up hearing him sing. When he sings *Die Winterreise* he is not its protagonist and not himself either. He is "the thing itself."

As Gelfant suggests, Lucy's identification with and desire for Sebastian is a desire to be in this condition, to be music itself, to "live on, having become . . . in essence, music." To live this other life, is, for Gelfant, inextricable from something she regards with alarm and finds embodied in Mockford; his "sinister nature seems melodramatically limned"; he "personifies . . . the parasitism of art." Gelfant says without saying what Woodress more baldly asserts, that Mockford is a "sinister homosexual."[31] Gelfant notes, too, that in addition to the triangle composed of Gordon, Sebastian, and Lucy, there also is the triangle composed of Mockford, Sebastian, and Lucy. But to her this conjunction can be only a "mockery, a travesty of love." Mockford is "indeterminate," akin for her to what she thinks of as a regressive antisexual bent in Cather toward "the hermaphrodite child."[32] Sexuality for Gelfant is heterosexuality, and she circles around without naming something that the novel, too, does not name more forthrightly, or perhaps does as "something," "it" or the "thing itself." These nominations, laying bare something beyond the categorical, also veil it by means of the "thing not said," which is the term by which Cather translates unspeakable, impossible sex into the aesthetic principle of "the thing not heard" that melodrama makes of the impossible.

Sedgwick wondered whether, ten years after the Wilde trial, Cather made her peace with him in "Paul's Case." She apparently did, but it was not the last time that Cather grappled with her (dis)identification with Wilde. Mockford is cast in the Wilde mold, and Lucy's response to him mirrors the narrator's in the first part of "Paul's Case," a mix of fascination and repulsion, just as his character includes something of Paul, "a mixture of timidity and cheek" (49). When Sebastian disappears for Lucy into the black cloud she has conjured up from "Der Doppel-

148 CHAPTER FOUR

gänger," all that is left behind onstage is Mockford. He remains Lucy's ghostly double, a white-faced creature that mirrors her existence. (She doubles him more prosaically as the pianist Sebastian has hired to replace him—temporarily at first, permanently, it is promised, but never to appear onstage with Sebastian.) Mockford's white face, which Lucy sees as a plaster cast or as a mask, also makes him appear naturally theatrical—as do his red hair and green eyes. He is what she would be if she were a boy, and in fact she is described several times as a boy in her looks and motion. The first time Gordon saw her she was "a slip of a girl in boy's overalls," he recalls late in the novel (190). Sebastian thinks of her as "rather boyish" (67) as he embraces her and takes her into his breath: "If he took her secret, he gave her his in return" (73). The secret of this other life is attached to a series of boys: his friend Larry McGowan, a boyhood companion whom he abandoned; the child Marius, whom he adopted into his childless marriage but whom his wife made him give up; Mockford, whom she supplied in his stead. Lucy doubles these boys.

Lucy, feeling intense antipathy for Mockford, wonders immediately whether she is jealous. (Familiarly and affectedly, Mockford calls Sebastian "Clément," while Sebastian calls him "Jimmy" and pronounces him a "queer, talented, trick boy" to whom he is indebted for some hints in his singing of Schubert [77].) Critics who pick up on Lucy's aversion to Mockford to draw invidious comparisons about sexuality ignore the complexity of identification and repudiation that Sedgwick explored imagining the moment when/if Cather could get past her "terroristic or terrorized season" (63), the possibility, that is, that she might not need to protect her own lesbian sexuality by disavowing male-male sexuality. These dynamics are played out in *Lucy Gayheart* as they had been earlier in *One of Ours* (1922) between that novel's protagonist, Claude Wheeler (an anagrammatic respelling of Willa Cather), and his love, David Gerhardt, a violinist (commentators don't notice the nominal connection to Gayheart, although they invariably link Lucy's name to a Cather neighbor named Gayhardt). They are played out again in *The Professor's House* between the suicidal professor and Tom Outland, who is killed, like Gerhardt, in the First World War. As Christopher Nealon has persuasively shown, these stories of failed, impossible love offer sites of painful denial that intimate desires impossible to name, secret desires likely to be repudiated.[33] This is the dynamic ignited by Wilde.

In *Lucy Gayheart*, Cather summons up aesthetic existence, living by and as music, as a way to figure this other life.

At the very end of the novel, Gordon visits Lucy's room, which has been preserved for years just as she left it. "The only thing . . . touched" in the twilit room is a picture of Sebastian, and "this Gordon put in his pocket" (194). Gordon's musicality, something in his voice, is what drew Lucy to him—that and the solidity of his body. There are, as it were, two Gordons, and it is both the seen and the unseen that drew her to him. Everyone is a doppelgänger. Harry Gordon, rejected by Lucy, rejects her and marries a Harriet; her name intimates the desire for a double, the sameness of the "thing itself." Gordon's marriage is "barren," childless. So, too, was Sebastian's. Instead of that mode of reproduction, Gordon takes the image of Sebastian as his legacy from Lucy's room. Sebastian has Marius, Larry, Jimmy, Lucy, and, of course, the music that constitutes his other life.[34]

Gordon's visit to Lucy's room recalls Der Doppelgänger outside the house where his beloved once was. Other rooms in the novel are places where music abides; for Lucy, Sebastian's study is associated with "Die Forelle," a Schubert song she thinks of as happy, although it involves a fish being pulled out of water and killed. This is her story in reverse, her story either way, for pulled down and out of life like Sebastian was by Mockford they are pulled into a life that endures beyond them—as Paul's shattered body is finally gathered "back into the immense design of things" (488). It is the life to which we attest when we speak or write of characters who exist only on the pages we read as if they were more than that. Gelfant, for example, condemns Cather for killing Lucy for the sake of some falsely romantic and melodramatic plot about the life of art. To indict an author for such a crime is to attest to the power of the author to make one believe in an existence on the page that extends further than that. The novel acknowledges how painful this can be when translated into terms that are more "realistic" when Cather allows Gordon the thought that perhaps Lucy, dying at twenty-one, had been spared: "Perhaps it was no great loss to have missed two-thirds of her life, if she had the best third, and had been young,—so heedlessly young" (187). It is very hard to countenance this "perhaps," although Gordon measures it against the "life sentence" (186) he has suffered by his responsibility for cutting Lucy's life short, denying her what she wanted from him, support to go on living. Gordon, with whom the novel ends sympathetically, is Mockford to Lucy; like virtually all the male characters in the novel, he leads a kind of double life even if he doesn't know it (this is true of Lucy's spinster sister Pauline, as well). Writing of Katherine Mansfield in an essay included in *Not Under Forty*, Cather had praised her stories for the ways in which they intimated the impossibility of the life with others that humans also crave, the "double life" that arises from the fact that "human relationships are the tragic necessity of human life."[35] Something akin to this, I have noted, is the point that Fassbinder drew from Sirk and reiterated in his own films. If melodrama has a message, it is about this other life that persists as aesthetic connection. Here is what Lucy thinks when she is in Sebastian's embrace: "She felt herself drifting again into his breathing, into his heart beats. She knew this could not last; in a moment she must gather herself up and be herself again. Yet she knew, too, that it would last a lifetime" (75).

This connection is not merely aesthetic: it is about something as real — as possible — as real life with its delimited sense of the possible. As in Wilde, "real" life is a double life that also has an existence separate from one's own, making a vital connection beyond oneself. From the first page of *Lucy Gayheart*, that life vibrates with motion. In Haverford (a place that perhaps names a ford in which Lucy is remembered?), "they still see her as a slight figure always in motion; dancing or skating, or walking swiftly with intense direction, like a bird flying home" (3). Lucy's figural existence, like the star that signals to her, suggests that she is both herself and a meaning that extends her particular existence. In herself, she may be "slight," but the motion that is hers is not hers alone. At the end of the second book of the novel, Lucy will again be described as going "home" (169). This motion — of a bird to its nest, of a corpse to its grave — complicates the "intense direction" of Lucy's incessant motion, for it is apparently a motion without end, a perpetual music. Moreover, the direction of this "intense direction" is complicated: Is Lucy running away from or toward something? As she runs back to the place where in past years she had skated, her thought is of escape: "She would get away from this frozen country and these frozen people, go back to light and freedom such as they could never know" (167). In that place of "freedom" — literally, Chicago — "the world seemed free and wide, like the Lake out yonder. She was not always struggling against something, she was going with something much stronger than herself"

(114). "Something" aversive meets "something" that carries her, like the wind on which a bird glides. Opposite motions are refused opposition. They join in the way William Empson describes the most intense form of ambiguity: "In so far . . . as you know that two things are opposites, you know a relation that connects them."[36] Freedom shares something with the frozen land. Lucy's thoughts continue: "It was not that this new life was without pain. But there was nothing empty or meaningless in it" (114). Cather's negatives abide in this "new life."

The precarity and pain of this new life, glimpsed but difficult to sustain, can be lost "as one can lose a ravishing melody" (86). The melody itself, the comparison suggests, still exists even if one can no longer recall it. Yet it is itself "ravishing," driving itself in only by driving something out — driving oneself out of oneself in an assault that one would if conscious resist. Yet even this forgetting gets described as a kind of remembering: the melody is lost to mind "as remembering the mood of it, the kind of joy it gave" is not; indeed, it is only by remembering the feeling that the melody continues, but without being heard or recalled exactly as itself. One is "unable to recall precisely the air. . . . And she couldn't breathe in this other kind of life. It stifled her." Yet the air she can't breathe is the one she is breathing, and the air (the aria) she can't recall is the one that she can feel or at least recall having felt; she can recall the feeling, if not the sound. "If only one could lose one's life and one's body and be nothing but one's desire," Lucy's thoughts at this moment conclude, "if the rest could melt away, and that could float with the gulls, out yonder where the blue and green were changing" (86). This desire for bodily annihilation is also a desire for incorporation into a life that never stops. It is a life of matter in motion. To "be nothing but one's desire" is perhaps to be the one desire beneath and in all things. It is to vibrate with a life that persists the way a melody does. This is Lucy's desire to be music, to live in the air.

One can't do it as oneself forever: "You couldn't, after all, live above your level; with good luck you might, for a few breaths, hold yourself up in that more vital air, but you dropped back" (99). In her grave she lies "like a bird shot down when it rises in its morning flight to the sun" (175). Yet when Gordon remembers her, and she is the best thing he has to remember, he recalls her "gathered up and sustained by something that would never let her drop into the common world" (181). This is not a memory of her after death, but in the life she led when she returned to Haverford after the deaths of Sebastian and Mockford. At the end, Gordon preserves a token of this in the picture of Sebastian that he pockets—a token of their shared desire.

He also seeks to preserve a sign of Lucy in motion: "marks in the cement" (193) made by Lucy as a little girl in boy's overalls, running; three footprints, "light, in very low relief; unless one were looking for them, one might not notice them at all" (191). Lucy's footprints are palpably an allusion to the marks on the page—the novel is divided into three books, each one shorter than the one before, as if becoming increasingly faint. These almost unnoticeable marks allude, too, to a practice of reading what one can easily miss, the thing not said, the melody not heard by the ear. They are "swift impressions." The words go by, but what they intimate abides in some other temporality. "For to Harry Gordon they did seem swift . . ." The words on the page are not moving, and yet something moves in them; "the print of the toes was deeper than the heel" (this low relief is nonetheless capable of being seen as anything but flat); "the heel was very faint, as if that part of the living foot had just grazed the surface of the pavement." Being there—being here— is a matter of scarcely making a mark. It is a sign of going with a motion that guarantees being alive. Cather allows Harry Gordon to express skeptical doubt about what he reads in these prints: "Was there really some baffling suggestion of quick motion in those impressions . . . , or was it merely because he had seen them made, that to him they always had the look of swiftness, mischief, and lightness?" Gordon's thoughts are a reading of the prints marked by the limit of his having witnessed them being made. That limit does not exhaust them, as is suggested by a final comparison he makes: "As if the feet had tiny wings on them, like the herald Mercury" (191). Mercurial Lucy is affirmed against her lame double Mockford, and yet as herself a tricky boy.

....

Working on *Lucy Gayheart* in 1933, Cather described its heroine in a letter as "a very silly young girl." Again, not long before her death, she wrote a letter in 1946 to her first biographer, E. K. Brown, agreeing with his assessment of the novel. "I don't think much about 'Lucy Gayheart' either," she said. But then there is a but: "But, strangely enough, I think it picks up after all the Gayhearts are safe in the family burial lot. I think the last chapters, which deal entirely with the effect of Lucy on the hard-boiled business man, are rather interesting."[37] Cather modestly affirms the afterlife of her writing in a double gesture in which she identifies with Harry Gordon (the novel does the same) against the silly girl in favor of her translation into something left unsaid (but which even a "hard-boiled business man" might get). More than a decade earlier, writing a letter to Dorothy Canfield Fisher, who had just published a profile of Cather while Cather was working on *Lucy Gayheart*, Cather told her that although she had no complaints about what Fisher had written, when she thought back on her life, she did not remember herself as being there: "I seem to have been a bundle of enthusiasms and physical sensations, but not a person."[38] It is just that existence that Cather imagines Clement Sebastian conveys when he sings, and that Lucy does as well in the prints that mark her existence. "I'm Not There" once again.

CODA

This book opens with a chapter on Beethoven's opera *Fidelio* that explores the two aspects of melodrama studied, for the most part separately, in the remainder of the book: the impossible plot situation, and the music that accompanies it. Combined, these two strands provide the etymology for the word "melodrama" (*melos* + drama). Combined, they offer the thesis this book explores: melodrama is an aesthetics of the impossible situation, where "of" means both "derived from" and "representing." In Beethoven's opera, Leonore is in an impossible situation. She is a wife who wishes to rescue her husband from unjust political imprisonment; to do that, she needs to disguise herself as a man: women do not have political efficacy. The disguise plot offers the hope that she will not be confined by gender limitation, but that is unlikely given the slogan that links liberty and equality to fraternity—that is, unless "fraternity" were capable of being understood beyond its gendered meaning. Leonore is able to become the jailer's helper and his daughter's fiancé, but salvation of her husband is accomplished by the arrival of a benign minister. He appears like a deus ex machina in a Greek tragedy at just the moment that Fidelio reveals that he is Leonore. She is returned to her position as wife, and whatever hopes the plot raises of relationships outside of heterosexual gender limitations seem to disappear in the supposed "happy ending" that restores a familiar social order.

As Fidelio descends into the prison depths to help dig the grave of the unjustly imprisoned man, Beethoven interrupts the separation of speaking voice and music that prevails in *Fidelio*, joining melos and drama together in a moment the score names technically, formally, as "Melodram"; spoken words are underscored, interrupted, punctuated by music that plays beneath, alongside the dialogue, music that offers itself in no necessary or predictable harmonic sequence. Musical invention in the Melodram intimates ways past the impasses of the impossible gender/political situation; it discovers new possibilities of relationality. So doing, it suggests that aesthetic enjoyment of the opera may transcend the ideology of gender difference on which its plot depends.

As a dramatic and literary form, melodrama is difficult to define: it is not a genre, and, following Peter Brooks, is usually taken to be a mode, a term whose literary meaning is elusive, although as a musical term "mode" defines various kinds of harmonic organization. The one formal feature that might be said to define melodrama, melos + drama, is thus named in its etymology. Nonetheless, how music and drama are to join always remains in question. There are rules of composition and of harmony, to be sure, but the music for drama is not usually a sustained piece of composition. It is interrupted, it plays for effect, or as a background to which one does not necessarily attend as closely as one might to words on a page, to dialogue, or to images onscreen.

The indeterminations of the remediated nature of melodrama allow for the possibilities in the impossible. That hope is more usually attached to what Brooks labels the "moral occult," vestiges of the distinction of good and bad that remain in the secular, enlightened modernity that invented melodrama. Followers of Brooks (most everyone who has written on melodrama since the 1970s) seem to have no trouble finding the moral truth of melodrama. Linda Williams, one of these critics, has a recently published book on the HBO series *The Wire* (2002–8) intent on seeing it as a melodrama that does not pander to a contemporary social imaginary that says we have gotten past race and have achieved, by way of neoliberal economic rationality, a well-running governing apparatus. Williams ties the TV series to melodrama because it can thereby be attached to its ideological origins in the drama of Beethoven's time, the promises of liberal society to "the universal right to pursue equal opportunity" belied by neoliberalism. She seems to think that salvation will come from the innocents who have been betrayed. Whereas the institutions surveyed in *The Wire*—the schools, journalism, the police, government—"morally fail," utopic hope remains; a familiar dynamic of the individual versus society is pinned on humane treatment of others, on some reconstituted home.[1]

No one—I include myself in this—could argue with the desire for human flourishing. However, the liberalism to which Williams clings is connected to the neoliberalism she deplores, and the moral distinctions of good and bad of which she is so certain cut across her bad institutions and innocent victims.[2] For Williams *The Wire* is a better form of journalism than the preachy variety David Simon practiced before he turned to TV: it brings moral reality closer to us, and closer to preconceived notions of good and bad. "*The Wire* is a systematic melodrama of the evils of unencumbered capital accumulation," we are told, as if those "evils" did not characterize the liberalism on which Williams builds her moral framework.[3] She states:

> *The Wire* is able to generate both sympathy and respect for a wide array of black characters who are *not* portrayed as victims of white villainy yet still are victims of the larger, economic and institutional whole. . . . Under these charged conditions of a majority-black culture and a rich array of black male characters (though a paucity of women), the series transmutes into a racially aware, class-aware, and even queer-aware (although oddly gender-unaware) network of interrelated stories. Yet unlike so many stories about race, we are not asked to hiss a white racist villain in order to feel racially just ourselves.[4]

So described, the series seems designed to assuage white guilt and massage white liberalism, as if its "black racial imaginary" had that as its task. It succeeds for Williams except in one crucial way: there are not enough black women with whom she can identify. Not even with Kima, the lesbian police detective whose story provides one of the complex overarching plots over the five years of the series. Kima is dismissed as "male-identified."[5]

Williams brings a machinery of the moral dichotomy of good/evil and applies it to race and gender, to humans and social institutions. Against this scorecard, I would compare another recent analysis of *The Wire*, the final chapter of Caroline Levine's *Forms*, which uses the TV series as a way of summing up the book's formalist analysis. For Levine, attending to form is a way of performing social analysis. Forms do not mirror the real, as they do for Williams; rather they provide a theoretical lens through which to comprehend the real. Terms like "race" and "gender" barely count for Levine, who instead prefers to think about "whole, rhythm, hierarchy, network," terms that subtitle her book to name the formal domains explored in separate chapters; all are brought to bear in her analysis of *The Wire*. The totality on offer, rather than a monolith composed of a crushing set of failed institutions, is made of "contending forces." Forms constrain, but they also enable: "Far from an ideologically coherent society with power lodged in the hands of a few, *The Wire* gives us a social world constantly unsettled by the bewildering effects of clashes among wholes, rhythms, hierarchies, and networks."[6] Everything is connected, but not in a predictable manner precisely because everything is not itself one thing; the relations between time and space, humans and institutions, while more often than not leading to misery, every now and then allow for openings in or relays between networks that make for happy endings that suggest possibilities for change. For Levine, humans have some agency as they make their way through and across networks that seem to be exercises of power whose endpoint is anything but equal access and equitable distribution. Although she does not think she offers a Foucauldian analysis (she understands his as a carceral view of the social), Foucault's dictum that power is everywhere registers resistance as the necessary other side of oppression, a vision of unending struggle incapable of revolutionary overthrow or of an end of power.

In attending to form as form, with no interest in labeling *The Wire* a melodrama, Levine seeks to find an opening to the social—to a way of understanding it and inhabiting it—that does not assume total social control. Form for her is a tool for understanding the social, not something made entirely from it or in conformity to it. However, just as Williams's analysis seems complicit with the social that she describes and seeks to make evident, Levine's vision may be similarly motivated. An earlier book of hers argues that art is necessary for democracy since it espouses minority viewpoints necessary against majority domination. *Forms* does not seem couched in those terms and may trace a movement in her thought from liberalism to neoliberal rationalization in a formalism abstracted from any vision of minority inclusion.

Where are the possibilities in impossible situations? Is our choice between a social overturning that is simply a reversal and a formalism that rests its hope on chance and accident? Williams and Levine (and many other commentators on *The Wire*) concur on at least one point: they locate possibility in the character of Omar Little. At an early stage in my thinking about this book, I had imagined writing a chapter on *The Wire* titled "Why Is Omar Gay?" Williams addresses this question through the pregiven tools of cultural analysis — the identity terms of race, class, gender, and sexuality. Her answer is his exceptionality; Omar belongs nowhere. Levine comes to a similar conclusion, although without mentioning race, gender, or sexuality. For her, Omar, too, is "comparatively free" (for Williams he is a "free spirit"), "the consummate outsider, refusing to join hierarchies and always escaping from enclosing shapes. But he works the networks all the same, showing us that he understands well how hierarchies and networks operate."[7] Where does this knowledge come from? From what outside?

For a moment, when she heeds Wendy Brown's argument on the impossibility of expecting liberalism to rebuff the neoliberal wedding of the state to capitalism, freedom to entrepreneurship, Williams sees that Omar does not have "any liberal democratic illusions."[8] To put this political position beside his erotic position allows us to understand how the designation "outsider" is a way society names him, attempting to draw a formal divide that one can easily see is illusory. The excessive machismo that Williams deplores in *The Wire* is a key to the fact that male-male relations are intense, fueled sometimes by homoerotic "joking" (between Bunk and McNulty, for example), often by overt homophobia among men who have little use for women. Williams treats Omar as the only one, ignoring homosocial complexity; he is not in the closet and he makes his outsideness work for him. He articulates his belonging to "The Game" that everyone plays, which levels the moral distinctions that Williams wants to maintain and refound through her analysis. Omar shows that the game has no outside, only a vocabulary of exclusions and negations that can be seized. The limit of his success is his mortality, his murder by someone too young to be in the game except insofar as it names the human condition of being born into a life that exceeds our own. The boy who kills Omar has no idea who he is. Death makes no distinctions of identity. Williams pins her hopes on "home" and images it in the orange couch dragged outside, on which drug dealers perch. It is hard to know why one would want to call this home except through a domestic drive that reminds me of where Beethoven's Leonore seems finally confined. Omar, although apparently gay, includes women in his gang and has strong affective ties to them. And Michael, the new Omar — for Omar is not the only one — cares for his brother in a way his mother could not.

Omar is gay not because his sexuality necessarily has any ties to disillusionment with liberal democracy but because his abjection could lead there. It could as easily lead to the desire for inclusion in the groups perceived to have power (this is the position of Rawls in *The Wire*, for example). As gay, Omar is represented as the queer lever who works the system against itself, exposing how opposition is possible without imagining the reform of institutions that seem to be impediments to human flourishing. The fact that so many commentators on *The Wire* are drawn to Omar suggests that his appeal does not have to do with his sexual identity per se. It may also be because his existence has more to do with what fiction delivers than reality can produce, but to say that is to deny that imagination has any role to play in social reality. Both Williams and Levine testify, in very different modes of analysis, that Omar is located at the place where impossibility and possibility meet, satisfying as easily Williams's belief that melodrama reveals the truth about sociality as Levine's that literary form offers a theoretical vantage on reality not readily available to those who derive their terms of analysis from the social. That perspective is, if we follow Thomas Elsaesser, what melodrama offers us even as it represents characters for whom social existence seems a trap with no exit.

Where is the possibility in impossibility? Alexander García Düttmann addresses that question in his book on Luchino Visconti's melodramas, *Visconti: Insights into Flesh and Blood*. From the first page on, he has in mind the opaque and tantalizing sentence with which Adorno ends the introduction of *Negative Dialectics* as the way to answer the question: "Utopia is blocked off by possibility, never by immediate reality." The sentence seems to put "possibility" in the place of what I have been calling "impossibility"; that is its dialectical point. Something can be understood to be possible because it is bounded by what is deemed impossible. The possible, in this understanding, is the given, the legal, the social, the rules of existence, all the forces that say that anything else is impossible. Understood that way, the aim of melodrama is not to find the possible in the impossible situation, but to surpass the possible, to realize what the possible deems impossible; this is what Adorno calls "immediate reality" and Düttmann terms "flesh and blood." What *is* exceeds what is possible. Or, following this line of thought, "possible" also can mean what does not yet exist, or what does exist but has been blocked; the possible — in the sense of something not yet deemed possible — must nonetheless be in the possible that blocks utopia. (Adorno may be contemplating the double meaning in utopia, the good place that also is no place.) In Adorno's dialectical account, the possible is also what is impossible — in both of the opposing meanings that inhabit these terms. Beside, outside, yet coincident with this reversible and blocked pair — the im/possible — there is what Adorno calls reality; for Visconti, Düttmann argues, it resides in passions that seem constrained by possibility and yet which pulse with a life beyond limit. Melodrama, as Düttmann understands it, works in the wedge between the possible and the real, in an opening in the dialectical dilemma, "toward the difference between possibility and reality." Seeking a philosophical term for this, he lights on a nonce word in the work of Nicholas of Cusa: *possest*, a Latin verb that means at once "it can be" and "it is," both possible and actual.[9]

Düttmann offers another word for this as well: "Homosexuality . . . understood as the form and content of melodrama."[10] Homosexuality is always mentioned whenever Visconti is discussed, Düttmann notes (the director was gay), but not because his films usually feature gay characters or, when they do, because these characters are necessarily central or heroes or "positive" images (in *Ossessione* [1942], Visconti's first feature, the (im)possible love betrayed by a character presumed to be gay; the gay orgy in *The Damned* [1969]; sexual obsession in *Death in Venice* [1970]). The films don't advocate gay identity, but the "eye" of the films, Düttmann argues, presents a gay worldview. He gives an example from *Senso* (1954): "The passion which overcomes Countess Sarpieri would then be seen as unmistakably homosexual; the conduct of the Austrian officer is unmistakably that of a deceitful gay sex object, a preening queer, who, by his own admission, inspects himself in every mirror to reassure himself, and who attracts interest precisely through his unstinting self-regard, . . . as if degradation and extortion were the price to be paid for such attention, since every mirror is exchangeable and the self-regarding self is a nonentity that withdraws from itself."[11]

Düttmann's fugal analysis, fueled, it appears, by vehement negations of the negativity he associates with homosexuality, finally empties an excoriated queerness into the opening in which melodrama resides when identity withdraws from being identified as such, and the reality of an unthought (im/possible) relationality can take place and take the place of conventional relations, existing where individual identity no longer exists, "the void beneath the surface" where I'm not there.[12] The countess has an affair with the enemy; she gives up her national and marital identities.

It is perhaps simply an accident that the Austrian officer in *Senso* was played by Farley Granger just a couple of years after he was Guy in Hitchcock's *Strangers on a Train* (1951); the part gives off queer vibrations that extend extradiegetically, much as Rock Hudson's performances do. Visconti's oeuvre, as Düttmann's analysis suggests, could have been a subject for this book even without Granger's role. The affair in the film starts at a performance of Verdi's *Il Trovatore*, and the filmic melodrama plays out an operatic plot (the plot of *Fidelio* reversed). What it further suggests, in ways that are not just a coincidence, are the many networks of coincidence (of Cusa's *possest*, a could be that is) that could be rearticulated among the films and texts discussed in this book as well as other examples where this book might have anchored its analyses.

It would be possible, for instance, to go from *Fidelio* to *Senso*, from Granger's role that bears the surname of the composer Mahler to Hitchcock; from there to Fassbinder, who once said that *The Damned* was the greatest film ever made, as Düttmann reports. In an interview included in *The Anarchy of Imagination*, Fassbinder says he saw Visconti's film thirty times.[13] Or to go from Visconti to Sirk, whose first star, Zarah Leander, appears (at least on the phonograph) in *The Damned*. My chapter connecting Sirk to Fassbinder and Haynes cleaves to the most obvious route of connection from *All That Heaven Allows* to *Ali: Fear Eats the Soul* to *Far from Heaven*. It might have begun quite differently. In *Fassbinder's Germany*, Elsaesser notes that Fassbinder first became aware of Sirk thanks to Peer Raben.[14] Raben was responsible for the music in virtually all of Fassbinder's films—the music having been written by him or chosen by him—in a range comparable to the catholicity of the score in Highsmith's novels, or the medleys that Dimitri Tiomkin provided for Hitchcock. The connection for Fassbinder that I took to start with Sirk was initiated by way of music; Raben also was a lover of Fassbinder's. Starting there, Sirk's *Interlude* (1956) would have had to come into the discussion, a film whose impossible love concerns an American woman in Europe and a married man there who is a conductor. It is based on a James M. Cain novel, thereby opening a different route to Haynes, who made an HBO mini-series of *Mildred Pierce* (2012) that stays closer to Cain's novel than the Joan Crawford vehicle of 1945, allowing for its queer focus to be on Veda, who succeeds as an opera singer; artistic triumph allows her to get away from her mother and to take her lover away as well (she is indifferent to him—how like a gay man, Düttmann might say). She doesn't kill him as she does in the Hollywood version.

When this book moves to its second part on melos, its path runs from Hitchcock to Highsmith and Cather. The underlying thread of argument is an aesthetic network of authorial transport, from Hitchcock's hidden pictures and musical touches to Highsmith's Tom typing her novels as he himself tries on a series of impersonations that include assuming the parts of a dead painter who goes on painting and a drag queen for whom Lou Reed's *Transformer* provides a necessary soundtrack. These forays into aesthetic life—the thematization of the aesthetic life that vibrates in the books we read, the films we see—ends with Cather. There is a path to her to be traced that would start differently, with Sirk's *The Tarnished Angels* (1957). In that film, after Burke Devlin (Rock Hudson) has offered his room to the "gypsy" flyer family, he returns to find Laverne Shumann (Dorothy Malone) reading a book of his; it is *My Ántonia*. In his interview with Jon Halliday, Sirk mentions this in tandem with Thoreau (as *Walden* is in *All That Heaven Allows*, the Cather book jacket is made visible): "As I remember it, *My Ántonia* is a novel about circularity: the hero comes back to the place where he started."[15] Indeed, the novel traces a series of circles and of authorial transports through them, circles that seem to mean no way out and which nonetheless are just that.

In the novel, Jim Burden leaves Nebraska but returns there to see the heroine at its close. The framework of the book catches him in the present, on a train crossing the prairies with a nameless I. The two reminisce about their shared past and a woman who mesmerized them. Jim produces a manuscript named "Ántonia" and then adds "My" to his—to Cather's—title. Sirk ends his film with Laverne returning to her roots in Iowa, Devlin's book in hand. The Cather connection that runs between them punctuates the film. Devlin talks of the book at first as one of a lost place and lost love. When he convinces Laverne not to sleep with the man who can provide a new plane for her husband to fly, he leaves her behind reading Cather while he goes off in her place to bargain with the man. The book substitutes for her sexual assignation; he stands in for her. These exchanges have their prompt in Cather when Wick Cutter (his name summons up Willa Cather) attempts to rape Ántonia only to find Jim where he expected her to be. After Laverne's husband dies in the plane he thinks she got for him, Laverne, guilty about the sexual transgression she avoided and the substitution she agreed to, is about to run away with the man she had not slept with. It is "Farewell, my Ántonia," Devlin intones, before he is able to convince her to return to Iowa. She boards the plane, taking his Cather with her, as the sign of the possibility that they may someday meet again. But they have met in the book that substitutes for and yet is the sexual relationship between them, a homosexual relationship of the kind Düttmann reads in Visconti's melodramas. "Last night something did go on between us," Devlin tells Laverne. The night in question is the one she spent reading Cather and he spent with the man she had agreed to sleep with. Cather's Jim gropes for the terms of what Ántonia might have been to him when he returns: "I'd have liked to have you for a sweetheart, or a wife, or my mother or my sister — anything that a woman can be to a man. The idea of you is part of my mind; you influence my likes and dislikes, all my tastes, hundreds of times when I don't realize it. You really are a part of me."[16]

Here is one route from Sirk to Cather, from Cather to Jim to Burke Devlin and Laverne Shumann (the three stars of Sirk's film — Robert Stack plays the flyer husband — reprise roles from *Written on the Wind* [1956], changing places). For a route from Haynes to Highsmith, we can now turn to his most recent film, *Carol* (2015), based on her lesbian pulp novel *The Price of Salt*, which was initially released under the pseudonym Claire Morgan. The novel most directly about herself and her own sexuality (and pronounced a failure on those grounds by Slavoj Žižek)[17] appeared as if not written by her. The film stars Cate Blanchett playing the object of obsession. Haynes last cast her as his closest lookalike to Bob Dylan in *I'm Not There* (2007; quite unlike the part Anthony Minghella created for her in his *Talented Mr. Ripley* [1999]). We could

164 CODA

get to the punchline about nonidentity with which I have allowed my-self to conclude in previous sections of this book in quite another way, however, as Leo Bersani does in his analysis of Haynes's *Safe* (1995) in *Thoughts and Things*. Bersani, whom I have invoked previously in this book, arrives at that film's mirror scene of self-love as the abyss of non-self-identity. By way of the Dylan song title, Bersani performs the leap into sameness that he has been writing about for the past several years and which approaches the terrain of the real blocked by im/pos-sibility that I have pursued here as the aesthetic quarry of melodrama. Carol's "shedding of identities"—as wife and homemaker, as victim, as disease-carrier, as a person—empties herself as a subject and empties the film's ostensible subjects. So doing, Bersani implies, it coincides with Dylan's aesthetic achievement, one that attaches to his name and yet leaves him behind. The crux is "a nonviable yet somehow also nec-essary self-negativizing."[18] In the impossible inhabitation of the self-hood that is the desired uniqueness of any of us and the sameness—the material alikeness—of all of us, Bersani locates the aesthetic in its im-possible conjunctions: the possibility of passions that do not cleave to conventional modes of social being opens an "affinity" in what the mind makes with the "nonhuman," "the inorganic nonhuman" that is our ori-gin and end.[19]

....

If I could just go back and start again with a film that beautifully real-izes the argument of this book about melos + drama and the aesthet-ics of impossibility, that film would be Terence Davies's *The Long Day Closes* (1992). The materials of its plot focus the impossible situation on a young boy, Bud, on the verge of adolescence. He is seen more often than not staring out the window of his tenement house in 1950s Liver-pool, framed by it or by the bars along the stairways inside and along-side the house. Bud suffers a loneliness that is exacerbated by the social domains outside the house that dominate his existence: the Catholic Church, where the life-size crucifix of a tortured hunky Christ comes to life to torment him; the school, where his head is picked for lice by a nurse who pronounces boys "nasty" and where a schoolmaster all but salivates as he beats the boys, while another drones on about erosion, offering education that is the mental equivalent to the physical torture meted out. His classmates taunt him. His only friend seems to drop

CODA 165

him. His numerous siblings are often too busy with their girlfriends to pay him any attention. His mother does, but she is frequently shown at work, cooking and cleaning, or socializing with other grownups, while Bud is usually watching on the side.

Against and alongside this misery there is Davies's extraordinary camera work, with scenes framed as tableaus or shot with a slow-moving camera that opens distance beyond Bud's constraints and allows for rhythms of attention to detail that also distance the boy's pain; it nonetheless remains palpable (Bud cries only once, near the end of the film; his mother, too, close to its opening). Then there is the extraordinary sound track, a mélange of quotations from other films and a variety of music—classical, orchestral, liturgical, popular, jazz. Much of the music is vocal: Nat King Cole is heard first, with Kathleen Ferrier soon thereafter and the resonant Isobel Buchanan later, as well as Doris Day, Debbie Reynolds, and Judy Garland. The first voice heard speaking on the sound track is Margaret Rutherford's from *The Happiest Days of Your Life* (1950): "Tap, Gossage, I said, 'tap'—you're not introducing a film," she says, introducing the film and its insistent juxtapositions of what we see and hear beside the plot elements. The one institution where the boy is at home is the cinema. Film and music transport him to an elsewhere that is not to be understood as escapism; his mother sends him to "the pictures—where else?," and once she starts singing, ten minutes into the film, she often is heard in song.[20] Indeed, everyone in the boy's immediate family and neighbors can be found breaking into song; at one moment, Bud and a sister entertain the family with a song-and-dance routine. This is the route the boy took to become the filmmaker Terence Davies.

In his book on Davies's oeuvre, Michael Koresky plausibly claims it for a queer aesthetic that constantly combines opposites: "love and joy are inextricable from their impossibility." Similarly, J. Hoberman, in a review in the *Village Voice*, praises the "controlled, perhaps depressed ecstasy" of *The Long Day Closes*.[21] Koresky worries that the autobiographical content of the film means that Davies, who has often reported his discomfort with his homosexuality, makes problems for queer analysis. Yet, as his exacting discussion of the film's camera work and sonic splendor also argues, the film's aesthetic—indeed, the fact that the film exists—belies and supplements the enduring misery that Davies claims as his own. "How do you come to terms with being in the world and then not being," Davies muses in an interview with Koresky.[22] His answer lies in recognizing that we are both at once. The temporality of *The Long Day Closes* achieves that double time, just as its juxtapositions of plot and melos do two things at once: a neighbor who often does impressions of movie actors sings Irving Berlin's "When I Leave the World Behind"; he sings and acts in this world, transporting it elsewhere. Koresky describes Bud at the film's end, while Sir Arthur Sullivan's partsong that titles the film swells, this way: "a constant object while life swirls around him, a still point in the turning world"; a boy in thought, contemplating the stars. "Some of those stars are dead—the light from them started out when Jesus was alive," Bud says, joining life and death together in an im/possible present.[23] He is one with the things in this world to which music and image provide a way beyond words.

NOTES

Preface

1 Brooks, *The Melodramatic Imagination* (1995), viii. Subsequent citations to this edition are given in parentheses in the text.

2 Berlant and Edelman, *Sex, or the Unbearable*, xvii.

3 Tereda, *Looking Away*, 3, 33, 9.

4 For an example, see Linda Williams, *Screening Sex*; where, for once, she considers same-sex sex, in *Brokeback Mountain* (Ang Lee, 2005). Taking issue with D. A. Miller, who has qualms about the film's representational strategies, Williams is sure that homosexuality in the film does not pre-exist homosexual sex (with what she terms its "threat of castration") and thereby shows that homosexuality is not a minority issue but "a fear, and a desire, sympathetically, and even melodramatically, felt by all" (238). "All" here seems to mean "all heterosexuals," and the parsing of minoritizing/universalizing that Williams takes from Eve Kosofsky Sedgwick's *Epistemology of the Closet* is bent in a straight direction.

5 Berlant, *The Female Complaint*, 268.

6 Mercer and Shingler, *Melodrama*, 1.

7 Mercer and Shingler, *Melodrama*, 7.

8 Brooks continually likens the melodramatic plot to psychoanalysis, offering a just-so story that brings analysis to the happy ending of recognition, a repudiation of the dark forces within.

9 Mercer and Shingler, *Melodrama*, 105.

10 Gledhill, "Rethinking Genre," 227.

11 Gledhill, "Rethinking Genre," 238, 240.

12 Foucault, *The History of Sexuality*, 93.

13 Gledhill, "The Melodramatic Field," 33.

14 Alfred Hitchcock, "Why I Make Melodramas" (1936), available at http://www.labyrinth.net.au/~muffin/melodramas_c.html (last modified March 31, 2000). Hitchcock notes that melodrama is a designation that as easily marks a theatrical milieu as a generic kind; that it often is attached to exaggerated emotional response but can as easily be found in ordinary re-

sponse. His films are plotted in a way that allies a heightened realism with unexaggerated response.

15 Berlant, *The Female Complaint*, 271.

16 Sedgwick, *Tendencies*, 6.

17 Halliday, *Sirk on Sirk*, 95, 93.

18 The three films are considered together, in a discussion that rarely goes further than plot summary, by Mercer and Shingler (*Melodrama*, 50–77).

1. Agency and Identity

1 The 1814 *Fidelio* was the third version of the opera; from Beethoven's sketchbook, it appears that the Melodram was in its 1805 and 1806 incarnations. See Kaleva, "Beethoven and Melodrama," 58.

2 Elsaesser, "Tales of Sound and Fury," 74.

3 Beethoven, *Fidelio*, 164. Subsequent citations to this edition are given in parentheses in the text.

4 Lischke, "Commentaire musicale et littéraire," 54.

5 Kaleva, "Beethoven and Melodrama," 59.

6 Kaleva, "Beethoven and Melodrama," 53.

7 Kaleva, "Beethoven and Melodrama," 56.

8 Schenk, "Über Tonsymbolik in Beethovens Fidelio," 245, quotes Willy Hess on this point: "In beiden Fallen die Steigerung der Gedanken und Gefühle des Gefangenen in eine lichte, schöne Vision—das einmal ist es das holde Bild seiner Gattin, das seine Sinne erfüllt, das zweitemal die Vision der Freiheit, der Engel der Freiheit mit den Zügen der Leonore."

9 Hull, *Sexuality, State, and Civil Society in Germany, 1700–1815*.

10 Foucault, *The History of Sexuality*, 89.

11 I have discussed Kant's positions on marriage, sexuality, and gender difference in *Tempest in the Caribbean*, 130–31. Isabel V. Hull, in *Sexuality, State, and Civil Society in Germany, 1700–1815*, 301–13, contextualizes Kant in a discussion of the ways in which the movement from an absolutist state to civil society repositioned women in marriage; Eric O. Clarke, in *Virtuous Vice*, 101–25, while ignoring gender in his analysis, points to the incoherence in Kant's position in relationship to male homosexuality. Beethoven is assumed to have some acquaintance with and interest in Kant; phrases from Kant's *Critique of Practical Reason* appear in his notebooks. See Kinderman, *Beethoven*, 5.

12 Joseph Kerman, in "Augenblicke in Fidelio," points out that in the 1805–6 version of the opera the reunion of husband and wife carried no assurance of a political solution: just the opposite, in fact; the 1814 opera collapses Florestan's freedom into recovery of his wife with a "suspicious alacrity"

that Kerman associates with the other moments ("Augenblicke") of magical instantaneity (133). These, I would suggest, are as often ideological collapses as they are unthinkable finesses of otherwise insuperable differences.

13 Derrida, *Politics of Friendship*, 279.

14 On this, see Pederson, "Beethoven and Masculinity." Rich's poem is in her *Poems: Selected and New, 1950–1974*, 205–6.

15 Robinson, *Ludwig van Beethoven, Fidelio*, 1, 2.

16 Robinson, *Ludwig van Beethoven, Fidelio*, 97.

17 I refer to Robinson, *Queer Wars*; the range of Robinson's interests is reflected in his volume of collected essays, *Opera, Sex, and Other Vital Matters*.

18 Sedgwick, *The Weather in Proust*, 183.

19 Elsaesser, "Tales of Sound and Fury," 86.

20 Carson, "Why I Wrote Two Plays about Phaidra by Euripides," in *Grief Lessons*, 309–12. For another classical connection, see Meisel, *Realizations*, connecting Leonora saving her husband to the "erotic and sacrificial possibilities" (304) of the figure of Roman Charity, the image of filial piety (a daughter offering her breast to her father) transferred to the husband-wife relationship.

21 Carson, "Why I Wrote Two Plays about Phaidra by Euripides," in *Grief Lessons*, 311.

22 Halliday, *Sirk on Sirk*, 93, 94–95.

23 Kaleva, "Beethoven and Melodrama," 52.

24 Halliday, *Sirk on Sirk*, 95.

25 Halliday, *Sirk on Sirk*, 95.

26 I cite line numbers of Richmond Lattimore's English translation of *Alcestis* in *Euripides I: Four Tragedies*, 44.

27 Lattimore, *Euripides I*, 3.

28 Lattimore, *Euripides I*, 5.

29 Carson, *Grief Lessons*, 247.

30 Elsaesser, "Tales of Sound and Fury," 89.

31 I cite the final chorus in Carson's translation, *Grief Lessons*, 306. Sirk quotes it, in a different translation, in Halliday, *Sirk on Sirk*, 132.

2. Identity and Identification

1 Halliday, *Sirk on Sirk*, 95. (I noted this at the end of chapter 1.) Subsequent citations to Halliday's book are given in parentheses in the text; page numbers refer to the 1972 edition unless otherwise noted.

2 Mark Shivas, *Behind the Mirror: A Profile of Douglas Sirk* (BBC2, 1979),

interview excerpted on *All That Heaven Allows*, DVD (Criterion Collection, 2001).

3 See Wyatt, "Cinematic/Sexual," 4, for Haynes's account of his high school film experience and his Brown identity as a painter. The latter is reflected in *Dottie Gets Spanked* (1994), where the child protagonist's drawings include ones made by Haynes as a child. *The Suicide* is available on the Criterion Collection DVD of *Safe* (2014).

4 Schmidt's documentary is available on the Criterion Collection DVD of *Magnificent Obsession* (2009).

5 In the interview with Schmidt, conducted in German, Sirk often offers English words, at one point even saying he can't think of the word he wants in German; this despite the fact that it was the language he spoke most of his life — he only learned English when he came to the United States when he was around forty years old.

6 Sirk's obituary for Fassbinder, "Rainer Werner Fassbinder — In Commemoration," appeared originally in *Nouvelles littéraires* on July 1, 1982.

7 Unless otherwise noted, all citations from Fassbinder are from the interviews, essays, and notes gathered in *The Anarchy of the Imagination*.

8 This identification can be seen in the twenty-five-minute film on which they collaborated, *Bourbon Street Blues* (1979). Sirk is the film's nominal director; Fassbinder plays a major role in it, a drunken failure articulating a brief for the aesthetic (his character is variously named Chekov and Shakespeare), identifying with a female protagonist who lives in a world of illusion (she is based on a Tennessee Williams character).

9 Julia Leyda, "'Something That Is Dangerous and Arousing and Transgressive': An Interview with Todd Haynes," *Bright Lights*, October 31, 2012, http://brightlightsfilm.com/something-that-is-dangerous-and-arousing-and-transgressive-an-interview-with-todd-haynes/.

10 Haynes, "*Far from Heaven*: Director's Statement," in *Far from Heaven, Safe, and Superstar: The Karen Carpenter Story*, xiii.

11 Haynes, "*Far from Heaven*: Director's Statement," xiv.

12 Noel Murray, "Todd Haynes," interview, *A.V. Club*, November 20, 2007, www.avclub.com/article/todd-haynes-14178.

13 Haynes, "Three Screenplays: An Introduction," in *Far from Heaven, Safe, and Superstar: The Karen Carpenter Story*, xii; Doane, "Pathos and Pathology," 5. Haynes's footnote actually refers to a talk Doane gave at Brown in 2003, which was published as "Pathos and Pathology: The Cinema of Todd Haynes," in issue 57 of *Camera Obscura* titled "Todd Haynes: A Magnificent Obsession." The issue initiated a growing academic concern with Haynes that includes a collection of essays edited by James Morrison (*The Cinema of Todd Haynes*) and monographs by Glyn Davis (*Far from Heaven and Superstar*), John Gill (*Far from Heaven*), and Rob White (*Todd Haynes*).

14 Haynes, "Three Screenplays: An Introduction," xii; Haynes, "*Far from Heaven*: Director's Statement," xiii.

15 Haynes's "Homoaesthetics and *Querelle*" is engaged by Reginald Shepherd in "What Remained of a Genet."

16 Haynes, "Homoaesthetics and *Querelle*," 75.

17 Sedgwick, *Tendencies*, xii. Queer is inextinguishable here because it is located across language, *troublant*, as Sedgwick writes, and because it is a movement across at its root. Where it ramifies, she takes up in the first essay in the book, "Queer and Now," 1–20, esp. 8–9. Wyatt, "Cinematic/Sexual."

18 Haynes, "Homoaesthetics and *Querelle*," 73, 74.

19 Haynes, "Homoaesthetics and *Querelle*," 75, 77, 78. In *Querelle*, division is also conveyed by insistent doubling: the same actor plays two parts; two men who don't look at all alike are nonetheless said to be identical twins. Doubling divides the same even as it refuses the difference of difference.

20 Haynes, "Homoaesthetics and *Querelle*," 97, 92. For a different take, however, see Edelman, "I'm Not There."

21 That is, it is possible to see Haynes at this point working from feminist paradigms of difference (Shepherd, "What Remained of a Genet," sees Laura Mulvey behind Haynes's theorizations, for example) and falling into the dilemmas in Kaja Silverman's work that Sedgwick underscores in *Tendencies*, 79–80, 97–98, where heterosexual presumption tied to female exclusion and difference limits its queer purchase.

22 Leyda, "'Something That Is Dangerous and Arousing and Transgressive.'"

23 Haynes, "Three Screenplays: An Introduction," viii.

24 Haynes, "Three Screenplays: An Introduction," viii.

25 Wyatt, "Cinematic/Sexual," 4; Haynes, "Three Screenplays: An Introduction," ix.

26 Haynes, "Three Screenplays: An Introduction," ix.

27 Haynes, "Three Screenplays: An Introduction," ix.

28 Leyda, "'Something That Is Dangerous and Arousing and Transgressive.'"

29 Haynes, "Three Screenplays: An Introduction," xi.

30 Haynes, "Three Screenplays: An Introduction," xii.

31 Haynes, "Three Screenplays: An Introduction," xi, xiv.

32 Haynes, "Three Screenplays: An Introduction," xii. The citation is from an interview with Christian Braad Thomsen in 1975 (Rayns, *Fassbinder*, 93).

33 Amy Kroin, "Movies Are Nothing until We Bring an Emotional Life to Them," *Salon*, November 11, 2002, www.salon.com/2002/11/11/haynes-2/. This is how Haynes explicates Fassbinder in an April 2005 interview that is the basis for Robert Fischer's 2006 Film Factory documentary, *A Powerful Political Potential: Todd Haynes on Fassbinder and Melodrama*.

34 Skvirsky, "The Price of Heaven," 113, 114.

35 Skvirsky, "The Price of Heaven," 95.

36 Richard Dyer, in "Reading Fassbinder's Sexual Politics," critiques Fassbinder for just what Skvirsky finds to fault in Haynes, what he calls, after Walter Benjamin, "left-wing melancholy" (55).

37 Skvirsky, "The Price of Heaven," 113.

38 J. Hoberman, "Signs of the Times," *Village Voice*, November 5, 2002, http://www.villagevoice.com/film/signs-of-the-times-6412283.

39 O'Brien, "Past Perfect."

40 Landy, "Storytelling and Information in Todd Haynes' Films," 22. As she affirms in "The Dream of Gesture," "Haynes's cinema does not affirm 'an illusion of the world' but confronts the impossible task of restoring 'belief in the world'" (139; she is citing Deleuze); thus his films "cannot be reduced to a meaning that confirms the social world as safe and manageable" (140).

41 Davis, *Far from Heaven*, 42.

42 Gill, *Far from Heaven*, 43, 46.

43 O'Brien, "Past Perfect."

44 Bennett, *The Enchantment of Modern Life*.

45 Davis, *Far from Heaven*, 62, 98.

46 Willis, "The Politics of Disappointment," 135.

47 Quoted in Gill, *Far from Heaven*, 28.

48 Joan Hawkins, in "The Sleazy Pedigree of Todd Haynes," sees well that Haynes is interested in the persistence rather than the supersession that liberalism dreams. Unlike Skvirsky, who explicitly doubts the liberalism underlying Willis's piece, Hawkins sees how close Haynes's politics are to Fassbinder's, not misrecognizing him as someone for whom class analysis has full explanatory force. As Hawkins avers, recalling Haynes's 1985 essay, "*Far from Heaven* seems to be — at least in part — Haynes's attempt to work out some of the homoaesthetics he attributes to Fassbinder" (211).

49 Gill, *Far from Heaven*, 37; Willis, "The Politics of Disappointment," 166.

50 Comeau, *Melodramatic License*, 5.

51 Gill, *Far from Heaven*, 27, 101.

52 Willis, "The Politics of Disappointment," 169.

53 Gill, *Far from Heaven*, 13.

54 DeFalco, "A Double-Edged Longing," 36.

55 Gill, *Far from Heaven*, 104.

56 Klinger, *Melodrama and Meaning*; Willis, "The Politics of Disappointment," 137; Davis, *Far from Heaven*, 7, 121.

57 The most compelling version of this argument is offered by Elena Gorfinkel in "The Future of Anachronism." Gorfinkel is alert to cinematic self-consciousness in Haynes, cannily summarizing Haynes's relation to Sirk this way: "This sort of presentation, as an opening into a film historical

imaginary, *inserts the historically and socially possible into the film historically impossible*" (158).

58 Berlant, *The Female Complaint*, 138. Nella Larsen's *Passing* is a well-studied example of cross-racial sexualization.

59 Rohmer and Chabrol, *Hitchcock*. I discuss their claims in my *Strangers on a Train*, 64–72.

60 Klinger, *Melodrama and Meaning*, 127.

61 Dyer, "Rock—The Last Guy You'd Have Figured" (this essay first appeared in 1985 in *Body Politic*, no. 121). To the examples of double entendres in Dyer and Klinger, I would add the plot of *Send Me No Flowers*, where Hudson's hypochondriacal character, sure he is close to death, is busy imagining his male friends as suitable new husbands for the Doris Day character, sizing up their sexual potential.

62 Meyer, "Rock Hudson's Body." Mann, *Behind the Screen*, amply demonstrates how widespread knowledge of sexuality was in Hollywood.

63 Meyer, "Rock Hudson's Body," 262.

64 Halliday, *Sirk on Sirk* (rev. ed.), 4. Further citations from this revised 1997 edition are given in parentheses in the text.

65 Mann, *Behind the Screen*, 322. As Cynthia Fuchs argues in "Split Screen," this is a masculinity that is not one. Fuchs builds her case on Dyer as well as theoretical models about performativity in the work of Judith Butler, Sedgwick, and Michael Moon.

66 Mann, *Behind the Screen*, 322.

67 More directly, it anticipates *Captain Lightfoot* (1955), a Sirk film that again pairs Hudson and Barbara Rush. This film also was shot on location (in Ireland). It is a historical costume drama set in 1815 about an Irish rebel who works underhandedly against the British and who at the end is about to marry the daughter of another rebel, John Doherty (Jeff Morrow), who, like Hudson's character Mike Martin, has a real name and a pretend one: Captain Thunder to Hudson's Captain Lightfoot. The film often looks like a western, lush green replacing desert; it involves doubling, mistaken identities, and a constantly deferred marriage plot. For all its supposed seriousness, it is mainly played for laughs; Hudson even sings a bit. He is hopelessly inept at being civilized or domesticated (but it turns out that the women he supposes are "ladies" aren't really that either); he is pledged to a higher cause of freedom that transcends singularity of identity— identification with the captain in whose footsteps he follows as second in command. Hudson's cross-identification here, including putting on an Irish accent, is another artificial performance, as when he models himself as an Indian.

68 Lee and Lee, *All That Heaven Allows*, 3, 12.

69 Mary Beth Haralovich, in *"All That Heaven Allows,"* notes how Wyman's cos-

tuming often fits her to the "monochromatic tones of the narrative space of her suburban home" (69).

70 Lee and Lee, *All That Heaven Allows*, 12.

71 Lee and Lee, *All That Heaven Allows*, 89.

72 Mulvey, "Notes on Sirk and Melodrama," 41, 43.

73 Mulvey, "Notes on Sirk and Melodrama," 42.

74 Lee and Lee, *All That Heaven Allows*, 5, 43.

75 Cottingham, *Fear Eats the Soul*, 26.

76 White, *Uninvited*.

77 Jackie Byars, in *All That Hollywood Allows*, notes moments of Cary and Sara's proximity (181), nominating the latter as her "substitute companion" (184), and observes the use of the two-shot, usually reserved for heterosexual lovers, for female-female encounters (205). For her, this female-female solidarity is in the service of heterosexual closure. Cottingham (*Fear Eats the Soul*, 26) says that Moorehead lends the film "invisible lesbianism," whatever that means.

78 Lee and Lee, *All That Heaven Allows*, 304.

79 Bosley Crowther, reviewing the film with mild distaste in the *New York Times* on February 29, 1956, gets at this in his dismissive accounts of Wyman's and Hudson's performances. "When she surrenders to Mr. Hudson . . . she does so with lady-like decorum and elegant restraint," he notes, recording the negative/positive affect Wyman conveys at every moment in her relationship to Hudson. "He, too, performs with perfect manners, barely speaking above a whisper for most of the time and giving a sterling imitation of a rustic stalwart who is passionate for trees." Crowther registers where his most positive affect resides — for trees — and can't take it seriously: "It is true that he bears a slight resemblance to L'il Abner of comic strip fame . . . but that isn't inappropriate to this film." Indeed, the border of absurdity is what keeps melodrama from tragic despair.

80 Warner, "Thoreau's Bottom" and "*Walden*'s Erotic Economy"; Coviello, *Tomorrow's Parties*.

81 Coviello, *Tomorrow's Parties*, 33.

82 Lee and Lee, *All That Heaven Allows*, 115.

83 Michael Töteberg, "All That Fassbinder Allows," translated by Stephen Locke, in liner notes for *Ali: Fear Eats the Soul*, DVD (Criterion Collection, 2003), 11–13; the essay is from the afterword in Töteberg's edited collection *Fassbinders Filme 3*, which reprints the script of *Fear Eats the Soul* from which I quote. Page numbers from this script are given in parentheses in the text.

84 Fassbinder's film is located in a time in the protagonist's life after Sirk's: the children are all married and have abandoned Emmi; this makes it easier for her to marry Ali but does not shield her from their wrath; in a

counterpoint to the scene in *All That Heaven Allows* where a TV substitutes for sociality, when Emmi tells her children what she has done, one of them smashes in the TV set, as if it should have been all she needed for company.

85 Frantz Fanon's "North African Syndrome" seems to be in Fassbinder's mind.

86 Sylvia Wynter's elaborate schemas of difference as the underlying truth of historical change might be a theory to put beside the film; see my *Tempest in the Caribbean*, 63–70, for a discussion of Wynter's schemas of classed, gendered, and racialized difference on a world-historical scale, as well as for a bibliography of her many essays and interviews on the subject.

87 Chris Fujiwara, "One Love, Two Oppressions," included in the notes for *Ali: Fear Eats the Soul*, DVD (Criterion Collection, 2003), 4–8.

88 I'm echoing Eve Kosofsky Sedgwick in *Epistemology of the Closet*, when she remarks on the "coarse axes of categorization" through which difference is explored: "gender, race, class, nationality, sexual orientation" ("Axiom 1: People are different from each other," 22).

89 Cottingham, *Fear Eats the Soul*. The pattern was repeated in *In a Year of Thirteen Moons* (1978), a film Fassbinder made to commemorate his lover Armin Meier, who committed suicide on Fassbinder's birthday, giving him what he seemed to want.

90 Cottingham, *Fear Eats the Soul*, 11.

91 See, for example, Elsaesser, "A Cinema of Vicious Circles (and Afterword)" and "A Cinema of Vicious Circles," for his continuous rethinking of his central insights on Fassbinder. His book *Fassbinder's Germany: History, Identity, Subject* consolidates the thesis in a historicizing direction, reading subjectivity as political subject formation. Subsequent citations to this book are given in parentheses in the text.

92 As Sedgwick writes in *Tendencies*: "Beyond the pressure of crisis or exception, it may be that there exists for nations, as for genders, simply no normal way to partake of the categorical definitiveness of the national, no single kind of 'other' of what a nation is to which all can by the same structuration be definitionally opposed" ("Nationalisms and Sexualities," 150).

93 Sedgwick, *Epistemology of the Closet*, 33.

94 Gorfinkel, "Impossible, Impolitic," 514. Gorfinkel offers a close reading of the opening scene against its reiteration. She concludes by summoning Dyer, "Reading Fassbinder's Sexual Politics," and Kaja Silverman's 1989 essay, "Fassbinder and Lacan: A Reconsideration of Gaze, Look and Image." The latter is included in Silverman's *Male Subjectivity at the Margins* (125–56), which also has an essay titled "Masochistic Ecstasy and the Ruination of Masculinity in Fassbinder's Cinema" (214–96). Silverman could be answering Laura Mulvey, who ends her brief 1974 consideration of "Sirk and Fassbinder" by saying that in both *All That Heaven Allows* and

Fear Eats the Soul "an active/passive role reversal is no solution. The man loses dignity, risking stereotyping as sex-object, for example" (47).

95 Rhodes, "Fassbinder's Work," 195.

96 "Todd Haynes: From Fassbinder to Sirk and Back," on *Ali: Fear Eats the Soul*, DVD (Criterion Collection, 2003).

97 Silverman, "Fassbinder and Lacan."

98 Sedgwick, *Epistemology of the Closet*, 32.

99 Director's commentary, *Far from Heaven*, DVD (Universal, 2003).

100 Davis, *Far from Heaven*, 119. Davis seconds Lynne Joyrich, who first proposed Cathy and Sybil as the "primary couple" in the film in her essay "Written on the Screen." This possibility is also embraced by Dana Luciano in "Coming Around Again"; Luciano has also pursued questions of temporality in Haynes in "Nostalgia for an Age Yet to Come," whose embrace of a posthuman vitality—and its distinction from global capitalism—complements the argument I make to close this chapter.

101 Haynes, *Far from Heaven, Safe, and Superstar: The Karen Carpenter Story*, 42.

102 The dynamic here matches that of Lora Meredith and Annie Johnson in *Imitation of Life*, while Haynes fetches the name of Sybil from the black maid in *The Reckless Moment*, who similarly keeps the house going effortlessly while the protagonist is doing her heroic best to do the same.

103 The picture is identified and discussed in an essay to which I am indebted: Bernier, "'Beyond the Surface of Things.'"

104 Wilde, *De Profundis and Other Writings*, 232, 252.

105 Jeanne Moreau channels Zarah Leander, as Alice A. Kuzniar suggests in *The Queer German Cinema*, 57–87.

106 Patricia Highsmith cites this passage as part of the epigraph to *Ripley Under Ground*.

107 Wilde said at his second trial, "'The love that dare not speak its name' in this century is such a great affection of an elder for a younger man as there was between David and Jonathan, such as Plato made the very basis for his philosophy, and such as you find in the sonnets of Michelangelo and Shakespeare"; quoted in Hyde, *The Trials of Oscar Wilde*, 201.

108 Oscar Wilde, "The Portrait of Mr W.H.," in *The Soul of Man under Socialism and Selected Critical Prose*, 91.

3. The Art of Murder

1 Alfred Hitchcock, "Why I Make Melodramas" (1936), available at http://www.labyrinth.net.au/~muffin/melodramas_c.html (last modified March 31, 2000).

2 The photo is reproduced in Goldberg, *Strangers on a Train*, 51.

3 Brett, "Musicality, Essentialism, and the Closet."

4 For a representative example, see Cooper, *Bernard Herrmann's "Vertigo."*

5 See Adorno and Eisler, *Composing for the Films*. The initial chapter of this book is an excoriating examination of the clichéd use of music in film and the kinds of automatic response it means to trigger. Horkheimer and Adorno, *Dialectic of Enlightenment*, makes similar arguments in the chapter "The Culture Industry: Enlightenment as Mass Deception," 120–67.

6 Adorno, "Punctuation Marks," 300.

7 The position is encapsulated in the brief "Statement" signed by S. M. Eisenstein, V. I. Pudovkin, and G. V. Alexandrov anthologized in Weis and Belton, *Film Sound*, 83–86. For a provocative statement of the affordances of filmic disparity, see Jacques Rancière, *The Intervals of Cinema*.

8 Elsaesser, "Tales of Sound and Fury," 70.

9 Elsaesser, "Tales of Sound and Fury," 74. It was with just this kind of Melodram in *Fidelio* that I began this book.

10 Elsaesser, "Tales of Sound and Fury," 74.

11 Granger, *Include Me Out*, 35.

12 Granger, *Include Me Out*, 41, 64, 243.

13 See Miller, *Place for Us*, 108–18, for Miller's meditation on Merman as a mother who is not a woman, and its relationship to the complex identifications and disidentifications involved in her adoration.

14 Miller, *Place for Us*, 68.

15 Sullivan, *Hitchcock's Music*, 146, 147. Compare Weis, *The Silent Scream*, where she writes that Philip's "ability to control his guilt—to control his emotions—is equated with his ability to continue playing a piece of music" (99).

16 Clifton, "Unravelling Music in Hitchcock's *Rope*," 64, 65.

17 Clifton, "Unravelling Music in Hitchcock's *Rope*," 64, 69, 70.

18 Schroeder, *Hitchcock's Ear*, 174. I refer to the thesis of Robin Wood's 1965 *Hitchcock's Films* included in and rethought after his coming out in his *Hitchcock's Films Revisited*.

19 Sullivan, *Hitchcock's Music*, 145.

20 Brett and Wood, "Lesbian and Gay Music," 353, 354.

21 Miller develops this concept in *The Novel and the Police*. In their essay, Brett and Wood cite Miller's definition of how the open secret works: "not to conceal knowledge, so much as to conceal the knowledge of the knowledge" (355, citing *The Novel and the Police*, 206).

22 Sullivan, *Hitchcock's Music*, 145.

23 Clifton, "Unravelling Music in Hitchcock's *Rope*," 67.

24 Clifton, "Unravelling Music in Hitchcock's *Rope*," 65, 69.

25 Sullivan, *Hitchcock's Music*, 146; Schroeder, *Hitchcock's Ear*, 172.

26 Laurent Bouzerau, "*Rope* Unleashed," on *Rope*, DVD (Universal, 2006).

27 Laurents, *Original Story*, 122, 130.

28 Miller has charted them in "Anal *Rope*"; Weis, *The Silent Scream*, 99, notes the confluence of camera technique and musical selection as "significant" but does not say what that significance might be.

29 Bosley Crowther, "'Strangers on a Train,' Another Hitchcock Venture, Arrives at the Warner Theater," *New York Times*, July 4, 1951, 13.

30 Adorno, "Punctuation Marks," 300, 305.

31 Gorbman, *Unheard Melodies*, 7.

32 Adorno and Eisler, *Composing for the Films*, 49.

33 Gorbman, *Unheard Melodies*, 6; Adorno and Eisler, *Composing for the Films*, 48; Horkheimer and Adorno, *Dialectic of Enlightenment*, 145.

34 Nancy, *Listening*, 40.

35 For a text of the John C. Palmer lyrics to "The Band Played On," see Messerli, *Listen to the Mockingbird*, 214–16; as Messerli notes, the piece was enormously popular in the first half of the twentieth century, through newspaper publication, a 1941 Guy Lombardo recording, and its use in films (216).

36 Miller, "Hitchcock's Hidden Pictures," 123n13. Weis, *The Silent Scream*, provides a list of about half of the Hitchcock films in which "music is an essential component of the story" (86), extending Miller's examples.

37 On this trope, see also Allen, *Hitchcock's Romantic Irony*, 208–13, on "the fairground in expressionist cinema"; Schroeder, *Hitchcock's Ear*, fastens Hitchcock's musicality to the influence of German expressionism, with two chapters devoted to the waltz; Sullivan, *Hitchcock's Music*, likewise comments on "the German expressionist tradition" of "the amusement park as nightmare" in which a waltz sounds "with terrifying indifference" (159).

38 Sullivan, *Hitchcock's Music*, 159.

39 Sullivan, *Hitchcock's Music*, 159.

40 Highsmith, *Strangers on a Train*, 78. Subsequent citations to this book are given in parentheses in the text.

41 Miller, *Place for Us*, 124.

42 Miller, *Place for Us*, 125.

43 Sullivan, *Hitchcock's Music*, 160.

44 Sullivan follows Christopher Palmer in *Dimitri Tiomkin* (material repackaged in *The Composer in Hollywood*), taking his notion that there is a theme associated with Guy, a weak theme befitting the character; Guy's theme "carries a mocking irony" at times—for example, when it sounds as "Guy slugs Bruno in the jaw, a kind of lover's spat to please the many viewers who find homoerotic subcurrents in their decidedly peculiar relationship" (*The Composer in Hollywood*, 158).

45 Sullivan, *Hitchcock's Music*, 157.

46 Adorno and Eisler, *Composing for the Films*, 91.

47 Sullivan, *Hitchcock's Music*, 161.

48 Raymond Chandler and Czenzi Ormonde, *Strangers on a Train*, October 1950, available on the Internet Movie Script Database (IMSDb), http://www.imsdb.com/scripts/Strangers-on-a-Train.html.

49 Frances Ferguson has attempted to puzzle this out in "Now It's Personal."

50 Tiomkin and Buranelli, *Please Don't Hate Me*, 225–26.

51 Mark Seltzer has read these as the insidious sign of the reflexive violence of reflexive modernity in a number of essays, beginning in *True Crime*, whose final chapter, "Vicarious Crime," takes Highsmith's *Strangers on a Train* as its focus, and most recently in "The Daily Planet," an essay that is part of a group on Highsmith (Seltzer mainly looks at *The Talented Mr. Ripley*) in the online journal *Post 45*, December 18, 2012, http://post45.research.yale.edu/2012/12/the-daily-planet/.

52 These dynamics of watching and being watched in the Ripley novels are traced in Peters, *Anxiety and Evil in the Writings of Patricia Highsmith*, chapter 3, "Tom Ripley: The *Sinthome* Writes Back."

53 *Ripley Under Ground*, in Highsmith, *The Talented Mr. Ripley, Ripley Under Ground, Ripley's Game*, 434. Subsequent citations to this volume are given in parentheses in the text.

54 The documentary is included on the Paramount Pictures DVD of *The Talented Mr. Ripley* (2000). Subsequent references to the DVD extras are to this edition.

55 Citations to the film are from Minghella, *The Talented Mr. Ripley: A Screenplay*, occasionally modified to match the final film version.

56 The credits in the film indicate that Sally Heath performs the Bach and Jared himself the Vivaldi transcription; almost certainly Gretchen Egolf, who plays the part of the classical singer, is being lip-synched by Mary Ann McCormick, while Toni Manoli is playing the piano.

57 Minghella, *The Talented Mr. Ripley: A Screenplay*, xiv.

58 Minghella, *The Talented Mr. Ripley: A Screenplay*, xiii.

59 For another account of the limits in the film's representation of homosexuality, see Stoddart, "The Talented Mr. Ripley."

60 Slavoj Žižek, "Not a Desire to Have Him, but to Be Like Him" (a review of Andrew Wilson's 2003 biography of Highsmith, *Beautiful Shadow*), *London Review of Books*, August 21, 2003, 13–14.

61 Žižek, "Not a Desire to Have Him, but to Be Like Him," 14.

62 I glance here at Michael Trask's "Patricia Highsmith's Method," which valuably enquires into the limits of recuperating her for usual notions of gay identity politics. Trask's method involves historicizing Highsmith in

ways that make hers a period piece in which the closet is the only way to explain both Dickie's and Tom's performances. This analysis reinstates the identities that Trask questions even though he acknowledges that Highsmith herself was no closet case. He ends his essay insisting on fantasy as a key in Highsmith's novels, a point congruent with my own conclusion.

63 Highsmith, *Plotting and Writing Suspense Fiction*, 76.

64 Žižek, "Not a Desire to Have Him, but to Be Like Him," 14.

65 Minghella, *The Talented Mr. Ripley: A Screenplay*, xv, xvi, xv.

66 Landowski appears on Brett and Wood's list of musical queers in "Lesbian and Gay Music," her status as high priestess of early music taken as a cover for her sexuality, much as Minghella makes Peter a professional church musician.

67 Walter Benjamin, "Theses on the Philosophy of History," in *Illuminations*, 256.

68 Jacques Rancière, "*Ars gratia artis*: Minnelli's Poetics," in *The Intervals of Cinema*, 71, 79.

69 Highsmith, *The Boy Who Followed Ripley*, 70. Subsequent citations to this book are given in parentheses in the text.

70 This phenomenon is studied as insidious in Peter Szendy's *Hits* and with more appreciation of the telepathic by Ned Schantz's reading of Hitchcock's *Shadow of a Doubt* (Tiomkin's score in this film making use of the "Merry Widow Waltz" as one of its devices for the telepathy that links one Charlie to another) in *Gossip, Letters, Phones*, 84–95.

71 See Schenkar, *The Talented Miss Highsmith*, 243, 464; Wilson, *Beautiful Shadow*, 372.

72 Was Henry James an inspiration for Highsmith in this? We know that *The Talented Mr. Ripley* takes its impetus from *The Ambassadors* because that is made explicit in the novel. Did Highsmith have access to the preface to the New York edition of *The Spoils of Poynton*, where James muses on the insufficiency of fact "excellent, for development, if arrested in the right place, that is in the germ" (25)?

73 For the counterargument, see Tom Perrin, "On Patricia Highsmith," *Post 45*, December 18, 2012, http://post45.research.yale.edu/2012/12/cluster -introduction-patricia-highsmith/.

74 See Highsmith, *Zeichnungen*, 107–8. Further citations in the text are translated or paraphrased from this German edition.

75 Elsaesser, "The Dandy in Hitchcock."

4. Wildean Aesthetics

1 See Oscar Wilde, "The Portrait of Mr W.H.," in *The Soul of Man under Socialism and Selected Critical Prose*, 193–212.

2 Oscar Wilde, "Pen, Pencil and Poison," in *The Soul of Man under Socialism and Selected Critical Prose*, 195.

3 See Eve Kosofsky Sedgwick and Michael Moon, "Divinity: A Dossier, a Performance Piece, a Little-Understood Emotion," in Sedgwick, *Tendencies*, 215–51.

4 Sedgwick, "Across Gender, Across Sexuality." At just the same time, Claude J. Summers published an essay with similar aims, "'A Losing Game in the End': Aestheticism and Homosexuality in 'Paul's Case.'" Like Sedgwick, Summers notes the shift in Cather's attitude toward Wilde. His main concern is to establish that Paul is gay and that the story aims to show that he could have reconciled with his father and, using his imagination in a Christian way toward social acceptance, avoided his sad ending. Summers is followed by David Halperin in *How to Be Gay*, 212–14, 226–28, demurring from a reading more akin to Sedgwick's in Scott Herring, *Queering the Underworld*, 67–103. Rather than offering a brief for gay identity, Herring sees the story as intimating a kind of social mobility. He concludes: "Queerness can move one beyond identifications" (101); "queer transients . . . fit in nowhere and everywhere" (103).

5 Sedgwick, "Across Gender, Across Sexuality," 70.

6 Sedgwick quotes these essays from Slote, *The Kingdom of Art*. These are not the only places in Cather's journalism where Wilde is mentioned, and disapproved; an 1894 piece, for example, refers to the "driveling effeminacy" of the school of Wilde (135); another review from 1895 excoriates Ouida novels for their "pitiable waste and shameful weaknesses" that "fill me with the same disgust that Oscar Wilde's books do" (409). These pieces also can be found in the more compendious selection of Cather's early journalism, Curtin, *The World and the Parish*.

7 Slote, *The Kingdom of Art*, 391.

8 Sedgwick, "Across Gender, Across Sexuality," 63.

9 Jewell and Stout, *The Selected Letters of Willa Cather*, 614.

10 Willa Cather, "Paul's Case," in *Stories, Poems, and Other Writings*, 470. Subsequent citations to this edition are given in parentheses in the text. This is the slightly revised 1920 version of this story from the collection *Youth and the Bright Medusa*; it first appeared as the final story in the 1905 collection *The Troll Garden*. Carpenter, "Why Willa Cather Revised 'Paul's Case,'" details the changes made to argue that they intensify the notion that Paul is

living a lie, in relation to art and at the Waldorf. Carpenter does not grasp the change in valuation that the story offers.

11 On this, see Kittler, "World-Breath." I discuss this essay in *Willa Cather and Others*, 77–78, in a chapter on Cather's relationship to Olive Fremstad in relation to *The Song of the Lark*; I draw on this chapter in the following discussion.

12 Sedgwick, "Across Gender, Across Sexuality," 65.

13 Jeff Nunokawa, in *Tame Passions of Wilde*, is preoccupied with the paradoxes of a love that "transcends bodily exhaustion" (56).

14 See Judith Butler, "'Dangerous Crossing': Willa Cather's Masculine Names," in *Bodies That Matter*, 166. Butler's essay is in conversation with Sedgwick's, stressing the difficulty of cross-identification as well as the figurative dimension of lesbian sexuality embodied in Paul. Following Christopher Nealon's discussion of the relationship between these two theorists in "Affect-Genealogy," I have further parsed their readings of "Paul's Case" in "Cather and Sexuality."

15 Cather, *My Ántonia*, 14.

16 Lewis, *Willa Cather Living*, 92.

17 Lewis, *Willa Cather Living*, 92.

18 Cather, "The Novel Démeublé," 50.

19 Cather, *The Song of the Lark*, xxxi–xxxii.

20 Jewell and Stout, *The Selected Letters of Willa Cather*, 218.

21 Hall, *The Wagnerian Romances*, vii–viii.

22 Jameson, *The Antinomies of Realism*, 161, at the conclusion of a chapter titled "Realism and the Dissolution of Genre."

23 See Stout, *Willa Cather*, for "valedictory" (262) opening a discussion of *Lucy Gayheart* that extends to page 274. The comparison to the 1911 story occurs on page 263. Woodress, *Willa Cather*, mentions the story on page 449, the opening page of a discussion of the novel that concludes on page 465.

24 Gelfant, "Movement and Melody," 261n18. Gelfant refers in this note to John J. Murphy, "'Lucy's Case': An Interpretation of *Lucy Gayheart*," *Markham Review* 9 (1980), and is citing Richard Giannone, *Music in Willa Cather's Fiction* (Lincoln: University of Nebraska Press, 1968), 46, on "Paul's Case." Giannone has a more recent essay on music in *Lucy Gayheart*, "Music, Silence, and the Spirituality of Willa Cather," which insistently translates questions of life into spiritual life. The missing sexual connection is delivered only in his spiritual autobiography, *Hidden: Reflections on Gay Life, AIDS, and Spiritual Desire*.

25 Woodress, *Willa Cather*, 461; Stout, *Willa Cather*, 265.

26 Gelfant, "Movement and Melody," 121.

27 Cather, *Lucy Gayheart*, 155. Subsequent citations to this book are given in parentheses in the text.

28 Gelfant, "Movement and Melody," 121.

29 Jewell and Stout, *The Selected Letters of Willa Cather*, 510.

30 Woodress, *Willa Cather*, 462.

31 Gelfant, "Movement and Melody," 127, 134; Woodress, *Willa Cather*, 462.

32 Gelfant, "Movement and Melody," 135, 131.

33 See Christopher Nealon, "Feeling and Affiliation in Willa Cather," in *Foundlings*, 61–97.

34 Lewis, *Willa Cather Living*, associates the writing of *Lucy Gayheart* with Cather's friendship with the musical prodigy Yehudi Menuhin and his sisters Hephzibah and Yaltah (168–73). She became their beloved Aunt Willa. Lewis recounts their final meeting with Cather before her death on the way to summoning up the renewed musicality that prompted the writing of *Lucy Gayheart*. As is usual with Lewis's writing, it is fine-tuned to the Cather she describes, a collaboration well explored in Homestead, "Willa Cather, Edith Lewis, and Collaboration."

35 Willa Cather, "Katherine Mansfield," 136.

36 Empson, *Seven Types of Ambiguity*, 196. I owe this citation to Sharon Cameron's discussion of Empson's Buddhism in *Impersonality*; Empson's pursuit of self-abandonment in the direction of an impersonal self beyond identity resonates with the aesthetic project I describe and with its personal painfulness and impossibility. As Cameron writes, the practice of impersonality must inevitably be impossible since it is done by persons.

37 Jewell and Stout, *The Selected Letters of Willa Cather*, 488, 667.

38 Jewell and Stout, *The Selected Letters of Willa Cather*, 487.

Coda

1 Williams, *On The Wire*, 100, 122.

2 For a related analysis of Williams, see Noah Berlatsky, "Building a Better Panopticon: 'The Wire' as Melodrama," *Los Angeles Review of Books*, August 18, 2014, http://lareviewofbooks.org/review/building-better-panopticon.

3 Williams, *On The Wire*, 81.

4 Williams, *On The Wire*, 176.

5 Williams, *On The Wire*, 189, 161.

6 Levine, *Forms*, 137, 149.

7 Williams, *On The Wire*, 197–98; Levine, *Forms*, 150.

8 Williams, *On The Wire*, 207.

9 Düttmann, *Visconti*, 87, 123.

10 Düttmann, *Visconti*, 91.

11 Düttmann, *Visconti*, 90.

12 Düttmann, *Visconti*, 91.

13 Düttmann, *Visconti*, 41; Fassbinder, *The Anarchy of Imagination*, 39.

14 Elsaesser, *Fassbinder's Germany*, 107.

15 Halliday, *Sirk on Sirk*, 100.

16 Cather, *My Ántonia*, 206.

17 Slavoj Žižek, "Not a Desire to Have Him, but to Be Like Him," *London Review of Books*, August 21, 2003, 13–14.

18 Bersani, *Thoughts and Things*, 35.

19 Bersani, *Thoughts and Things*, 82, 83.

20 Quotations from the script in Davies, *A Modest Pageant*, 137, 141.

21 Koresky, *Terence Davies*, 61; J. Hoberman, "The Rapture," *Village Voice*, June 1, 1993.

22 Koresky, *Terence Davies*, 126.

23 Koresky, *Terence Davies*, 123; Davies, *A Modest Pageant*, 185.

BIBLIOGRAPHY

Adorno, Theodor. "Punctuation Marks." Translated by Shierry Weber Nicholsen. *Antioch Review* 48, no. 3 (summer 1990): 300–305.

Adorno, Theodor, and Hanns Eisler. *Composing for the Films*. London: Continuum, 1947.

Allen, Richard. *Hitchcock's Romantic Irony*. New York: Columbia University Press, 2007.

Beethoven, Ludwig von. *Fidelio*. New York: Dover, 1984.

Benjamin, Walter. *Illuminations*. Edited by Hannah Arendt. Translated by Harry Zohn. New York: Schocken, 1969.

Bennett, Jane. *The Enchantment of Modern Life: Attachments, Crossings, and Ethics*. Princeton, NJ: Princeton University Press, 2001.

Berlant, Lauren. *The Female Complaint*. Durham, NC: Duke University Press, 2008.

Berlant, Lauren, and Lee Edelman. *Sex, or the Unbearable*. Durham, NC: Duke University Press, 2014.

Bernier, Celeste-Marie. "'Beyond the Surface of Things': Race, Representation and the Fine Arts in *Far from Heaven*." In *The Cinema of Todd Haynes: All That Heaven Allows*, ed. James Morrison, 122–31. London: Wallflower, 2007.

Bersani, Leo. "Sociality and Sex." *Critical Inquiry* 26, no. 4 (summer 2000): 641–56.

Bersani, Leo. *Thoughts and Things*. Chicago: University of Chicago Press, 2015.

Brett, Philip. "Musicality, Essentialism, and the Closet." In *Queering the Pitch: The New Gay and Lesbian Musicology*, 2nd ed., ed. Philip Brett, Elizabeth Wood, and Gary C. Thomas, 9–26. New York: Routledge, 2006.

Brett, Philip, and Elizabeth Wood. "Lesbian and Gay Music." In *Queering the Pitch: The New Gay and Lesbian Musicology*, 2nd ed., ed. Philip Brett, Elizabeth Wood, and Gary C. Thomas, 351–89. New York: Routledge, 2006.

Brett, Philip, Elizabeth Wood, and Gary C. Thomas, eds. *Queering the Pitch: The New Gay and Lesbian Musicology*. 2nd ed. New York: Routledge, 2006.

Brooks, Peter. *The Melodramatic Imagination: Balzac, Henry James, Melodrama, and the Mode of Excess*. 1976. New Haven, CT: Yale University Press, 1995.

Butler, Judith. *Bodies That Matter*. New York: Routledge, 1993.

Byars, Jackie. *All That Hollywood Allows: Re-reading Gender in 1950s Melodrama.* Chapel Hill: University of North Carolina Press, 1991.

Cameron, Sharon. *Impersonality.* Chicago: University of Chicago Press, 2007.

Carpenter, David A. "Why Willa Cather Revised 'Paul's Case': The Work in Art and Those Sundry Afternoons." *American Literature* 59, no. 4 (December 1987): 590–608.

Carson, Anne. *Grief Lessons: Four Plays.* New York: New York Review of Books, 2006.

Cather, Willa. "Katherine Mansfield." In *Not Under Forty,* 123–47. Reprint, Lincoln: University Press of Nebraska, 1988.

Cather, Willa. *Lucy Gayheart.* New York: Vintage, 1995.

Cather, Willa. *My Ántonia.* 1918. Boston: Houghton Mifflin, 1988.

Cather, Willa. "The Novel Démeublé." In *Not Under Forty,* 43–51. Reprint, Lincoln: University Press of Nebraska, 1988.

Cather, Willa. *The Song of the Lark.* 1915. Boston: Houghton Mifflin, 1988.

Cather, Willa. *Stories, Poems, and Other Writings.* Edited by Sharon O'Brien. New York: Library of America, 1992.

Clarke, Eric O. *Virtuous Vice: Homoeroticism and the Public Sphere.* Durham, NC: Duke University Press, 2000.

Clifton, Kevin. "Unravelling Music in Hitchcock's *Rope.*" *Horror Studies* 4, no. 1 (April 2013): 63–74.

Cohan, Steven. *Masked Men: Masculinity and the Movies in the Fifties.* Bloomington: Indiana University Press, 1997.

Comeau, Vance. *Melodramatic License: The Re-imagining of Douglas Sirk's "All That Heaven Allows" by Rainer Werner Fassbender [sic] and Todd Haynes.* Saarbrüken: VDM Verlag Dr. Müller, 2011.

Cooper, David. *Bernard Herman's "Vertigo."* Westport, CT: Greenwood, 2001.

Cottingham, Laura. *Fear Eats the Soul.* London: BFI, 2005.

Coviello, Peter. *Tomorrow's Parties: Sex and the Untimely in Nineteenth-Century America.* New York: NYU Press, 2013.

Curtin, William M., ed. *The World and the Parish.* Lincoln: University of Nebraska Press, 1970.

Davies, Terence. *A Modest Pageant: Children, Madonna and Child, Death and Transfiguration, Distant Voices, Still Lives, and The Long Day Closes.* London: Faber and Faber, 1992.

Davis, Glyn. *Far from Heaven.* Edinburgh: Edinburgh University Press, 2011.

Davis, Glyn. *Superstar: The Karen Carpenter Story.* London: Wallflower, 2008.

DeFalco, Amelia. "A Double-Edged Longing: Nostalgia, Melodrama, and Todd Haynes's *Far from Heaven.*" *Iowa Journal of Cultural Studies* 5 (fall 2004): 26–39.

Derrida, Jacques. *Politics of Friendship.* Translated by George Collins. London: Verso, 1997.

Doane, Mary Ann. "Pathos and Pathology: The Cinema of Todd Haynes." *Camera Obscura* 19, no. 3 57 (2004): 1–21.

Düttmann, Alexander García. *Visconti: Insights into Flesh and Blood*. Translated by Robert Savage. Stanford, CA: Stanford University Press, 2009.

Dyer, Richard. "Reading Fassbinder's Sexual Politics." In *Fassbinder*, ed. Tony Rayns, 54–64. London: BFI, 1980.

Dyer, Richard. "Rock—The Last Guy You'd Have Figured." In *You Tarzan: Masculinity, Movies and Men*, ed. Pat Kirkham and Janet Thurman, 27–34. New York: St. Martin's, 1993.

Edelman, Lee. "I'm Not There: The Absence of Theory." *differences* 21, no. 1 (2010): 149–60.

Elsaesser, Thomas. "A Cinema of Vicious Circles." In *Rainer Werner Fassbinder*, ed. Laurence Kardish with Juliane Lorenz, 15–27. New York: Museum of Modern Art, 1997.

Elsaesser, Thomas. "A Cinema of Vicious Circles (and Afterword)." In *Fassbinder*, ed. Tony Rayns, 24–53. London: BFI, 1980.

Elsaesser, Thomas. "The Dandy in Hitchcock." In *Alfred Hitchcock: Centenary Essays*, ed. Richard Allen and S. Ishii-Gonzalès, 3–13. London: BFI, 1999.

Elsaesser, Thomas. *Fassbinder's Germany: History, Identity, Subject*. Amsterdam: Amsterdam University Press, 1996.

Elsaesser, Thomas. "Tales of Sound and Fury: Observations on the Family Melodrama" (1972). Reprinted in *Imitations of Life: A Reader on Film and Television Melodramas*, ed. Marcia Landy, 68–91. Detroit: Wayne State University Press, 1991.

Empson, William. *Seven Types of Ambiguity*. New York: New Directions, 1966.

Fanon, Frantz. "The North African Syndrome." In *Toward the African Revolution*, trans. Haakon Chevalier, 3–16. New York: Grove, 1967.

Fassbinder, Rainer Werner. *The Anarchy of Imagination*. Edited by Michael Töteberg and Leo Lansing. Translated by Krishna Winston. Baltimore: Johns Hopkins University Press, 1992.

Ferguson, Frances. "Now It's Personal: D. A. Miller and Too-Close Reading." *Critical Inquiry* 41 (spring 2015): 521–40.

Foucault, Michel. *The History of Sexuality: An Introduction*. Translated by Robert Hurley. New York: Pantheon, 1978.

Frank, Marcie. "At the Intersections of Mode, Genre and Media: A Dossier of Essays on Melodrama." *Criticism* 55, no. 4 (fall 2013): 535–45.

Fuchs, Cynthia. "Split Screen: Framing and Passing in *Pillow Talk*." In *The Other Fifties*, ed. Joel Forman, 224–51. Urbana: University of Illinois Press, 1997.

Gelfant, Blanche. "Movement and Melody: The Disembodiment of Lucy Gayheart." In *Women Writing in America: Voices in Collage*, 117–43. Hanover: University Press of New England, 1984.

Giannone, Richard. *Hidden: Reflections on Gay Life, AIDS, and Spiritual Desire.* New York: Fordham University Press, 2012.

Giannone, Richard. "Music, Silence, and the Spirituality of Willa Cather." *Renascence* 57, no. 2 (winter 2005): 123–49.

Gill, John. *Far from Heaven.* London: Palgrave Macmillan / BFI, 2011.

Gledhill, Christine. "The Melodramatic Field: An Investigation." In *Home Is Where the Heart Is*, ed. Christine Gledhill, 5–39. London: BFI, 1987.

Gledhill, Christine. "Rethinking Genre." In *Reinventing Film Studies*, ed. Christine Gledhill and Linda Williams, 221–43. London: Arnold, 2000.

Goldberg, Jonathan. "Cather and Sexuality." In *The Cambridge Companion to Willa Cather*, ed. Marilee Lindemann, 86–100. Cambridge: Cambridge University Press, 2005.

Goldberg, Jonathan. *Strangers on a Train.* Vancouver: Arsenal Pulp, 2012.

Goldberg, Jonathan. *Tempest in the Caribbean.* Minneapolis: University of Minnesota Press, 2004.

Goldberg, Jonathan. *Willa Cather and Others.* Durham, NC: Duke University Press, 2001.

Gorbman, Claudia. *Unheard Melodies.* London: BFI, 1987.

Gorfinkel, Elena. "The Future of Anachronism: Todd Haynes and the Magnificent Andersons." In *Cinephilia: Movies, Love and Memory*, ed. Marijke de Valck and Malte Hagener, 153–67. Amsterdam: Amsterdam University Press, 2005.

Gorfinkel, Elena. "Impossible, Impolitic: *Ali: Fear Eats the Soul* and Fassbinder's Asynchronous Bodies." In *A Companion to Rainer Werner Fassbinder*, ed. Brigitte Peucker, 505–15. Chichester: Wiley-Blackwell, 2012.

Granger Farley, with Robert Calhoun. *Include Me Out.* New York: St. Martin's Griffin, 2007.

Hall, Gertrude. *The Wagnerian Romances.* 1907. New York: Alfred A. Knopf, 1942.

Halliday, Jon. *Sirk on Sirk.* New York: Viking, 1972.

Halliday, Jon. *Sirk on Sirk.* Rev. ed. London: Faber and Faber, 1997.

Halperin, David. *How to Be Gay.* Cambridge, MA: Harvard University Press, 2012.

Haralovich, Mary Beth. "*All That Heaven Allows*: Color, Narrative Space, and Melodrama." In *Close Viewings*, ed. Peter Lehman, 57–72. Tallahassee: Florida State University Press, 1990.

Hawkins, Joan. "The Sleazy Pedigree of Todd Haynes." In *Sleaze Artists*, ed. Jeffrey Sconce, 189–218. Durham, NC: Duke University Press, 2007.

Haynes, Todd. *Far from Heaven, Safe, and Superstar: The Karen Carpenter Story: Three Screenplays.* New York: Grove, 2003.

Haynes, Todd. "Homoaesthetics and *Querelle*." *subjects/objects* 3 (1985): 71–99.

Herring, Scott. *Queering the Underworld.* Chicago: University of Chicago Press, 2007.

Highsmith, Patricia. *The Boy Who Followed Ripley*. 1980. New York: Random House, 1993.

Highsmith, Patricia. *Plotting and Writing Suspense Fiction*. New York: St. Martin's, 1983.

Highsmith, Patricia. *Strangers on a Train*. 1950. New York: Norton, 2001.

Highsmith, Patricia. *The Talented Mr. Ripley, Ripley Under Ground, Ripley's Game*. 1955, 1970, 1974. New York: Knopf Everyman's Library, 1999.

Highsmith, Patricia. *Zeichnungen*. Zürich: Diogenes, 1995.

Homestead, Melissa J. "Willa Cather, Edith Lewis, and Collaboration: The Southwestern Novels of the 1920s and Beyond." *Studies in the Novel* 45, no. 3 (fall 2013): 408–41.

Horkheimer, Max, and Theodor Adorno. *Dialectic of Enlightenment*. Translated by John Cumming. New York: Continuum, [1944] 2001.

Hull, Isabel V. *Sexuality, State, and Civil Society in Germany, 1700–1815*. Ithaca, NY: Cornell University Press, 1996.

Hyde, H. Montgomery. *The Trials of Oscar Wilde*. New York: Dover, 1962.

James, Henry. *The Spoils of Poynton*. London: Penguin, 1987.

Jameson, Fredric. *The Antinomies of Realism*. London: Verso, 2013.

Jewell, Andrew, and Janis Stout, eds. *The Selected Letters of Willa Cather*. New York: Knopf, 2013.

Joyrich, Lynne. "Written on the Screen: Mediation and Immersion in *Far from Heaven*." *Camera Obscura* 19, no. 3 57 (2004): 187–218.

Kaleva, Daniela. "Beethoven and Melodrama." *Musicology Australia* 23, no. 1 (2000): 49–75.

Kerman, Joseph. "Augenblicke in *Fidelio*." In *Fidelio*, ed. Paul Robinson, 132–44. Cambridge: Cambridge University Press, 1996.

Kinderman, William. *Beethoven*. Berkeley: University of California Press, 1995.

Kittler, Friedrich. "World-Breath: On Wagner's Media Technology." In *Opera through Other Eyes*, ed. David J. Levin, 215–35. Stanford, CA: Stanford University Press, 1992.

Klinger, Barbara. *Melodrama and Meaning: History, Culture, and the Films of Douglas Sirk*. Bloomington: Indiana University Press, 1994.

Koresky, Michael. *Terence Davies*. Urbana: University of Illinois Press, 2014.

Kuzniar, Alice A. *The Queer German Cinema*. Stanford, CA: Stanford University Press, 2000.

Landy, Marcia. "The Dream of Gesture: The Body of/in Todd Haynes's Films." *boundary 2* 30, no. 3 (fall 2003): 123–40.

Landy, Marcia. "Storytelling and Information in Todd Haynes' Films." In *The Cinema of Todd Haynes: All That Heaven Allows*, ed. James Morrison, 7–24. London: Wallflower, 2007.

Lattimore, Richmond, ed. and trans. *Euripides I: Four Tragedies*. Chicago: University of Chicago Press, 1955.

Laurents, Arthur. *Original Story*. New York: Applause, 2000.

Lee, Edna, and Harry Lee. *All That Heaven Allows*. New York: G. P. Putnam's Sons, 1952.

Levine, Caroline. *Forms: Whole, Rhythm, Hierarchy, Network*. Princeton, NJ: Princeton University Press, 2015.

Lewis, Edith. *Willa Cather Living*. 1953. Lincoln: University of Nebraska Press, 2000.

Lischke, André. "Commentaire musicale et littéraire." *Fidelio, L'Avant Scène Opéra*, no. 164 (1995): 10–78.

Luciano, Dana. "Coming Around Again: The Queer Momentum of *Far from Heaven*." GLQ 13, no. 2–3 (2007): 249–72.

Luciano, Dana. "Nostalgia for an Age Yet to Come: *Velvet Goldmine*'s Queer Archive." In *Queer Times, Queer Becomings*, ed. E. L. McCallum and Mikko Tuhkanen, 121–55. Albany: SUNY Press, 2011.

Mann, William J. *Behind the Screen: How Gays and Lesbians Shaped Hollywood, 1910–1969*. New York: Viking, 2001.

Meisel, Martin. *Realizations*. Princeton, NJ: Princeton University Press, 1983.

Mercer, John, and Martin Shingler. *Melodrama: Genre, Style, Sensibility*. London: Wallflower, 2004.

Messerli, Douglas, ed. *Listen to the Mockingbird: Folksongs and Popular Music Lyrics of the 19th Century*. Los Angeles: Green Integer, 2005.

Meyer, Richard. "Rock Hudson's Body." In *Inside Out: Lesbian Theories, Gay Theories*, ed. Diana Fuss, 259–88. New York: Routledge, 1991.

Miller, D. A. "Anal *Rope*." *Representations* 32 (fall 1990): 114–33.

Miller, D. A. "Hitchcock's Hidden Pictures." *Critical Inquiry* 37 (autumn 2010): 106–30.

Miller, D. A. "Hitchcock's Understyle: A Too-Close View of *Rope*." *Representations* 121 (winter 2013): 1–30.

Miller, D. A. *The Novel and the Police*. Berkeley: University of California Press, 1988.

Miller, D. A. *Place for Us*. Cambridge, MA: Harvard University Press, 1998.

Minghella, Anthony. *The Talented Mr. Ripley: A Screenplay*. New York: Hyperion, 1999.

Morrison, James, ed. *The Cinema of Todd Haynes: All That Heaven Allows*. London: Wallflower, 2007.

Mulvey, Laura. "Notes on Sirk and Melodrama." In *Visual and Other Pleasures*, 39–43. Bloomington: Indiana University Press, 1989.

Mulvey, Laura. "Sirk and Fassbinder." In *Visual and Other Pleasures*, 45–48. Bloomington: Indiana University Press, 1989.

Nancy, Jean-Luc. *Being Singular Plural*. Translated by Robert Richardson and Anne O'Byrne. Stanford, CA: Stanford University Press, 2000.

Nancy, Jean-Luc. *Listening.* Translated by Charlotte Mandell. New York: Fordham University Press, 2007.

Nealon, Christopher. "Affect-Genealogy: Feeling and Affiliation in Willa Cather." *American Literature* 69, no. 1 (March 1997): 5–37.

Nealon, Christopher. *Foundlings: Lesbian and Gay Historical Emotion before Stonewall.* Durham, NC: Duke University Press, 2001.

Nunokawa, Jeff. *Tame Passions of Wilde.* Princeton, NJ: Princeton University Press, 2003.

O'Brien, Geoffrey. "Past Perfect." *Artforum International* 41, no. 3 (November 2002): 152–56.

Palmer, Christopher. *The Composer in Hollywood.* London: Marion Boyars, 1990.

Palmer, Christopher. *Dimitri Tiomkin.* London: T. E. Books, 1984.

Pederson, Sanna. "Beethoven and Masculinity." In *Beethoven and His World*, ed. Scott Burnham and Michael P. Steinberg, 313–31. Princeton, NJ: Princeton University Press, 2000.

Peters, Fiona. *Anxiety and Evil in the Writings of Patricia Highsmith.* Farnham, UK: Ashgate, 2011.

Peucker, Brigitte, ed. *A Companion to Rainer Werner Fassbinder.* Chichester: Wiley-Blackwell, 2012.

Rancière, Jacques. *The Intervals of Cinema.* Translated by John Howe. London: Verso, 2014.

Rayns, Tony, ed. *Fassbinder.* London: BFI, 1980.

Rhodes, John David. "Fassbinder's Work: Style, Sirk, and Queer Labor." In *A Companion to Rainer Werner Fassbinder*, ed. Brigitte Peucker, 181–203. Chichester: Wiley-Blackwell, 2012.

Rich, Adrienne. *Poems: Selected and New, 1950–1974.* New York: Norton, 1974.

Robinson, Paul. *Fidelio.* Cambridge: Cambridge University Press, 1996.

Robinson, Paul. *Opera, Sex, and Other Vital Matters.* Chicago: University of Chicago Press, 2002.

Robinson, Paul. *Queer Wars: The New Gay Right and Its Critics.* Chicago: University of Chicago Press, 2005.

Rohmer, Eric, and Claude Chabrol. *Hitchcock: The First Forty-Four Films.* Translated by Stanley Hochman. New York: Frederick Ungar, 1979.

Schantz, Ned. *Gossip, Letters, Phones: The Scandal of Female Networks in Film and Literature.* Oxford: Oxford University Press, 2008.

Schenk, Erich. "Über Tonsymbolik in Beethovens Fidelio." *Beethoven-Studien* (1970): 223–50.

Schenkar, Joan. *The Talented Miss Highsmith.* New York: St. Martin's, 2009.

Schroeder, David. *Hitchcock's Ear: Music and the Director's Art.* New York: Continuum, 2012.

Sedgwick, Eve Kosofsky. "Across Gender, Across Sexuality: Willa Cather and Others." *SAQ* 88, no. 1 (winter 1989): 53–72.

Sedgwick, Eve Kosofsky. *Epistemology of the Closet*. Berkeley: University of California Press, 1990.

Sedgwick, Eve Kosofsky. *Tendencies*. Durham, NC: Duke University Press, 1993.

Sedgwick, Eve Kosofsky. *The Weather in Proust*. Edited by Jonathan Goldberg. Durham, NC: Duke University Press, 2011.

Seltzer, Mark. "The Official World." *Critical Inquiry* 37, no. 4 (summer 2011): 724–53.

Seltzer, Mark. *True Crime: Observations on Violence and Modernity*. New York: Routledge, 2007.

Shepherd, Reginald. "What Remained of a Genet: On the Topic of *Querelle*." *GLQ* 4, no. 3 (1998): 453–70.

Silverman, Kaja. *Male Subjectivity at the Margins*. New York: Routledge, 1992.

Sirk, Douglas. "Rainer Werner Fassbinder — In Commemoration." In Rainer Werner Fassbinder, *Querelle: The Film Book*, ed. Dieter Schidor and Michael McLernon, trans. Arthur Wensinger and Richard Wood, 180. Munich: Schirmer / Mosel, 1982.

Skvirsky, Salomé Aguilera. "The Price of Heaven: Remaking Politics in *All That Heaven Allows*, *Ali: Fear Eats the Soul*, and *Far from Heaven*." *Cinema Journal* 47, no. 3 (spring 2008): 90–121.

Slote, Bernice, ed. *The Kingdom of Art*. Lincoln: University of Nebraska Press, 1966.

Stoddart, Scott F. "The Talented Mr. Ripley: A '50s Homme Fatal for the New Millennium." In *Queer Love in Film and Television*, ed. Pamela Demory and Christopher Pullen, 219–31. New York: Palgrave Macmillan, 2013.

Stout, Janis. *Willa Cather: The Writer and Her World*. Charlottesville: University of Virginia Press, 2000.

Sullivan, Jack. *Hitchcock's Music*. New Haven, CT: Yale University Press, 2006.

Summers, Claude J. "'A Losing Game in the End': Aestheticism and Homosexuality in 'Paul's Case.'" *Modern Fiction Studies* 36, no. 1 (spring 1990): 103–19.

Szendy, Peter. *Hits: Philosophy in the Jukebox*. New York: Fordham University Press, 2012.

Terada, Rei. *Looking Away: Phenomenality and Dissatisfaction, Kant to Adorno*. Cambridge, MA: Harvard University Press, 2009.

Thomsen, Christian Braad. *Fassbinder*. Translated by Martin Chalmers. London: Faber and Faber, 1991.

Tiomkin, Dimitri, and Prosper Buranelli. *Please Don't Hate Me*. Garden City, NY: Doubleday, 1959.

Töteberg, Michael, ed. *Fassbinders Filme 3*. Frankfurt am Main: Verlag des Autoren, 1990.

Trask, Michael. "Patricia Highsmith's Method." *American Literary History* 22, no. 3 (summer 2010): 584–614.

Warner, Michael. "Thoreau's Bottom." *Raritan* 11, no. 3 (winter 1992): 53–79.

Warner, Michael. "*Walden*'s Erotic Economy." In *Comparative American Identities*, ed. Hortense J. Spillers, 157–74. New York: Routledge, 1991.

Weis, Elisabeth. *The Silent Scream: Alfred Hitchcock's Sound Track*. Rutherford, NJ: Fairleigh Dickinson University Press, 1982.

Weis, Elisabeth, and John Belton, eds. *Film Sound*. New York: Columbia University Press, 1985.

White, Patricia. *Uninvited: Classical Hollywood Cinema and Lesbian Representability*. Bloomington: Indiana University Press, 1999.

White, Rob. *Todd Haynes*. Urbana: University of Illinois Press, 2013.

Wilde, Oscar. *De Profundis and Other Writings*. Harmondsworth: Penguin, 1973.

Wilde, Oscar. *The Soul of Man under Socialism and Selected Critical Prose*. Edited by Linda Dowling. London: Penguin, 2001.

Williams, Linda. *Hard Core: Power, Pleasure, and "the Frenzy of the Visible."* Berkeley: University of California Press, 1989.

Williams, Linda. "Melodrama Revisited." In *Refiguring American Film Genres*, ed. Nick Browne, 42–88. Berkeley: University of California Press, 1998.

Williams, Linda. *On The Wire*. Durham, NC: Duke University Press, 2014.

Williams, Linda. *Playing the Race Card: Melodramas of Black and White*. Princeton, NJ: Princeton University Press, 2001.

Williams, Linda. *Screening Sex*. Durham, NC: Duke University Press, 2008.

Willis, Sharon. "The Politics of Disappointment: Todd Haynes Rewrites Douglas Sirk." *Camera Obscura* 18, no. 3 54 (2003): 131–75.

Wilson, Andrew. *Beautiful Shadow*. New York: Bloomsbury, 2003.

Wood, Robin. *Hitchcock's Films Revisited*. New York: Columbia University Press, 2002.

Woodress, James. *Willa Cather: A Literary Life*. Lincoln: University of Nebraska Press, 1987.

Wyatt, Justin. "Cinematic/Sexual: An Interview with Todd Haynes." *Film Quarterly* 46, no. 3 (spring 1993): 2–8.

INDEX

Adams, J. B., 73

Adorno, Theodor, 86–87, 95–98, 105, 160–61

agency: melodrama and, 39–44; in "Melodram" of Beethoven's *Fidelio*, 4–21

Alcestis/Alkestis (Euripides), 17–20, 23

Ali: Fear Eats the Soul (film), xvi, 162; Haynes's discussion of, 68–73; music in, 96–97; queer relations in, 56–67, 67–73, 84; reality and melodrama in, 36–44, 176n84

All That Heaven Allows (film), xvi, 18, 26–28, 40; *Fear Eats the Soul* compared with, 56–58, 67, 162, 176n84; Haynes's discussion of, 67–68, 72, 163; queer desire and, 44–55, 176n77; reality and melodrama in, 36–44

All That Heaven Allows (Lee), 48

Anarchy of Imagination, The (Fassbinder), 162

Angst Essen Seele Auf. See *Ali: Fear Eats the Soul* (film)

antinomy, Sirk's discussion of, 24–26

Arabian Nights, The, 136, 139

artistic life, in Highsmith's Ripley novels, 125–32

Assassins: A Film Concerning Rimbaud (film), 23–24

Bach, Johann Sebastian, 112, 115, 119–25

"Ballad of Reading Gaol, The" (Wilde), 77–79

"Band Played On, The" (song), 87, 98–107, 180n35

Barthes, Roland, 30, 43

Beethoven, Ludwig van, xvi, 105; *Fidelio* composed by, 3–21, 105, 155–56

Benjamin, Walter, 120

Berlant, Lauren, x–xi, xv, 44

Berlin Alexanderplatz (Döblin), 27–28, 69

Berlin Alexanderplatz (television series), 27–28, 64

Bersani, Leo, 31, 126, 165

binarism, homoaesthetics and, 30–32

Black Skin, White Masks (Fanon), 59–60

Blanchette, Cate, 112, 134

Boetticher, Budd, 47–48

Bohemian Girl (Balfe), 146–47

Bouilly, J. N., 9

Bourbon Street Blues (film), 172n8

Bouzerau, Laurent, 92–93

Boy Who Followed Ripley, The (Highsmith), 120–32

Brecht, Bertolt, 23

Breton, Jules, 141

Brett, Philip, 85–86, 91–94

Brokeback Mountain (film), 169n4
Brooks, Peter, ix–xv, 33; on force of
   moral truth, 12–13; on identity in
   melodrama, 8–9; "moral occult"
   concept of, x, 76, 156–57; Skvirsky
   and, 36
Brown, E. K., 153–54
Brown, John, 106–7
Brown, Wendy, 159
Butler, Judith, 31, 138, 184n14
Byars, Jackie, 176n77
Byrd, James, 42

Cain, James M., 163
Call Me Madam (musical), 85
Captain Lightfoot (film), 175n67
Carmen (Bizet), 123–24
Carol (film), 164–65
Carousel (musical), 102–3
Carson, Anne, 17, 20
Cather, Willa, xvi; fiction of, 138–48,
   163–67; on Wilde, 134–35, 137,
   148–54, 183n6. *See also specific titles*
Cavani, Liliana, 124–26
Chabrol, Claude, 44
Chandler, Joan, 89
Christopher and His Kind (Isherwood),
   123
civil rights movement, 40–41
Clarke, Eric O., 170n11
class politics: in Fassbinder's *Fear
   Eats the Soul*, 57–67; melodrama
   and, 36–37, 41–44; in *The Talented
   Mr. Ripley* (film), 114–18
Clément, René, 118
Clifton, Kevin, 90–94
Comeau, Vance, 41
Composing for the Films (Adorno and
   Eisler), 179n5
Cottingham, Laura, 50–51, 58–59,
   176n77

Coviello, Peter, 54
cross-citations concerning melodrama, 29–30
cross-racial desire: in Fassbinder's
   Fear Eats the Soul, 59–67; in
   Haynes's films, 40–44, 73–77; in
   Imitation of Life, 44–55; in Sirk's
   films, 46–55
Crowther, Bosley, 94, 176n79

Damned, The (film), 161–62
Damon, Matt, 111–18
Davies, Terence, 165–67
Davis, Glyn, 38–39, 41–44, 73–74,
   178n100
Death in Venice (film), 161
DeFalco, Amelia, 43–44
Deleuze, Gilles, 31
Derrida, Jacques, 14–16
Desert Island Discs (radio show), 124
Diamond, David, 124
Die Winterreise (Schubert), 147–48
"Director's Statement" (Haynes),
   29–30
Doane, Mary Ann, 29
Döblin, Alfred, 27–28
Dombey and Son (Dickens), 138
Douglas, Alfred (Lord), 78
drowning death, as melodramatic
   plot device, 141–42
Düttmann, Alexander García, 160–
   63
Dyer, Richard, 45, 66–67, 174n36,
   175n61
Dylan, Bob, 32

Edelman, Lee, x
eindeutig, Sirk's discussion of, 25, 32,
   70–71
Eisenstein, Sergei, 86
Eisler, Hanns, 86, 97–98, 105

Elliott, Laura, 99–100

Ellmann, Richard, 131

Elsaesser, Thomas, xi–xii; on Fassbinder, 64–66, 162, 177n91; on film music, 86–87; film theory and, 29; Haynes's films and, 33, 67–68; on Hitchcock, 99; on melodrama, 3–4, 17, 20–21, 132

Empson, William, 152, 184n36

Epistemology of the Closet (Sedgwick), 66, 69, 134, 169n4, 177n88

Euripides, 17–21

Fanon, Frantz, 59–60

Far from Heaven (film), 29, 33, 35, 162; art show scene in, 72–77, 84; queer relations in, 67–79, 84; reality and melodrama in, xvi, 36–44

Fassbinder, Rainer Werner, xii, xiv, xvi, 16, 23, 127; Haynes's discussion of, 29–35, 67–73; music in films of, 162–63; reality in films of, 36–44; sexual relations in films of, 56–67, 84; Sirk and, 25–28, 56–67, 151, 172n7; on Visconti, 162; Wilde's poetry in films of, 77–79. *See also specific films and other works*

Fassbinder's Germany: History, Identity, Subject (Elsaesser), 64, 163, 177n91

Fear Eats the Soul. See Ali: Fear Eats the Soul (film)

feminist film theory: Haynes's homoaesthetics and, 31, 33–34, 68–73; Sirk's melodramas and, 29

Fidelio (Beethoven), xvi, 155–56; first act quartet in, 16–17; "Leonore motif" in, 10–11; "Melodram" section of, 3–21, 105; *Senso* (film) and, 162; "shiver motif" in, 10

film studies, evolution of melodrama and, xii–xiv

Fisher, Dorothy Canfield, 140, 154

Forbstein, Leo F., 92

Forms (Levine), 157–59

Foucault, Michel, xiii–xiv, 30; on discipline and identity, 11–12

Fox and His Friends (Faustrecht der Freiheit) (film), 69–70

Frank, Marcie, xi

freedom: in Cather's *Lucy Gayheart*, 151–54; in *Fidelio*, 12–16

Fremstad, Olive, 138–40

From UFA to Hollywood: Douglas Sirk Remembers (documentary), 24

Fuchs, Cynthia, 175n65

Fujiwara, Chris, 57–59, 61

Gates, Henry Louis, Jr., 42

gay politics, reality vs. melodrama and, 41–44

Gelfant, Blanche, 141–42, 148, 150

gender: ambiguity in *Fidelio*, 13–21; melodrama and, xii–xiii

Gender Trouble (Butler), 31

Genet, Jean, 30, 34, 78–79

Giannone, Richard, 141–42

Gill, John, 39, 41–43

Gledhill, Christine, xii–xiv, 73

Gorbman, Claudia, 96–97

Gorfinkel, Elena, 66–67, 174n57, 177n94

Granger, Farley, 85–94, 98–102, 112, 162

Guattari, Félix, 31–32

Hall, Gertrude, 140

Halliday, Jon, xv, 18, 23–25, 45, 50, 53, 68, 163

Happiest Days of Your Life, The (film), 166

INDEX 199

Has Anybody Seen My Gal? (film), 46

Hawkins, Joan, 174n48

Hayes Code, 43

Haynes, Todd, xii, xiv, xvi, 16, 23–24, 127; on Fassbinder, 67–73; on gender and film, 28–35; *Mildred Pierce* mini-series by, 163; queer relations in *Far from Heaven* and, 67–79, 84; on reality, 36–44; Wilde's work and films of, 78–79, 134. *See also specific films*

Herrmann, Bernard, 86

heterosexuality: in *Fidelio*, 14–21; in Sirk's films, 49–55

Highsmith, Patricia, xiv, xvi; Cather and, 134; Haynes and, 164–65; Hitchcock and, 84, 87, 89–90, 100–107, 125–33, 163–69; identity and relationality in Ripley novels of, 118–25; male coupling in novels of, 85; musicality of, 124; music in novels of, 98, 109–18, 162; painting in Ripley novels of, 125–32. *See also specific titles*

History of Sexuality: An Introduction, The (Foucault), xiii–xiv, 12

Hitchcock, Alfred, xiv, xvi, 20, 44–45; cameo appearances by, 94–96, 98–99; films in "homosexual triptych," 45; Highsmith and, 84, 87, 89–90, 100–107, 125–32, 163–69; melodrama in films of, 83–84, 87, 169n14; music in films of, 89–94, 98–107, 162. *See also specific films*

Hoberman, J., 37–38, 166

homoaesthetics: in Fassbinder's films, 77–78; Haynes's articulation of, 29–35, 68–73, 173n19

"Homoaesthetics and *Querelle*" (Haynes), 30

homosexuality: in Cather's *Paul's Case*, 135–36, 183n4; in *Far from Heaven*, 73–77; Fassbinder's *Fear Eats the Soul* and, 58–67; feminist theory and, 31; in Highsmith's Ripley novels, 118–25; in Hitchcock's *Rope*, 88–94; music and, 88–94; politics and, 16–18; in *The Talented Mr. Ripley* (film), 113–18; in Visconti's films, 161–62; Williams's discussion of, 169n4; in *The Wire*, 157–60

Hudson, Rock, 18, 23–25, 45–55, 61, 68, 84, 162, 163, 175n61, 175n67

Hull, Isabel V., 11–12, 170n11

Hunter, Ross, 46

identification: in Cather's *Paul's Case*, 134–36; Haynes's discussion of, 33–35; in Highsmith's Ripley novels, 126–32; music and, 85–86; Wilde's theatricalization and, 133

identity: in Fassbinder's *Fear Eats the Soul*, 57–67; in melodrama, 33–35; melodrama and, 39–44; in "Melodram" of Beethoven's *Fidelio*, 6–21; Sirk's discussion of, 24–25; in *Strangers on a Train* (film and novel), 104–7, 108–9; in *The Talented Mr. Ripley* (film and novel), 115–16

Imitation of Life (film), 18, 26–28, 40, 134, 178n102

"Imitation of Life: On the Films of Douglas Sirk" (Fassbinder), 26–28

I'm Not There (film), 32, 34, 134, 164

Importance of Being Earnest, The (Wilde), 136

In a Year of Thirteen Moons (film), 177n89

Inside The Talented Mr. Ripley (documentary), 111–12

Interlude (film), 26–28, 163

I Only Want You to Love Me (film), 65
Irigaray, Luce, 31
Isherwood, Christopher, 123

James, Henry, 23, 134, 182n72
Jameson, Fredric, 141
Jared, Gabriel, 111
jazz, in *The Talented Mr. Ripley* (film), 113–18
"Joy of Nelly Deane, The" (Cather), 141
Joyrich, Lynne, 178n100

Kafka, Franz, 23
Kaleva, Daniela, 7, 9–10, 18
Kant, Immanuel, 12–13, 16, 170n11
Kerman, Joseph, 170n12
Klinger, Barbara, 44, 45
Koresky, Michael, 166–67
Kramer, Lawrence, 14
Kristeva, Julia, 31–32
Kroin, Amy, 36

Landy, Marcia, 38, 174n40
Lattimore, Richmond, 20
Laurents, Arthur, 90, 92–93
Leander, Zarah, 25, 89, 162
Lee, Edna, 48
Lee, Harry, 48
Léonore, ou L'amour conjugale (Bouilly), 9
Levine, Caroline, 157–60
Lewis, Edith, 134, 138–39, 184n34
Leyda, Julia, 28–29, 33–35
Lischke, André, 4
Lola (film), 64
Long Day Closes, The (film), 165–67
Love Is Colder Than Death (film), 27–28, 65
Lover Come Back (film), 45
Loving v. Virginia, 62
Luciano, Dana, 178n100

Lucy Gayheart (Cather), xvi, 141–54
Lyotard, Jean-François, 31–32

Magnificent Obsession (film), 18, 23–25, 46, 51
Mahler, Gustav, 162
"Making Gay Meanings" (Sedgwick), 16
Mann, William J., 46–48
Mansfield, Katherine, 151
Marillier, H. C., 78
marriage: Kant's discussion of, 12–13, 16, 170n11; in Sirk's films, 53–55
Marriage of Maria Braun, The (film), 64
masculinity: in *Fidelio*, 11–12, 14–21; in Sirk's films, 45–55, 175n65
McClary, Susan, 14
McClung, Isabelle, 136
melodrama, historical evolution of, ix–xv
Melodramatic Imagination: Balzac, Henry James, Melodrama and the Mode of Excess, The (Brooks), ix–xi; identity discussed in, 8–9
Menuhin, Yehudi, 185n34
Mercer, John, xi–xii
Merchant of Four Seasons, The (film), 62
Merman, Ethel, 85, 88–89, 179n13
Meyer, Richard, 45
Mildred Pierce (film), 163
Mildred Pierce (HBO mini-series), 163
Miller, D. A. (David A.), xv, 30, 67, 169n4; on Granger, 86; on Hitchcock, 85, 88–90, 94–97, 101–7, 180n28; musicality of, 124; on open secrets, 179n21
Miller, Perry, 54
Minghella, Anthony, 111–18, 124, 130, 164
Minnelli, Vincente, 120

INDEX   201

Mira, Brigitte, 39, 58, 66
Miracle in the Rain (film), 71
Miró, Joan, 73–74, 78, 84
Moon, Michael, 78, 134
Moore, Julianne, 39
Moorehead, Agnes, 51, 84, 176n77
"moral occult," x
Mouvements Perpétuels (Poulenc),
    90–94, 96–97, 103
Mulvey, Laura, 45, 49–51, 173n21,
    177n94
Murder! (film), 45
murder, male coupling and, 85
Murray, Noel, 29
music: in Cather's fiction, 138–54;
    film and, 83–87, 96–98; Granger's
    discussion of, 88–94; in Haynes's
    films, 33–35; in Highsmith's Ripley
    novels, 109–25; in Hitchcock's
    films, 98–107; in *The Long Day
    Closes* (film), 166–69; in *The Tal-
    ented Mr. Ripley* (film), 111–18
My Ántonia (Cather), 138–39, 163–64

Nagel, Conrad, 55
Nancy, Jean-Luc, 42, 98
Native Americans, in Sirk's films,
    45–55
Nealon, Christopher, 149–50, 184n14
Negative Dialectics (Adorno), 160–61
*Nightingale's Song at Midnight and the
    Morning Rain, The* (Miró), 73–74
"Ninth Symphony of Beethoven
    Understood at Last as a Sexual
    Message, The" (Rich), 14
novel, melodrama and, xi
Novel and the Police, The (Miller),
    179n21
"Novel Démeublé, The" (Cather), 139

O'Brien, Geoffrey, 38–39
One of Ours (Cather), 149

Ophüls, Max, 29, 72
Ossessione (film), 161

painting: in Cather's *Paul's Case*,
    136; in Highsmith's Ripley novels,
    125–32
Palmer, Christopher, 180n44
Paradine Case, The (film), 99
Parker, Charlie, 115
Parsifal (Wagner), 140
Pater, Walter, 140
patriarchy, sexuality and, 49–51
"Paul's Case" (Cather), 134–39, 141–
    44, 148–50, 183n4
Picture of Dorian Gray, The (Wilde),
    139–40
Pillow Talk (film), 45
Plein Soleil (film), 118
Plotting and Writing Suspense Fiction
    (Highsmith), 116–17
Poison (film), 34, 78–79
politics: domestic in, 11–12; of libera-
    tion, 15–16; reality and melodrama
    and, 40–41
Poulenc, Francis, 90–94, 96–97, 103
power, Foucault's discussion of, xiii–
    xiv
Price of Salt, The (Highsmith), 164–65
Professor's House, The (Cather), 134,
    149–50
Proust, Marcel, 134
psychoanalysis, melodrama and,
    169n8

queer theory: identity and, 43–44;
    melodrama and, xiii–xiv
Querelle (film), 30–32, 34, 66, 77–78,
    173n19
Querelle (Genet), 30, 173n21

Raben, Peer, 162–63
race and sexuality: in *Far from*

Heaven, 73–77; in Fassbinder's *Fear Eats the Soul*, 58–67; melodrama and, 38–44

Raffaëlli, Jean-François, 136

Rancière, Jacques, 120

reality, melodramatic relations and, 36–44

Reckless Moment, The (film), 72, 178n102

Reed, Lou, 121–24, 163

referentiality: in Fassbinder's *Fear Eats the Soul*, 58–67; in melodramatic film, 37–44

Reisz, Toby, 111–12

relationality: *eindeutig* and, 79; film music and, 98; in Haynes's films, 30–35, 84–86; in Highsmith's Ripley novels, 111–18, 126–32; in melodrama, 39–40, 61–67; in Sirk and Fassbinder films, 27–28, 30, 71–72

Rhodes, John David, 67

Rich, Adrienne, 14

Ripley novels of Patricia Highsmith: identity and relationality in, 118–25; male coupling in, 85; music in films based on, 109–18; painting in, 125–32

Ripley's Game (film), 124–25

Ripley's Game (Highsmith), 110, 118–25

Ripley Under Ground (Highsmith), 110, 122–33

Ripley Under Water (Highsmith), 121, 125, 128–29, 131

Robinson, Paul, 14–16

Rohmer, Eric, 44

Rope (film), xvi, 45, 84; male coupling in, 85; music in, 89–94, 96–97, 112

"*Rope* Unleashed" (documentary), 92

Rush, Barbara, 46, 175n67

Rutherford, Margaret, 166

sadomasochism, Haynes's discussion of, 31–32

Safe (film), 33–34, 165

Salem, El Hedi ben M'Barek Mohamed, 39, 58, 66, 68, 84

same-sex desire: in *Far from Heaven*, 40; Fassbinder's discussion of, 28; in *Fidelio*, 15–16; in Hitchcock films, 44–45; trouser roles and, 14

Schenk, Erich, 10–11

Schenkar, Joan, 124

Schmidt, Eckhart, 24

Schroeder, David, 90–91

Schubert, Franz, 121, 144–45, 147–50

Sedgwick, Eve Kosofsky, xv, 16, 66, 69, 78; on Cather, 134–37, 148–49, 184n14; on difference and categorization, 177n88, 177n92; on homoaesthetics, 30–31; on queer theory, 173n17

Seltzer, Mark, 108, 181n51

Send Me No Flowers (film), 45, 175n61

Senso (film), 162

Sex, or the Unbearable (Berlant and Edelman), x

sexuality: in Cather's fiction, 147–54; homoaesthetics and, 30–31; politics and, 16–21; in Sirk's films, 44–55

Shadow of a Doubt (film), 20, 107

Shakespeare, William, 23; Wilde on, 133

Shepard, Matthew, 42

Shingler, Martin, xi–xii

Shivas, Mark, 23

Silverman, Kaja, 67, 68, 173n21, 177n94

Simon, David, 147

Sirk, Douglas, xii, xiv, xv, 16, 127, 163; on Euripides's *Alcestis*, 23; Fassbinder's work and, 25–28, 61–67, 151, 172n7; on filmmaking, 24–26, 172n5; Haynes's discussion of, 29–35, 67–73; influence on Haynes of, 37–38, 76–77; melodrama in films of, 3–4, 17–18; queer relations in films of, 44–55; reality in films of, 43–44; Wilde's influence on, 134; women in films of, 27–28, 31–32, 50–55, 70–71, 89. *See also specific films*

Sirk on Sirk, 45

Skvirsky, Salomé Aguilera, 36–38, 40–41, 49, 174n48

Song of the Lark, The (Cather), 139–41

Spellbound (film), 99

Stewart, James, 89–90

Stout, Janis, 141–42

Strangers on a Train (film), xvi, 45, 84, 117, 162; carousel scene in, 87, 99; Hitchcock's cameo in, 95–96; Miller's essay on, 94; music in, 98–107, 114

Strangers on a Train (Highsmith), xvi, 84, 100–109, 117, 131

Suicide, The (film), 23

Sullivan, Jack, 90–92, 100, 104–5, 180n44

Summers, Claude J., 183n4

Superstar: The Karen Carpenter Story (film), 33–34

Talented Mr. Ripley, The (film), 111–18, 130, 164

Talented Mr. Ripley, The (Highsmith), 110, 112–18, 128, 182n72

"Tales of Sound and Fury: Observations on the Family Melodrama" (Elsaesser), xi, 3–4, 86–87

Tarnished Angels, The (film), 24, 163–64

Taza, Son of Cochise (film), 45–46

telepathic power, 182n70; in Highsmith's Ripley novels, 110

Tendencies (Sedgwick), xv, 31, 173n21, 177n92

Tereda, Rei, x

Thoreau, Henry David, 53–55, 163

Three Faces of Eve, The (film), 71

Time to Love and a Time to Die, A (film), 26–28

Tiomkin, Dimitri, 98, 104–7, 162

"Todd Haynes: From Fassbinder to Sirk and Back" (Haynes interview), 67–73

Töteberg, Michael, 56

touch, Hitchcock's use of, 94–96

Transformer (Reed album), 124, 126, 163

Trask, Michael, 181n62

trouser role, in *Fidelio*, 13–14

understatement, Hitchcock's discussion of, 83–84

Velvet Goldmine (film), xvi, 34, 78, 134

Veronika Voss (film), 64

Vertigo (film), 86, 99

Village Voice, 37–38, 166

Virtuous Vice (Clarke), 170n11

Visconti, Luchino, 160–62. *See also specific films*

von Platta, Anna, 130–31

Wagner, Richard, 140–41

Wainewright, Thomas Griffith, 133–34, 138

Walden (Thoreau), 53–55, 163

Walker, Robert, 98–102

Warner, Michael, 54

Weis, Elisabeth, 90, 96, 180n28
Wenders, Wim, 125
White, Patricia, 44, 51
"Why I Make Melodramas" (Hitchcock), 83–84
Wilde, Oscar, 32, 77–79, 109; aesthetics of melodrama and, 133–54; influence on Cather of, 134–35, 137, 148–54, 183n6; influence on Highsmith and Hitchcock of, xvi, 131–32
Williams, Linda, xii–xiv, 36, 156–60, 169n4; on melodrama, 37
Willis, Sharon, 40–44, 174n48
Wilson, Andrew, 124
Wire, The (television series), 156–60

Wittgenstein, Ludwig, 24–25
women: Haynes's homoaesthetics and, 31–35; in Sirk's films, 27–28, 31–32, 50–55, 70–71
Wood, Elisabeth, 91–94
Wood, Robin, 90
Woodress, James, 141–42
Written on the Wind (film), 17–18, 24, 26–28, 164
W. W. Norton, 130
Wyatt, Justin, 31, 33
Wyatt, Thomas (Sir), 55
Wyman, Jane, 55, 68, 71
Wynter, Sylvia, 177n86

Žižek, Slavoj, 115–16, 164